Executed: But was James Hanratty Innocent?

Executed: But was James Hanratty Innocent?

A Damning Indictment of the DNA Evidence Used to Condemn Him

Robert Harriman

First published in Great Britain in 2023
by Pen & Sword True Crime
An imprint of
Pen & Sword Books Limited
Yorkshire - Philadelphia

Copyright © Robert Harriman, 2023

ISBN 978 1 39904 493 6

The right of Robert Harriman to be identified as Author of this work has been asserted by him in accordance with the Copyright, Designs and Patents Act 1988.

A CIP catalogue record for this book is available from the British Library

All rights reserved. No part of this book may be reproduced or transmitted in any form or by any means, electronic or mechanical including photocopying, recording or by any information storage and retrieval system, without permission from the Publisher in writing.

Typeset in INDIA by IMPEC eSolutions
Printed and bound in the UK by CPI Group (UK) Ltd, Croydon, CR0 4YY

Pen & Sword Books Limited incorporates the imprints of Atlas, Archaeology, Aviation, Discovery, Family History, Fiction, History, Maritime, Military, Military Classics, Politics, Select, Transport, True Crime, Air World, Frontline Publishing, Leo Cooper, Remember When, Seaforth Publishing, The Praetorian Press, Wharncliffe Local History, Wharncliffe Transport, Wharncliffe True Crime and White Owl.

For a complete list of Pen & Sword titles please contact
PEN & SWORD BOOKS LIMITED
47 Church Street, Barnsley, South Yorkshire S70 2AS, United Kingdom
E-mail: enquiries@pen-and-sword.co.uk
Website: www.pen-and-sword.co.uk

or

PEN AND SWORD BOOKS
1950 Lawrence Rd, Havertown, PA 19083, USA
E-mail: Uspen-and-sword@casematepublishers.com
Website: www.penandswordbooks.com

For the Hanratty family, still waiting.

With thanks to Paul Foot who carried the torch with honour.
Without whom, along with Kate Bohdanowicz, Malachy Muinzer
and my wife Judith, this work would not exist.

Contents

Introduction	viii
Preface	x
Some Reasons for the Controversy	1
The Liverpool Alibi	9
The BBC Horizon Programme	24
The Court of Appeal Judgment	37
Expert Witnesses in English Courts	59
Statistics and DNA	66
DNA Profiling Issues	84
Introducing the Transcripts	112
Monday, 22 April 2002	121
Tuesday, 23 April 2002	136
Wednesday, 24 April 2002	169
Conclusion	189
Points for the Criminal Cases Review Commission	193
Bibliography	198
References	200
Index	205

Introduction

Caveat Emptor

This is not a light read in the manner of a crime thriller. Instead, it details my research into an area of our criminal justice system that is rife with confusion, misrepresentation, and outright obfuscation but which is, nonetheless, of importance to us all. I have endeavoured to make this book worthwhile and easy to follow. However, as we are dealing with subject matter which is at the intersection between the English legal system – with its arcane language and strictures – and cutting-edge science, some sections will inevitably require some effort on your behalf. For this I can only apologise and beg your understanding as I place these no doubt controversial and unpopular findings into the public domain.

This book documents the woeful 'miscarriage of justice' that is the James Hanratty case, dealing primarily with the blatantly erroneous way that it was handled by the Court of Appeal in 2002, when the DNA evidence was pronounced to have proved his conclusive guilt. An extraordinary amount of effort to prove his innocence had been undertaken by many people over several decades to culminate in that hearing. Much of their work is in the public domain, in the form of books and articles, and this material is, to say the very least, sufficient to give the impartial reader a sense of unease. My intention is to avoid unnecessary repetition of their work, while allowing the uninitiated reader a clear understanding of my reasons for believing the verdict to be unsupported by the evidence. My work builds upon their efforts and covers new ground but could never have existed without them. I owe them all a huge debt of gratitude.

'What the thinker thinks the prover proves'

Author, Robert Anton Wilson

This aphorism describes the way we work as human beings, whether we be scientist, Court of Appeal judge or man in the street. We cannot help but work this way, for it is part of our fundamental approach to dealing with the world. It means we seek the evidence that conforms to the way we view things and tend to ignore the rest – unless it is so overwhelming that we are forced to change our opinion. Consider this as you read the following.

Preface

Hanratty – the name alone is sufficient to invoke strong emotions in people of a certain age. In many ways it is an unfortunate name that has been forever scarred by its association with one of the most contentious criminal cases in British legal history. Having studied it in depth, I realise that the emotions it arouses – of passion or venom depending on your position – are disproportionate to the historical significance of the case.

It appears to have taken on the status of a mythic quest for those who passionately believe in the innocence of the man called James Hanratty; a man they believe was failed by the judicial system that tried and executed him. Then there are those who believe, just as passionately, in his guilt and wish this ruthless killer would stop being lauded as an innocent.

I have often wondered what it was about this case that created this level of emotional, and often far from rational, debate. Whatever it might be, it has always been clear to me that by putting my head above the parapet in this case, I risk unleashing considerable opprobrium.

I am of an age that I can remember some of the build-up to Hanratty's execution at Bedford in 1962, and I must admit that it made a far greater impression on me than any other case of capital punishment, before or since. I remember seeing a picture in a newspaper of those keeping vigil outside the gates of the prison and reading that he had maintained his innocence to the end. Although the death penalty was abolished just three years later, I know people were executed after Hanratty, although I have absolutely no recollection of their cases. There was something about Hanratty's circumstances that resonated with me even then, long before I became aware of any campaign to prove his innocence. I don't recall knowing the details of the actual crime that resulted in Hanratty being sentenced to death. I just remember the media, specifically newspapers, chronicling his impending and actual execution and it left me with a strange sense of disquiet over the intervening years. It seems that I was not alone.

You may rightly say, 'Wasn't this case definitively resolved, in favour of Hanratty's guilt, by the Court of Appeal in 2002? Didn't the DNA scientists prove conclusively that he was guilty?' This was widely reported at the time, most notably by the BBC, who devoted an edition of their flagship scientific programme *Horizon* to discuss how the science had finally put the debate to rest. While that may very well have been the case, it didn't alter the fact that, after forty years of campaigning and investigation by the likes of journalists Paul Foot and Bob Woffinden, the Criminal Cases Review Commission (CCRC) deemed the evidence gathered before the DNA tests sufficient to refer the case back to the Court of Appeal. Surely the CCRC wouldn't have done that without a considerable body of evidence pointing towards the case against Hanratty being unsound?

I saw nothing in the media reports of the judgment about how the court had considered any of the evidence other than the DNA. This left me with considerable unease as to how the English legal system deals with such cases, when the DNA stands in direct opposition to other evidence. Was that other evidence just discounted in the face of this triumphant DNA result? Does this mean all evidence, *other than DNA evidence*, should be ignored from here on? If so, what safeguards are in place to ensure that the DNA evidence's veracity is unequivocal?

This is how I felt twenty years ago, in 2002. Yet, as had been the case for the previous forty years, I felt there was nothing I could do to 'scratch the itch' that had been exposed. Hanratty was guilty. End of story. However, in 2006 I began studying for an Honours Degree in Forensic Computing. It included modules in law and forensic principles, and as part of these I had to produce a paper detailing the impact of forensic science on a legal case of my choice. Here was my chance to potentially scratch that itch and so, unsurprisingly, I chose to focus on this infamous case. Little did I realise that what I was about to uncover was not only going to exacerbate my concerns over the way this case had been handled, but that it would also raise grave concerns about the way DNA forensic evidence is still being handled by the English legal system.

As I began my investigations into a project that was only due to last for a matter of weeks, I realised I was becoming involved in a case with far more than its fair share of obfuscation, and with very little of the relevant information in the public domain. For the duration of my university project, the only documents available to me were the judgment from the Appeal proceedings and the transcript from the previously mentioned *Horizon* programme.

Unfortunately, my attempts to elicit further information, from either the FSS, in the form of answers to my questions, or the court service, in the form of access to the transcript of the hearing, were blocked. Both organisations simply referred me to the judgment. Since academic projects require reputable sources of information, this paucity of data meant that I could not obtain answers to all the questions concerning me. It is only now, with the passing of several more years, that I have been able to collect the necessary information to enable me to return to this investigation, and to formulate my arguments sufficiently to consider placing them in print.

Human nature being what it is, especially in view of the emotional baggage with which this case is burdened, I very much doubt my efforts will persuade the die-hards on the 'Hanratty was guilty' side of the debate. Nor will they prove popular with the political and legal establishment. Nevertheless, I would like to point out that the burden of proof in the English criminal justice system has always been 'beyond reasonable doubt'. This has very recently been replaced by the instruction for jurors to be 'satisfied that they are sure', as the former was felt by some to be unclear. This is no small hurdle that needs to be cleared to justify a guilty verdict, especially if that carries a death penalty. The courts are supposed to be arenas in which the arguments are fully aired and, as far as possible, considered rationally. Nevertheless, I know it is impossible for a legal system run by human beings to entirely remove human emotions and prejudices from its deliberations. We will see that this clearly applies in the way the case was handled by the Court of Appeal in 2002, much to the Hanratty family's detriment. The long-standing and well-known history of the case also had a major influence on the outcome some four decades later.

Unfortunately, those self-same courts tend to be treated by their highly paid denizens as gladiatorial battlegrounds, where truth is often an inconvenience to be discredited at all costs, and where the dispensing of 'justice' relies on the combative and presentational skills of the participants. Such is our flawed 'adversarial' legal system which, despite its litany of past mistakes, still tries to present itself as being the best. If you then add highly contentious, little understood, and mostly unverified science to this potent mix is it any wonder things can go awry, especially when attempting to persuade a jury of the veracity of the arguments?

When one is dealing with the Court of Appeal – peopled by the some of the highest members of the legal profession, who should be well-versed in the legal jousting between the teams representing the Crown (the respondent) and Hanratty (the appellant) – how far can one have faith that the verdict will be sound? As we will see, it was the DNA evidence that was seemingly crucial in reaching the verdict that was delivered. I say seemingly because, having looked at how this evidence was presented and handled, it is impossible to escape the feeling that the forces behind the long running obduracy with which this case is plagued were still at play.

Unfortunately for us all, the English legal system is yet to fully come to terms with the implications of DNA Low Copy Number (LCN) forensics (of which more later), nearly two decades after James Hanratty's guilt was, supposedly, completely resolved. To this day his family remains failed by our political authorities, our media, our courts, and supposedly clear-cut scientific evidence.

Some Reasons for the Controversy

James Hanratty, a petty-crook and occasional car thief, was executed on 4 April 1962, having been convicted on 17 February of murdering Michael Gregsten in a lay-by at Deadman's Hill on the A6 in Bedfordshire six months earlier. He was just 25. He had previously led a feckless life and been in and out of prison for housebreaking and theft, and there is little doubt that he would have continued to do so, but there was nothing in his criminal history to suggest he was capable of murder or rape. Because shortly after shooting Gregsten, a 36-year-old married father of two, the killer had then raped, shot, and seriously wounded Gregsten's lover, 22-year-old Valerie Storie, in the same lay-by, leaving her for dead. He then proceeded to drive away in the couple's car, having committed the crime in the early hours of Wednesday, 23 August 1961.

The couple had been surprised by a man with a gun some hours before, at about 9.30pm on the evening of Tuesday, 22 August, during a lover's tryst in their car in a cornfield near Dorney Reach, a few miles west of Slough in Buckinghamshire. It later became known that their affair had been going on for quite a while and that Gregsten, who worked as a scientist in a laboratory where Storie worked as an assistant, had hoped to divorce his wife Janet for her; though his wife stated at the time that she had no intention of accepting a divorce. The lovers had then endured several terrifying hours during which they were held at gunpoint and forced to drive around a large swathe of southern England, before being made to stop in that fateful lay-by. Despite the fact her assailant shot her several times, Valerie Storie survived the attack, although she was paralysed from the waist down and was subsequently confined to a wheelchair.

2 Executed: But was James Hanratty Innocent?

Like many other murder cases, it immediately caught the interest of the media and soon attained a considerable level of notoriety, containing as it did both elements to which they are most attracted, namely sex and violence. It also added an extra frisson to that heady cocktail by appearing, at least initially, to be motiveless. And the story continued to intrigue the public. The murder weapon was discovered on the evening of Thursday, 24 August, hidden under the backseat of a number 36A London bus, wiped clean of fingerprints, and wrapped in a handkerchief. The police had been tipped off about the weapon by a criminal associate and former friend of Hanratty, Charles 'Dixie' France, who claimed Hanratty told him that if he ever needed to get rid of anything, he would hide it under the backseat of a bus, and who would suspiciously commit suicide just prior to Hanratty's execution.

The initial prime suspect was a man called Peter Alphon, a drifter, who was later implicated in another attack on a woman, and who confessed to being the murderer for many years, until changing his story.

On 11 September, two cartridge cases that matched the bullets used were found in a bedroom of the Vienna Hotel in Maida Vale, London. A hotel employee, William Nudds, a man with a long criminal record, claimed the last person in that room was called James Ryan. Alphon had also stayed that the hotel the same night, but Valerie Storie failed to pick him out of an identity parade. Nudds told police that when he left the hotel, 'Ryan' had asked about the whereabouts of the 36A bus stop. Ryan would turn out to be Hanratty. Valerie Storie later picked Hanratty out of an identity parade (in which he was asked to speak to see if she could recognise his voice) and his fate was sealed. This is despite overwhelming evidence that he was innocent, including eyewitness accounts placing him at the other end of the country on the evening of the attacks, and the fact that France and Nudds, who helped implicate him, were themselves criminals and thus not the most reliable of witnesses.

Conspiracy theorists have suggested that Mrs Janet Gregsten and/or her later lover William Ewer conspired to hire a hitman to either frighten Michael Gregsten into returning to the marital fold, or to kill him so they could be free to have a relationship. To my knowledge, these theories have been without supportive evidence and remain speculation. In view of the following, I certainly consider Janet Gregsten to be as much a victim of the crime as her errant husband and his lover. Sadly, she died in 1995, but before her death she spoke to journalist Bob Woffinden for his book *Hanratty: The Final Verdict*, and said she was keen to assist with any enquiries into the case as for years following Hanratty's execution there were questions (including from herself) as to whether there had been enough evidence to convict him. She was particularly vexed regarding the issue of disclosure and whether the defence had been provided with all the evidence. She said:

> The defence has the right to have all the information. That's very important, because that's a part of the justice system which is all wrong in this country. If the defence has access to all the information, then maybe the end result would often have been different. I think the legal system stinks and what the police are doing stinks. If I can be involved in helping to put that right, I would be happy to do so.

If she had lived a year longer, she would, no doubt, have been dismayed by Home Secretary Michael Howard's introduction of the 1996 Criminal Procedure and Investigations Act, which allowed the police, once again, to decide what information to pass on to the defence and what not to disclose.[1] The police said that this Act was, at least in part, brought in to aid the position of informers. In other words, to protect the odious activities of career criminals, such as France and Nudds, upon whose evidence the prosecution built much of their case against Hanratty. The media interest in the police investigation was intense with great pressure and scrutiny, which may go some way to explaining the questionable tactics and actions that ensued. The baleful influence of the press may also go some way to explain the apparently inexplicable, and fatal for Hanratty, actions of the politicians who were in the Home Office at the time.

These continued until 1997, when, after thirty-five years of public questions and raised doubts about Hanratty's guilt, the CCRC was given the task of reviewing the case with a view to referring it back to the Court of Appeal. Unfortunately, several well-known politicians, of different political persuasions, were actively involved in the extraordinary litany of prevarication and obfuscation that had characterised the Home Office's responses to all attempts to review the case. These have included, among others, 'Rab' Butler, Reginald Maudling, Roy Jenkins, James Callaghan, and Michael Howard – all 'scions' of the political establishment.

In view of the fact the authorities had managed to grant a posthumous pardon to Timothy Evans, who was wrongly hanged for the murder of his wife and infant daughter, the reasons for the obstructive reticence in this case deserve an explanation. Surely it could not be on the grounds of setting a precedent. Could it have been treated in its overly secretive fashion merely because, unlike the Evans' case when serial killer John Christie was responsible, the Crown didn't have a suitable candidate for the murderer if Hanratty was exonerated? Whatever the reason, it didn't appear to be party political, as both Conservative and Labour Home Secretaries were involved. It should be noted that not one of these has deigned to discuss their reasons publicly – a fact which has only added to suspicions over the years.

The eventual involvement of the CCRC in 2002, some forty years after Hanratty was executed, was due to the efforts of tireless and highly vociferous campaigners, such as journalists Paul Foot and Bob Woffinden, neither of whom are still alive. They chronicled at great length, and in forensic detail, the weaknesses of the case against Hanratty, as well as the unedifying actions of the police, politicians, and the legal establishment in their attempts to shore up the original conviction (more of which later). They were helped by many other less well-known but equally committed and tireless campaigners, whose parts in the saga should not go unrecorded, such as members of the A6 Murder Committee and the Hanratty family. While I cite media interest as contributing to the pressures and notoriety of this case, I also want to point out that parts of that self-same media also played a full and valuable role in attempting to get the case reviewed. Such is life!

I have no intention of repeating the astonishing weaknesses in the case against Hanratty in full; although I would heartily recommend anyone with sufficient interest in this case to read at least one of the books in the bibliography, where the many flaws are laid out and to which I shall refer throughout my work.

I defy anyone who has read any of these books to be able to say that they did not harbour serious misgivings about the way the case was handled, by the legal and political elite of this country, for forty years until the second appeal hearing. I was astonished by the amount of information the campaigners' extraordinary efforts had managed to extricate from an obdurate establishment. For example, consider the following letter to Foot in late 1969 from the private secretary of Home Secretary James Callaghan in Foot's book *Who Killed Hanratty?*

Dear Mr Foot,

The Home Secretary has asked me to thank you for your letter of 21st November about the case of A6 murder and to say that he is sorry you have not had an earlier reply.

All Home Office criminal case papers are closed to public inspection for a period of 100 years under the provisions of the Public Records Acts and the Orders made by the Lord Chancellor under section 5(1) of the Act of 1958. At the inquest into the death of Mr Charles France the coroner decided that the letters he left before he died should not be made public, although two Members of Parliament have been permitted to see copies of them at the Home Office as an exceptional measure and against assurances that they would not disclose their contents. They do not however cast any doubt on the veracity of the evidence he gave at Hanratty's trial. The Home Secretary would be prepared to extend that concession to you on receipt of a similar assurance; but after careful consideration he regrets that he does not feel able to go further than this. You will appreciate that Home

Office papers on capital cases have been disclosed only in the most exceptional circumstances and never in a case as recent or controversial as this. Similarly it would be contrary to long established practice for officials to discuss an individual capital case in the way you envisage.

It should be noted that Section 5 (1) of the 1958 Act, referred to in this letter, as enacted, was drafted as follows:[2]

(1) Public records in the Public Record Office, other than those to which members of the public had access before their transfer to the Public Record Office, shall not be available for public inspection until they have been in existence for fifty years or such other period, either longer or shorter, as the Lord Chancellor may, with the approval, or at the request, of the Minister or other person, if any, who appears to him to be primarily concerned, for the time being prescribe as respects any particular class of public records.

This Act was later replaced by the Freedom of Information Act 2000.

The implications of this letter to Foot are quite staggering. It seems that, as a matter of course, the Home Office retained any documents that fell under the auspices of the Act for a period of 100 years without public access. Despite the Act stipulating that a period of fifty years would be normal, it was so widely drafted that the authorities could, should they choose, hide any documentation that they wished, for any length of time. Such a length of time seems inordinate anyway, especially since it does not appear to be an issue of national security, but what implications does this have for the Hanratty case?

One could reasonably ask what documentation is being hidden and why? It seems that some letters by France, which are related to this case, are being withheld. He is one of the pivotal characters in the whole story. In view of the claim that these do not cast any doubt on the veracity of the evidence he gave at Hanratty's trial, why are they *still* being withheld? What other documentation, which might be pertinent to the case, is also being kept hidden? In view of the long-lived interest in this case, it is hard to imagine that the Home Office has not reviewed this hidden documentation. To my knowledge, it has not only refused to release any of these materials, but it won't even provide a list of what documents are included. It is possible that, with the handover of this case to the CCRC, some, or all, of these documents may have been released, though I have no confirmation of this. In view of the fact none of the major participants in this case are still alive, one can reasonably ask whose interests are being served by this prohibition. Certainly not James Hanratty's.

Those who believe in his guilt will say that Mr Lewis Hawser QC was granted access to this documentation when he wrote a report in 1975, at the behest of the Home Secretary, which found the case against Hanratty 'overwhelming'. Unfortunately, when conducting his investigations, Mr Hawser was alone in being granted access to the documentation and gave no indication of what it contained. Strictly speaking, as highlighted in the letter to Foot, two MPs had earlier been granted access to France's letters, which he had left following his mysterious suicide a couple of weeks before Hanratty's execution, but only on the condition that they never revealed their contents. Mr Hawser also interviewed his witnesses in secret. Although the Hanratty campaigners were able to make submissions to him, they could not see any of this evidence or in any way cross-examine the witnesses he relied upon to compile his report. In addition, Foot highlights a series of 'blatant errors and innuendos' in the report that consistently overstated the case against Hanratty. Likewise, Woffinden referred to 'the many failings and unjustified bias' contained within the report. He also highlights that two legal journals, *Justice of the Peace,* and *New Law Journal*, were equally withering and condemnatory in their assessment of this report. Therefore, I feel that an unbiased observer would be hard put to consider this report as a definitive statement on the validity of the case against Hanratty; although, as we will see, this was not what the Court of Appeal thought in 2002.

It is interesting to note that Detective Chief Superintendent Roger Matthews was also asked by the Home Office to review the case when lawyer Geoffrey Bindman and Woffinden submitted their evidence of a mistrial to them in 1994. Like Hawser, he was able to review all the evidence held by the Home Office and, unlike Hawser, concluded that Hanratty was innocent and, furthermore, that he no longer supported capital punishment as a result. It was after this that the Home Office sent the case to the CCRC. It's also worth noting that the Court of Appeal subsequently ignored the evidence of this high-ranking police officer in contrast to its acceptance of the whole dubious police case throughout, which is a notable contradiction that is redolent of Wilson's aphorism at work.

When the case was finally again referred to the Court of Appeal, the hopes of those campaigning for the exoneration of Hanratty were high. After almost four decades of struggle, it seemed possible that the legal establishment was, at last, about to concede defeat, and acknowledge that Hanratty was innocent of this crime and had been fatally wronged. As we now know, those hopes were about to be dashed. The Forensic Science Service (FSS) produced a DNA 'rabbit out of the hat' which enabled the establishment to finally put the case to bed, having achieved its apparent aim of keeping the rationale behind its actions secret. A cynic might say, 'How convenient!' I, however, wanted to convince myself that it was the result of verified science, and therefore not open to question. It was in the light of this pitiful history of prevarication that I began my investigation into the case in 2007.

The Liverpool Alibi

I have no intention of trying to solve the vexed questions of who murdered Michael Gregston and raped and attempted to murder his girlfriend, Valerie Storie, whether there was a conspiracy behind the attack, and if so, who was behind it. At this stage, with all the protagonists dead, the chances of confirming these are vanishingly small. So much time has now passed that we will probably never know the truth of what happened, or who was responsible. I am, therefore, not interested in such imponderables; although the suicide of France, just prior to Hanratty's execution, still requires a satisfactory explanation. He was a previously friendly criminal associate of Hanratty who became a witness for the prosecution at the trial. It was he who told the police about the gun's hiding place, and whose final letters have been hidden away for at least 100 years by the Home Office, in an act that looks suspicious to say the least. Nevertheless, I am just interested in the single question of whether it has been proved 'beyond reasonable doubt' that James Hanratty was the assailant.

Although it is far from the only weakness in the case against Hanratty, I shall confine my discussion to a single area of argument – the Liverpool alibi. It contains what I consider to be irrefutable evidence for his innocence, regardless of any claims to the contrary.

This is pivotal because if it is confirmed – and to my mind it is – any subsequent DNA finding on Miss Storie's knickers must be the result of something other than the reason ascribed to it by the FSS (which, as we will see later, attributed the DNA to Hanratty being the rapist and appeared to dismiss the presence of DNA of another blood group, and the chance of contamination). This issue is the crux of the whole case and anything else pointing to Hanratty's guilt, including Miss Storie's often reiterated insistence that he was justly executed, is mistaken and an irrelevance. This is because, if Hanratty was in Liverpool on the evening of Tuesday, 22 August, no realistic mechanism existed for him to get to Dorney Reach by 9.30pm that evening. The only form of transport that might have managed this would have been a helicopter, and although the prosecution made some outrageous claims, and relied on some dubious criminals to furnish their case, not even they claimed that Hanratty could have had access to one of these.

Hanratty changed his alibi, from saying he had been in Liverpool for some days, to claiming that he travelled from Liverpool to Rhyl for some of the time, catching the bus at approximately 7.30pm on the evening of the attack. Unfortunately, he did this in the middle of the trial itself, which severely damaged his cause. It was at the trial that he provided the following account.[1]

He left the Vienna Hotel in London on the morning of 22 August at about 9.00am, having stayed there the previous night, and walked to Paddington Station. One 'key' witness for the prosecution, William Nudds, confirmed that Hanratty had indeed stayed there the previous night, and several witnesses, including another key prosecution witness, Dixie France, confirmed Hanratty's presence in London on August 21.

When Hanratty arrived at Paddington, he realised this was the wrong station for trains to Liverpool, so he got a taxi to Euston Station. After buying a return train ticket, he bought some magazines and stayed in the platform cafe awaiting the next train. There is some confusion about the precise train he caught, although he said it had a restaurant car. He said it left Euston at 10.55am or 11.55am, although the actual leaving times that morning, were 10.20am, 10.35am and 12.15pm, with subsequent arrivals at 2.22pm, 3.25pm and 4.45pm; in other words, the journey was approximately four hours. The reason for this discrepancy has not been confirmed but may simply be because Hanratty was trying to remember details of an event from several weeks earlier when giving his statements. It should also be borne in mind that he was known to have had a history of low educational standards. In his original statement he said that he arrived at about 3.30pm, although in court he revised that to between 4.00pm and 5.00pm. He had a wash and brush up, followed by a cup of tea, and then went to the left-luggage office to leave his case containing some stolen jewellery, which he hoped to sell on to some criminal associates he knew in the city. He described the left-luggage assistant as having a withered or turned hand.

After leaving the station he enquired about a Carlton Avenue or Tarlton Avenue, which he thought was the name of the street where his former cellmate Terry McNally lived. He thought McNally might be interested in the gems. A woman told him it was a two-penny bus ride up Scotland Road, so he caught the bus, alighted a few stops from Scotland Road, and went in to a sweet shop to make further enquiries. In his original statement to his solicitor, he said:

> Went into sweetshop and tobacconist. I asked for Carlton Avenue or Tarlton Avenue. She said no Carlton Road around there. Woman and young girl. I had pin-striped suit on. Woman came to the door of the shop and showed me the bus stop which was near it. The sweet shop is in the Scotland Road, opposite a picture house. A woman and young girl there. I asked them the way to Talbot Road, then said Carlton Road. The woman said this is Bank Hall and you have to get on a bus and go into town. Bank Hall joins Scotland Road. I did not get to Carlton Road.

He abandoned his search for Carlton Road, choosing instead to walk back into town and go to Lyons Café for a meal. On leaving Lyons, he approached a man on the steps leading up to a billiard hall and tried to sell him a gold watch, which was refused. The man tried to prevent Hanratty from going up the stairs, saying that the premises were licensed, although he did let him go inside to use the toilet.

This account highlighted three or four potentially corroborative witnesses: the left-luggage man with the turned or withered hand, the sweet shop lady and girl, as well as the billiard hall man. Again, unhappily for Hanratty's defence team, enquiries about these people were initially performed by the police, and the method of their investigation, as so often in this case, clouded the result with doubt. I shall take each of these key components of Hanratty's alibi in turn.

Lime Street Station

In the case of the man with the withered hand,[2] a Detective Chief Inspector (DCI) Harold Whiffen of Bedfordshire Constabulary had been present, for unknown reasons, when Hanratty first spoke at length to his solicitor about his defence. According to DCI Whiffen, Hanratty said the man had a withered *arm*, yet this was not what the solicitor, Mr Kleinman, heard, and in all the other statements made by Hanratty he said it was a withered or turned hand. DCI Whiffen, apparently without regard to solicitor interview confidentiality, reported this to his superiors, with the result that the police started investigating the left-luggage department in Lime Street Station. They found a regular attendant called Peter Usher, who was missing two fingers from his left hand. However, another employee called Peter Stringer, who normally worked in the gentlemen's toilet, would from time to time help in the left-luggage department, and he had an artificial arm. On the week in question, Mr Usher was supposedly on duty from 6.00am until 2.00pm, while Mr Stringer worked from 2.00pm till 10.00pm. However, the latter told the police it was not his custom to take the names of people who gave him luggage, as Hanratty had reported. He also said that he usually only helped in the left luggage after 8.30pm. Anyway, at the trial, although not at the earlier hearing, the prosecution produced Mr Stringer, who said he remembered nothing of Hanratty, though he had been on duty that day. In his summing up, Graham Swanwick, who was leading the prosecution, asked the jury to accept Mr Stringer as the man with the withered arm.

In the meantime, the defence representative had spoken to Mr Usher who *did* remember Hanratty. The representative, Mr Gillbanks, reported back by telephone that Mr Usher spoke about his name being on the ticket, mentioning the name 'Ratty', with an initial N or J, and that he was wearing a cap and a blue or dark suit. Mr Usher identified Hanratty from photographs, shown by the defence, and signed the one of Hanratty on the back. However, he said that the meeting probably took place between 11.00am and 12.30pm.

The timing was wrong, and so was the name given, since Hanratty's statement said that he used the name J. Ryan. However, Usher recognised Hanratty, and he fitted the description of the man with the withered hand. Foot, who interviewed Usher in 1970, wrote:

> Usher said he was interviewed by a senior officer from Liverpool police who came to interview him and showed him several books of photographs. He picked out five or six photographs of the man who had left the case with him. He asked the policeman if he had picked the right man and the officer replied 'We're neutral'. When Usher asked if he should be going to the trial instead of, or as well as, Stringer the officer said 'No we've got the man we want.' [Usher said] 'I'm sure that if I'd gone to trial I'd have identified Hanratty as the man. I certainly recognised him when his photograph was published in the papers after the trial.

So, why didn't the defence call Mr Usher? Foot says that, according to Mr Gillbanks' reports, he was keen to 'get in' on the courtroom scene, so they were worried about his performance. And of course, despite evidence to positively identify Hanratty at the left-luggage department, the times didn't fit. When discussing the train departure from Euston at 10.55am or 11.55am, Hanratty expressed a preference for the latter. Another fast train left earlier, at 10.20am, which arrived at 2.22pm, and like the 12.15pm train, this also had a restaurant car. The slower 10.35am train stopped at Crewe, which Hanratty thought his had done, and arrived at 3.25pm. This ties in most closely with Hanratty's original statement, in which he said he thought he arrived at about 3.30pm. I am unable to confirm if it also had a restaurant car, though if it did, it would seem to be the most likely train. In his 1970 interview with Foot, Usher explained that the hours he, Stringer and others worked at Lime Street were never very exact, with overtime ranging from half an hour to four hours being common. I have been unable to confirm whether he mentioned this point to Gillbanks. Whether he did or not, the failure to call Usher as a witness is, I believe, an unfortunate error on the part of Hanratty's team.

It appears that his left-luggage alibi was discounted due to a combination of police incompetence, or duplicity, and the inability of both Hanratty and Usher to be definite about the time of their interaction at Lime Street. Yet equally, if Usher is to be believed, he met a man who looked like Hanratty, who left a case and asked for the name Ratty N, or J, to be written on the left-luggage ticket, on the day in question. I find it hard to posit a scenario that explains these circumstances, other than the obvious one – that Hanratty and Usher did meet, regardless of the apparent anomalies between their individual accounts. The reader should understand that both were attempting to recount the details of a very fleeting meeting from several weeks earlier.

The Sweet Shop

On 16 October 1961, Detective Superintendent (DSU) Robert Acott, the officer in charge of the murder investigation team, wrote to the chief of Liverpool CID. The third paragraph was as follows:[3]

> Hanratty says that after he left Lime Street station he called at a sweet shop in Scotland Road, Liverpool, where he asked a woman who was accompanied by a child, to direct him to Carlton Road or Talbot Road. The purpose of this inquiry by Hanratty is not known.

As a result of this letter, Liverpool police soon found the sweet shop – one of twenty-nine they visited in all – at 408 Scotland Road. Although she was not the owner of the shop, the woman who had been working there that day was Mrs Olive Dinwoodie. She told them that she did indeed remember a young man coming into the shop, while she was serving, and asking the way to Carlton or Tarlton Road, or something of the kind.

Again, the police failed to do their job correctly. Procedure required them to show Mrs Dinwoodie several photographs of various men, but only one of Hanratty, to see if she would pick him out. Instead, they just showed her one photograph of Hanratty. Later, she was shown a requisite selection of photographs, including a different one of Hanratty, and she promptly picked him out again as being the man who came into her shop. Nevertheless, this procedural error allowed her identification of Hanratty to be subsequently 'questioned' by the prosecution at the trial.[4]

She confirmed that she had only worked two days that week, because she'd been taken ill. She worked Monday 21 August, from approximately 12.00pm until 6.00pm, and Tuesday 22 August, when she served all day. She had fallen ill that Tuesday evening after work and didn't return that week, so meeting Hanratty could only have happened on one or other of these two days. However, at this point, the police brought up the girl from Hanratty's statement. This caused her to say, albeit uncertainly according to Foot, that the discussion must have taken place on Monday 21 August. This was because her 13-year-old granddaughter, Barbara Ann Ford, had helped her in the shop 'all day' on the Monday.

When interviewed later by the police, Miss Ford also remembered that someone had come in and had been asking directions to Carlton Road. She also confirmed that she had been in the sweet shop helping her grandmother 'all day' on the Monday. You will see that both Mrs Dinwoodie and Miss Ford used the term 'all day' for their working time on the Monday, and that Mrs Dinwoodie's day was from 12.00pm to 6.00pm. However, Miss Ford's start time is not noted, so her actual working hours that day remain unconfirmed.

She said that on Tuesday, she went to Liverpool city centre, with her friend Linda Walton, to buy dress material, and on the way back they had called in at the shop at 4.45pm for approximately half an hour. So, like Mrs Dinwoodie, she said the meeting must have been on Monday for the same reason – she only worked in the shop that day. When the police interviewed Miss Walton, she confirmed that she and Barbara had been into the town centre for dress material, and that they had stopped off at the sweet shop on their return. However, she thought they got there just after 4.00pm and stayed rather longer, for about an hour.

Liverpool police duly wrote to DSU Acott on 24 October and detailed these findings. He, in yet another piece of abject – if not criminal –

police behaviour, didn't inform Hanratty's defence team. Instead, for some reason, he sat on this crucially important news. He waited until the committal proceedings where, under heated cross-examination from Mr Sherrard, he eventually admitted that Hanratty had been identified by Mrs Dinwoodie as calling at her shop on either 21 or 22 August.[5] After this delay, the defence team of Mr Kleinman and Mr Gillbanks set to work, and obtained statements from Mrs Dinwoodie, and both Barbara Ford and Linda Walton. Unlike the statements to the police, these were made available to Paul Foot. In his book, Foot says that, as inferred by DSU Acott at the committal proceedings at Ampthill, there was still considerable doubt in the minds of all three about the date of Hanratty's visit. However, Mrs Dinwoodie's statement explains, that while she couldn't have said whether it was the Monday or Tuesday, her mind had been made up by Hanratty's mention of there being a girl with her.

> I thought he meant the girl was serving with me. ...It must have been Monday or Tuesday. It could not have been any other day as I was not in for a fortnight from the Tuesday night. If it had not mentioned to me that a young girl was serving in the shop I would not have known which day it was. However, I do remember the man coming in.

Barbara Ford's statement assigned the visit to the Monday for the same reason: 'I think it was the Monday because I was serving on the Monday and not the Tuesday,' she said.

However, Linda Walton's short statement read:

> I was in town all day with my friend Barbara Ford. We had been to buy some green dress material and we got back to the shop about four or quarter past. Mrs Dinwoodie was serving. She was by herself. I don't know Mr John Cowley [the shop owner was Mr David Cowley]. People were coming in and out of the shop – men and women. Quite a number of men came in, some in groups, some by themselves. Some of the men I knew but

others I could not recognise. We stayed a good bit – about an hour I think. She, Barbara was standing in front of the counter most of the time with me, **but when children wanted serving she went behind the counter to serve them.**[6]

[My use of bold]

This was crucial, because in addition to extending the time the girls were in the shop, it meant that despite what Mrs Dinwoodie and Barbara Ford had said about Hanratty's visit *'definitely'* being on the Monday because Barbara had only served on the Monday, she had been behind the counter for a short period on the Tuesday. As it hadn't been 'work', neither party had recalled it.

However, these statements to the police claiming Hanratty had visited the sweet shop on the Monday were giving the prosecution a serious headache. This was because several of their other witnesses had already testified at the committal proceedings that Hanratty was in London on Monday 21 August, which meant that, if they were right, Hanratty could not have visited the sweet shop on Monday. To have acknowledged that they were wrong, at this stage, would have damaged large sections of the prosecution case. The prosecution would have probably fallen apart. Remember, if he was in Liverpool on the Tuesday evening when the attack happened, the case against him had no foundation and he must be innocent.

The evidence for Hanratty being in London on the Monday is overwhelming, and unchallenged, as detailed by Foot. Firstly, he put his green suit into the cleaners at Burtol's in Swiss Cottage at about 11.00am, as confirmed by their register. Then Dixie France, along with his wife and one of their daughters, confirmed that Hanratty visited them at their flat in Boundary Road, just off the Finchley Road, about 2.30pm and stayed until about 6.30pm, ostensibly to collect some washing that he had left with Mrs Charlotte France the day before (she seemed to have been unaware of her husband and Hanratty's criminal activities). They all remembered the day because Carol, the daughter, had been to the dentist to have a tooth out and was lying recovering on the sofa. The dentist, Dr Hillman, confirmed the time of the extraction as 2.00pm on Monday 21 August.

It should be noted that the France family, although friends with Hanratty before his arrest, refused to have anything to do with him, or his defence team thereafter, and France was central to the sending of Hanratty to the hangman's noose, so their corroboration of his story is worth a little consideration. Although Foot doesn't mention the possibility, a cynic might say that they colluded with Hanratty to back up his story. However, this should be considered in the light of France's suicide prior to Hanratty's execution, and the fact he was a key witness for the prosecution. Although I believe France to have been capable of severe dishonesty, I think this part of the story is more likely to be true than not.

Thereafter, Hanratty visited the Rehearsal Club in Archer Street, Soho, twice, as confirmed by Ann Pryce, who was a waitress at the club. He had bought her a drink and chatted with her, mostly about the fact that his hair had recently been dyed black by Carol France. He first arrived at about 5.30pm and left at about 7.00pm, before returning somewhere between 8.00pm and 9.30pm and staying until approximately 10.00pm. From there, he caught a taxi to Baker Street and went to the Broadway House Hotel, where he was seen by the manager at approximately 11.30pm. This hotel was the master hotel for a group of four other hotels and he went to one of them – the Vienna Hotel –where the register contained his signature, and where the habitual criminal William Nudds, another of the prosecution's 'star' witnesses, confirmed seeing him arrive at about midnight. Again, there seems to be little advantage to Nudds to make up testimony that supported Hanratty's explanation of his whereabouts. This is especially so since he had a close and, some would say, murky involvement in the subsequent finding of the empty cartridge cases from the murder weapon in the room that Hanratty had occupied, although it is not beyond the realms of possibility. However, since the manager of the Broadway House Hotel corroborated his story, it would seem to have been true.

While this is a long list of confirmed sightings, it does have a couple of hours missing between the two visits to the Rehearsal Club. Hanratty said he went to Hendon dog track, followed by a trip to Leicester Square Underground Station, to collect a pigskin briefcase containing the stolen goods he hoped to sell on to a fence in Liverpool the next day. He then made a short visit to a prostitute, of whom he was a regular client, in a room over a club near the Palace Theatre. There are no witnesses to his movements in these two hours, at least none that I can find. However, as his alibi checks out in so many other details, I see no reason to assume that Hanratty did anything other than what he said he did.

This list of sightings accounts for most of the day, and I can see nowhere that contains a gap large enough for Hanratty to have fitted in a visit to Liverpool. Especially when you consider this was 1961, and that the transport system was more primitive than today. According to Woffinden, Mr Swanwick claimed, during questioning of DSU Acott, that it would have been possible to get from Liverpool to Dorney Reach by either an air or train service, though no evidence to corroborate this was ever produced. As noted, the one-way train journey from Liverpool to London would have taken at least four hours, and that is without the necessary onward journey to Dorney Reach. It is unlikely the same journey would have taken less time by car. To me, this is the strongest possible confirmation that Hanratty visited Liverpool on the Tuesday, and that Olive Dinwoodie and Barbara Ford were mistaken in assigning the visit to the Monday.

In response to this apparent collapse of their case against Hanratty, the police made frantic enquiries in December 1961 and the first weeks of January 1962, and managed to unearth a new witness, Albert Cecil Harding, whose evidence was not served on the defence until after the trial had begun. He was a friend of the Cowley family, the sweet shop owners, and he worked as a supervisor in a small delivery firm. Every morning and evening, on his way to and from work, he would visit the sweet shop for cigarettes, and, occasionally, to help serve. He said that on Monday 21 August, he had come back from work at about 5.30pm to find Olive Dinwoodie and Barbara Ford in the shop, and Mrs Dinwoodie had told him about a man asking for 'Tarleton Road'. Then, on the Tuesday, he had gone into the shop at 7.00pm and Mrs Dinwoodie was not there.

Yet his logbooks, which were supplied to the defence with his statement, did not tally with this. According to Foot, his 'daily record of hours worked', showed that on Monday he finished at 6.00pm, and on Tuesday at 5.45pm. So, on the Monday, he apparently visited the sweet shop thirty minutes before he left work, while, on the Tuesday, he took an hour and a quarter to cover the three minutes' journey from his workplace to the sweet shop.

As an attempt to escape the horns of their dilemma – how to prove Hanratty could be in Liverpool on Monday 21 August when many of their own witnesses had confirmed he was in London – the prosecution resorted to what is probably the most far-fetched claim of all. In his summing up, Mr Swanwick said there were two possible scenarios to explain things: either it was not Hanratty in Liverpool on the Monday but someone who looked like him, or that the France family could have been mistaken when they said he had been to their house for four hours on the Monday; and so, by inference, were all the other witnesses who attested to his presence in London that day. Rather than attack his own witnesses, he preferred the explanation that it had been a case of mistaken identity in Liverpool. He then claimed that Hanratty *bought* the information about this sweet shop visit to use as his alibi. To spell out how absurd this is – which it seems Mr Swanwick did not do – it means that Hanratty, on discovering he is wanted for murder, travels to Liverpool to buy an alibi, and that one man there, who looks remarkably like Hanratty, is found, and furnishes him with the alibi. This alibi requires this unknown lookalike being able to say, several weeks later, 'I remember on that day, going into a sweet shop in Scotland Road to ask the way to Tarleton Road. A lady was there with a child. She told me to go back into town. You can pretend this was you, which will help with your alibi.'

There is one final point about this preposterous claim that needs to be considered carefully: why on earth would Hanratty buy an alibi for the wrong day? The obvious situation here, which I suspect even DSU Acott, Mr Swanwick and Mr Justice Gorman, who presided over the case, knew perfectly well, was this: Hanratty was in Liverpool at the sweet shop at around 5.00pm on Tuesday 22 August. As the sweet shop witnesses have corroborated his story, it would seem to have been true. There is no other viable explanation. His alibi was watertight.

The Billiard Hall

Hanratty claimed that after leaving the sweet shop he travelled back to town, and then, after a few more desultory inquiries about Carlton Road, decided to give up the search and go for a meal and a cup of tea in Lyons Cafe, next door to Lime Street Station. After this, he made a languid attempt to sell his gold wristwatch to a man on the steps of a billiard hall who declined the offer, and who also told Hanratty that he could not go upstairs to the billiard hall as it was a licensed premises. However, he did let Hanratty briefly enter the hall to go to the toilet. The defence team made enquiries and located Mr Kempt, the proprietor of Reynolds Billiard Hall in Lime Street. He agreed that it was his usual practice to stand on the steps outside the hall between 6.00pm and 7.00pm when the hall was less busy. He confirmed that a man had tried to sell him a watch, and that he had initially refused him access to the hall, before relenting to let him use the bathroom. He could not confirm the date, but he said it was before 26 August as that was when his holiday had started. He could not identify the young man, though he said he was in his mid-twenties.[7] Here, again, another part of Hanratty's story seems to be corroborated, unless, as a cynic might say, he bought this alibi as well. Mr Kempt confirms that Hanratty was in Lime Street, Liverpool at some time between 6.00pm and 7.00pm, on the Tuesday evening that he was supposed to be in Dorney Reach in Buckinghamshire less than three hours later.

I have explained the pivotal nature of this alibi to show why the Rhyl alibi, despite its undoubtedly contentious handling by the courts, is not the crux of the case. (As noted earlier, Hanratty changed his story during the trial, possibly in panic, to state that he caught a bus to Rhyl at about 7.30pm that Tuesday evening and subsequently stayed in a bed and breakfast in that Welsh resort. Several witnesses from Rhyl supported this claim in court).

I hope to have shown 'beyond reasonable doubt' that Hanratty was in Liverpool on the early evening of Tuesday 22 August. The chances of these witnesses – Mr Usher, Mrs Dinwoodie, Miss Ford, Miss Walton, and Mr Kempt – *all* lying or being mistaken, are vanishingly slim. The chances that he could have travelled to Liverpool and back again, at some unspecified time on the Monday, are even slimmer. Claiming that he *bought* the sweet shop alibi, but did so for the wrong day, is just preposterous.

The fact that a combination of lamentable police work and positively outrageous tactics from the prosecution led the trial jury to not understand the importance of this question, can be laid at the door of the judge in this case, Mr Justice Gorman. He, alongside DSU Acott and Mr Swanwick, should be held responsible for the hanging of an innocent man. It is obvious from the note of incredulity in his summing up, he knew perfectly well where the truth lay, but he did nothing to stop the jury from being bamboozled and misled by an outrageous prosecution case. He said:

> It is suggested that this is an invented or bought enquiry. You have to consider the position and you have to determine what view you form, because the prosecution has not hesitated to say – and I make no comment; I make no complaint – that this alibi at Liverpool was the result of a journey made to Liverpool at some time by this man, seeking to buy an alibi with the £250 which he is supposed to have told Dixie [France] that he had in the railway embankment. That was put to him as a suggestion. Now it merits very anxious consideration.[8]

If this is all that the judge is going to say about an obviously flawed prosecution case when a man's life is at stake, it doesn't say a great deal about the merits of the English judicial system.

The Hawser Report

I shall finish this – in my opinion – clear evidence for Hanratty's innocence, by highlighting how the 'definitive' report by Lewis Hawser

QC, compiled in 1975, more than a decade after the execution, dealt with this whole Liverpool alibi. Regarding the sweet shop discussion, Hawser conceded that it must have happened, and that if it had taken place on the Tuesday then Hanratty could not be guilty.[9]

But he fails to consider this, adding, 'This is so unlikely that it can be ignored. My assessment is that the incident occurred on Monday.' That's it. No explanation for this conclusion, or for the fact that he completely ignored all the witness statements for the prosecution that put Hanratty in London at the time, is provided. This is the level of forensic scrutiny exhibited throughout what was obviously a flawed investigation.

And then we come to the much-trumpeted DNA evidence, which stands in direct opposition to this overwhelming case for Hanratty being in Liverpool only two to three hours before the attack at Dorney Reach. How can this possibly be? As no realistic mechanism existed for him to have been able to be in both places, one of these contradictory *proofs* must be wrong. Those who still profess doubts about this alibi, including, as we will see, Lord Justice Leveson, need to explain how Hanratty managed this feat without access to a helicopter. I would love to hear their explanations as I am unable to offer a realistic suggestion, though I always remain willing to be enlightened.

So how sound is the DNA finding from the Court of Appeal 2002 hearing? To put it simply, for this verdict to be correct required Hanratty to have access to a helicopter to achieve the otherwise impossible feat of travelling from Liverpool to Dorney Reach in under 3 hours. The answer to this fundamental question, as this work will show, is not sound at all.

The BBC Horizon Programme

When I started that fateful university project, my knowledge of the Hanratty case was limited to a single reading of Bob Woffinden's book. As noted, I was more than a little perturbed by the media reporting of the Court of Appeal judgment, where the DNA finding had emphatically trumped all evidence from the CCRC and the appellant's team. It made me wonder how both the DNA and non-DNA evidence had been assessed and weighed against each other. What criteria had been used for discounting all the other evidence? Was the court saying that the other evidence gathered was not in good faith? Did the judges consider this evidence to be genuine but mistaken, or had they just ignored it? Even more importantly, considering the credence that was being attached to the DNA evidence, what procedures had been followed by the court to ensure that this DNA evidence was valid and safe?

As I pondered these important questions, I considered the fact that the judiciary operates a system of precedent, where the reasoning employed by a higher court almost always determines how lower courts will treat similar situations. Therefore, the implications of this ruling could spread far wider than just this single case.

Before considering the judgment in some detail, I obtained copies of the book by Paul Foot, as well as *Deadman's Hill: Was Hanratty Guilty?* by Lord Russell of Liverpool. After reading these, I formulated an outline of the concerns, which I have detailed thus far. I had seen the BBC *Horizon* programme when it was broadcast more than four years earlier, and from that I had gained the strong impression that the deciding factor in the case had been the presence of Hanratty's

DNA on Valerie Storie's knickers, and that no other male DNA was present.

How could this DNA evidence be correct if Hanratty was in Liverpool? The die-hard Hanratty opponents will say that DNA can never lie, and that the science should be trusted. For obvious reasons I was not so sure. I knew that DNA forensic attribution is far from a cut-and-dried scientific certainty, as I shall explain later. Instead, it requires 'interpretation' by the expert practitioner to be placed within the correct context. Could there be something wrong with the DNA evidence, or its interpretation, which had been relied on so heavily by this Court of Appeal? I began to review the transcript of *Horizon*, which was broadcast on 16 May 2002,[1] very shortly after the Court of Appeal judgment was published. It is clear it must have been in production for some time prior to the hearing. However, in view of the judgment in this case, the important area to consider is this: what did the programme say about the DNA evidence that was furnished by the scientists from the FSS?

The FSS was a government-owned British company that applied forensic science techniques to evidence retrieved in criminal or civil cases to prove or disprove methods used, identify guilty parties, and rule out the innocent. It was dissolved in 2012, with the government citing monthly losses of £2 million. Regarding DNA testing, on which the FSS relied heavily, here are the dates of when various types of DNA tests became available. The information is taken from *Factsheet Number 2* titled 'What is DNA?' from the FSS website, which has since been taken down:

1990 – Single Locus Profiling (SLP) replaces the less sensitive Multi Locus Profiling.

1994 – Short Tandem Repeat (STR) technique introduced.

1995 – Second Generation Multiplex (SGM) used to generate the first profiles for the NDNAD [National DNA Database]. It looked at (six STR Loci, plus a sex indicator area) to generate a profile. The average discriminating power of a full SGM profile is in the order of one in fifty million.

1999 – June SGM Plus® replaced SGM testing. It looks at (ten STR loci plus a sex indicator area). The average discriminating power of a full SGM Plus is less than one in a billion.

DNA Low Copy Number is an extension of the SGM Plus profiling technique. It is more sensitive and enables scientists to produce DNA profiles from samples containing very few cells even if they are too small to be visible to the naked eye.

Please note, the dates given here for the introduction of the SGM and SGM Plus® tests – 1995 and 1999 – will contradict the dates implied in *Horizon* and in the Court of Appeal hearing. This is just one of several examples of confusing, and possibly incorrect, FSS documentation that we will encounter.

Initial Testing

In 1961, when the murder of Michael Gregsten and the rape and attempted murder of Valerie Storie were being investigated, there was no such thing as forensic DNA testing, so the testing that could be done was minimal. Here is an extract from *Horizon*, in which Roger Mann, a scientist from the FSS, was being interviewed:

> ROGER MANN: Exhibit 26, Valerie Storie's knickers. There was semen found on those at the time. It was possible in those days to obtain a blood group from a semen sample and a blood group was obtained from the semen on Valerie Storie's knickers. Now this was found to be Group O. Michael Gregsten was not a Group O, so this established that the semen didn't, in fact, come from him.

> NARRATOR: This routine test ruled out Valerie Storie's boyfriend, Michael Gregsten, but in 1961 forensic science could go no further than blood typing and a group O blood type still included 40% of the male population, so Exhibit 26, with its telltale trace of the killer, was filed away and forgotten.

Gregsten's blood type was group AB, as was reported by DSU Acott, following tests done at the Metropolitan Police Laboratory. As we will see later, some group AB seminal fluid was also recovered from Miss Storie's underwear, and was assumed to belong to her boyfriend, Gregsten. However, the use of an assumption to describe this attribution means that this was not confirmed. It thus opens the door to the possibility that this AB semen belonged to the rapist and was not from Gregsten at all. I shall return to this point later.

DNA Testing

Decades later, after the advent of the science of DNA profiling, originally developed by Professor Sir Alec Jeffreys at Leicester University in the mid 1980s, the possibility of making a breakthrough in this highly contentious case began to be explored. More from *Horizon*:

> NARRATOR: Scientists knew that Exhibit 26 could hold a vital clue to the killer's identity if only they could resurrect DNA from the decayed thirty-year-old evidence. The tiny piece of fabric was immersed in sterile solution, shaken and centrifuged. Chemicals were added to destroy any cellular debris, the DNA-rich fluid refined to produce a clear, colourless liquid containing pure DNA. Each drop of refined solution will usually contain hundreds of strands of DNA, but with evidence as old as this the question was if the minute amount of DNA extracted would be enough to create a profile.
>
> SCIENTIST, JOHN BARK: The fabric was taken, DNA was extracted from it and the technology at the time was applied, but unfortunately no profile was obtained.

It will be confirmed later that the test applied in 1995 was the STR/QUAD test, as opposed to the SGM test, which was introduced in 1995 according to the FSS website. However, the science was moving forward at considerable speed, and a new development in 1997 enabled the FSS scientists to revisit the case again.

> NARRATOR: In 1997 DNA work began again on the Hanratty case. Scientists were prompted to start retesting because a new piece of evidence, called Exhibit 35, had emerged from the police files. The murder weapon and ammunition found in the bus had been wrapped in a man's white handkerchief. Now scientists decided to renew their attempts at DNA profiling, testing the handkerchief and also the remaining fragments of Valerie Storie's underwear. They had failed two years earlier but were now hopeful because of advances in a DNA copying technique called PCR.

This is slightly misleading in that it cannot mean the introduction of polymerase chain reaction (PCR), since the Cetus Corporation team had developed the first commercial PCR typing kit for forensic use (DQA1), in 1988.[2] I must assume that it refers to the introduction of the SGM technique in 1995. This would seem to raise the question of why SGM wasn't used in the 1995 testing, though this may just be down to the timing of the test versus the introduction of the procedure. However, what is not clear is which technology the 1997 test used. The implication from what follows is that it was LCN, and yet the FSS website gave the date of introduction of SGM Plus® as 1999, with no date for the introduction of LCN, though, as explained earlier in FSS *Factsheet Number 2*, it will have been after the introduction of SGM Plus®. Back to *Horizon*:

> NARRATOR: Sometimes called molecular photocopying the polymerase chain reaction is a remarkable technique used to magnify small quantities of DNA. ...Each cycle of PCR doubles the target DNA. By repeating the process scientists can soon have billions of exact copies of the DNA they want to test. **The minute quantities of DNA extracted from both exhibits**

were subjected to thirty-four separate cycles of PCR magnification and this time there were results.

SCIENTIST, JONATHAN WHITAKER: When we generated profiles from the handkerchief and the knickers, the first observation we saw was that these DNA profiles matched each other and this is what we would expect to find if they'd originated from the same person.

NARRATOR: The same matching DNA profile appearing on both exhibits meant that for the first time evidence had been linked forensically – **science suggesting that the person who had raped Valerie Storie had also handled the murder weapon.**

I have stressed, in bold type, a couple of statements in this section of the transcript. Firstly, that the testing involved thirty-four cycles of PCR magnification. This is of the utmost importance because it confirms that the test applied was the highly contentious version of the SGM Plus® test, developed by FSS scientists, and known as LCN testing. Standard SGM Plus® testing only performs twenty-eight cycles of magnification. LCN testing is intended to reduce the size of the sample of DNA from which the scientists can isolate a usable profile. The problem is the smaller the size of the DNA sample, the greater the likelihood of problems with the results, as will be detailed later. The second point, which suggests that Valerie Storie's rapist had handled the murder weapon, and which was critical in the handling of the 2002 hearing, is incorrect and will be discussed in the next chapter.

The programme then stated that FSS scientists took DNA samples from James Hanratty's brother Michael in November 1997, and from his mother, Mary, in April 1998. Finally, on 22 March 2001, Hanratty's body was exhumed, and DNA material was recovered from him. In view of the revelation at the 2002 hearing that the actual DNA samples taken from him, and subsequently tested, were composites, which means they came from more than one sample of Hanratty's DNA material, one must ask why was this the case, and what does this say about the reliability of the FSS case against Hanratty?

It should be noted that the only peer-reviewed papers published by the FSS into its controversial LCN testing were:

'An investigation of the rigor of interpretation rules for STRs derived from less than 100 pg [picogram] of DNA', the abstract of which reads:

> By increasing the PCR amplification regime to 34 cycles, we have demonstrated that it is possible routinely to analyse <100 pg DNA. ...The analysis of mixtures by peak area measurement becomes increasingly difficult as the sample size is reduced. Laboratory-based contamination cannot be completely avoided, even when analysis is carried out under stringent conditions of cleanliness. A set of guidelines that utilises duplication of results to interpret profiles originating from picogram levels of DNA is introduced. ...The method used is complex, yet can be converted into an expert system. We envisage this to be the next step.[3]

The second paper, 'A comparison of the characteristics of profiles produced with the AMPFlSTR(R) SGM Plus(TM) multiplex system for both standard and low copy number (LCN) STR DNA analysis', notes that:

> DNA STR profiles have been generated from 1 ng and low copy number (LCN) templates using 28 and 34 cycles of amplification, respectively. ...Analysis of the data allows us to develop sets of guidelines appropriate for interpreting both single and mixed DNA profiles.[4]

There is no information regarding who peer reviewed these papers, which in view of the storm of criticism this technique provoked in the global forensic DNA community raises further questions about the acceptability of its use on Hanratty's exhumed remains, especially considering the clear proximity of these publication dates with the exhumation. How much validation testing of the technique had been performed to confirm its reliability for use in this case? Serious concerns are being glossed over here.

While the test in March 1995 used the STR/QUAD technique, the 1997/1998 tests, including those involving Hanratty's relatives, involved the SGM technique, seeming to contradict the Horizon program transcript above, as will be confirmed by the test results shown later. In other words, the test looked only at six loci and had a discriminatory power of roughly one in 50 million. However, the post exhumation tests used SGM Plus® or LCN, as described in *Horizon*, with a discriminatory power of – supposedly – more than one in a billion. Although not discussed in the programme, this more powerful test was also seemingly run against the samples from Michael and Mary, but it is not clear whether these entailed further swabs being taken from them both. We will see that confusion concerning the sample sources and the type of testing involved continues in the Court of Appeal. Nevertheless, regarding these tests, Dr Whitaker, speaking on *Horizon*, said:

> JONATHAN WHITAKER: We calculated that it was 2.5 million times more likely of obtaining the DNA profile from the underwear and the handkerchief if it had originated from a son of and a brother of Mary and Michael, as compared to somebody unknown and unrelated to them.

There is no evidence in the public domain regarding how such a figure had been arrived at, so how could I attach any credence to it? And more to the point, what did it mean considering the supposed discriminatory powers involved? The use and understanding of these statistical likelihoods are another area that is mired in controversy, as will be discussed later.

I am assuming that the 2001 test on James Hanratty's remains involved the use of the LCN profiling technique, in view of the references to the minute size of the original sample and the thirty-four cycles of PCR, with a proposed discriminatory power of one in a billion.

But strangely this is not confirmed anywhere within the programme, or the Court of Appeal transcripts. Back to *Horizon*:

> JOHN BARK: We were able to obtain DNA from the remains and when we compare that DNA point by point with the DNA that we'd found on the handkerchief and on the knickers we found no discrepancies. We had a match there and therefore this considerably strengthened the evidence that we were looking at DNA from James Hanratty rather than anybody else in the population.
>
> NARRATOR: The DNA found on the exhibits was hundreds of millions of times more likely to have come from James Hanratty than a random member of the public.

As we will see, Dr Whitaker confirmed at the Court of Appeal hearing that Hanratty's exhumed DNA was a composite. Whatever he might have meant by such a statement, which unfortunately was not examined further during his testimony, this raises additional questions regarding the results of such testing, and what they could be said to mean. We will also see that the DNA profiles recovered from the knickers and handkerchief were nowhere near fully matching *each other*, let alone Hanratty as stated by Mr Bark. Also, from the statements made in this programme, it appears that the testing was the LCN test and, as we will see, this is a technique mired in controversy. Back to *Horizon*:

> NARRATOR: So those who believed James Hanratty to be innocent now had to explain how else, apart from at the murder itself, his DNA profile can have got onto the crime scene evidence and as they began to look into the science of DNA it did seem as though there were serious grounds to question the results. **What scientists call contamination is a genuine and alarming outcome of PCR** … . But the forensic scientists are absolutely confident that their DNA results are unaffected by contamination … . Their confidence stems from a simple act of

logic. **If James Hanratty is not the killer then where is the killer's DNA? For scientists can only find one male profile on the exhibits.**

ROGER MANN: We only have one profile. That profile matches James Hanratty. If that was a contaminant, if that was due to contamination we would expect two profiles, one from James Hanratty due to the contamination and one from the original killer.

NARRATOR: But the DNA undoubtedly is James Hanratty's and the theory this DNA was deposited there by contamination does not explain why only a single male profile, Hanratty's, has been found on the crime scene exhibits. For the police this is conclusive.

As this programme provided virtually no information regarding how this *certainty* was arrived at, I went to the FSS itself for an understanding of this crucial information. As I have already stated, the FSS was unwilling to furnish answers to my questions, so I sought information from its website. As the government had closed the FSS and hived off its work to private sector suppliers in March 2012, the information from its now-removed website is no longer verifiable at all. This is unfortunate, as one of my priorities is to ensure that my sources are attributable and repeatable. Nevertheless, I shall continue to detail the information that was on the FSS site as of 2007.

Firstly, it provided several case studies of high-profile criminal cases where DNA profiling had been crucial to the outcome. These ranged in time, from the murders of Linda Mann and Dawn Ashworth by Colin Pitchfork (convicted in 1988), through to the murders of Holly Wells and Jessica Chapman by Ian Huntley (convicted in 2005). The Pitchfork case was the first in the world where DNA evidence led to the conviction. The testing in that case was performed by Professor Jeffreys, the inventor of DNA profiling, at Leicester University. Interestingly, the FSS did not publish a case study for the Hanratty conviction which, considering its notoriety, is at the least surprising, if not suspicious, especially in view of the FSS's involvement with the *Horizon* program on this case. There was no mention of the case at all, nor was any mention made of the specific tests involved. However, in addition to the information in *Factsheet Number 2*, detailed above, the FSS made the following comments about the LCN technique in its *Factsheet Number 6*:

> As with all forensic evidence, the context and interpretation need to be considered carefully. This is even more important with DNA LCN, due to its sensitivity and the possibility that the DNA detected is unconnected with the offence under investigation.
>
> DNA LCN has the same discriminating power as the routine technique – about one in a billion. This means that if the DNA found at a crime scene matched a suspect, then the chance of obtaining the profile if it had originated from someone other than and unrelated to that suspect, is approximately one in a billion.

What is not made clear here is that the LCN test is an extremely controversial extension of the SGM Plus® test, which the manufacturer limits to twenty-eight cycles only. It was developed by among others Dr Whitaker and his colleague Dr, now Professor, Peter Gill, at the FSS, and, as noted, requires a smaller size of usable DNA sample, which means there can be greater problems with the results. The technique is so controversial it is only authorised for use in criminal courts in Great Britain and a few other countries. Interestingly, this did not stop prosecutors, in countries where it is not approved, from outsourcing the work to the FSS for considerable sums of money. As the FSS seemed to regard LCN as its default test from Hanratty forwards, the likelihood is that this science was being presented in many of these cases, which raises many questions. For example, another equally controversial case that utilised this technique was the Amanda Knox case in Italy, which just confirms how contentious this technique is among the global forensic community. As this is outside the scope of my work, I have not pursued this line of enquiry.

The FBI and the American courts still do not accept it as valid.[5] The Scientific Working Group on DNA Analysis Methods had led the criticism of the FSS and this method, and its 2014 document just referenced lists the acceptance criteria that American laboratories would need to pass to be able to use such testing. These are far beyond the standards applied by the FSS. Unfortunately, our political and judicial authorities for unclear reasons ignored this controversy and allowed this technique to be used unquestioningly for many years after the Hanratty hearing.

Conclusion

The woefully uncritical and potentially misleading *Horizon* programme tells us virtually nothing about the actual testing that was done. Nor does it provide any justifications for the scientific certainty exhibited by Dr Whitaker and Mr Mann regarding the veracity of the attribution of the DNA to Hanratty, nor, and potentially far more importantly, for their critical discounting of contamination. It seems that their whole argument for Hanratty's guilt, relied on finding one male DNA profile on the fragment of Valerie Storie's knickers which, as I explain later, is blatantly untrue. They make virtually no mention of the DNA found on the handkerchief, which seems of secondary importance to these scientists. Yet, as will be shown in the next chapter, it was the DNA found on the handkerchief that played a pivotal, and completely misunderstood, role in the deliberations of the Court of Appeal.

I shall revisit a number of these areas in more detail later, but for now, having failed to unearth any reliable information from the FSS concerning the testing that it had performed, I decided to turn my attention to the Court of Appeal judgment. Remember, I was trying to understand how the court regarded the wealth of evidence pointing to Hanratty's innocence, against this 'startling' DNA result, and what this might mean for future cases where DNA information contradicts other evidence. How could the court be so sure that the DNA testing was valid? Had it subjected the evidence to proper scrutiny? Had the testing been externally verified by suitably trained forensic specialists? Had the court understood the importance of the Liverpool alibi, and the wealth of other evidence that runs counter to the DNA result, or had it, like the courts before, become bogged down in irrelevant details?

The Court of Appeal Judgment

The version of the judgment that I am considering here is from the website of the British and Irish Legal Information Institute (www.bailii.org), and is subject to Crown copyright.[1] I understand this to mean that it may be reproduced free of charge in any format or medium, provided it is reproduced accurately and not used in a misleading context, and also provided that the source of the material is identified and the copyright status acknowledged. All bold type, used to stress a point, is mine.

The hearing was held before three judges: The Lord Chief Justice of England and Wales, who at that time was Lord Justice Harry Woolf, Lord Justice Charles Mantell and Mr Justice, later Lord Justice, Brian Leveson. The last of these chaired the inquiry into media standards, set up by the government in response to the *News of the World* phone hacking scandal.

I would ask the reader to consider the contents of this chapter in the light of my earlier comment regarding the undoubted presence of human bias and prejudice in the deliberations of our judicial system.

The Summary Judgment

The judgment is laid out in full and is followed by a summary provided by the court. If the summary is a fair reflection of the way the court viewed things, several points become clear quite quickly. In the summary (paragraphs 3 and 4) the court states:

> A police enquiry into the alibi in 1976 declared the conviction safe, and, in 1975, Lewis Hawser QC considered the case against

James Hanratty 'overwhelming'. ...On 26 March 1999, the Commission referred the conviction to the Court of Appeal on the statutory ground that there was a real possibility that the conviction would not be upheld.

It was contended by the prosecution that the DNA evidence proves conclusively that James Hanratty was, indeed, the murderer. Mr Hanratty's family argue that the DNA evidence was not admissible on the appeal and, in any event, the Court cannot exclude the real possibility that the results are due to innocent contamination from articles of James Hanratty's clothing and from a suitcase of his belongings seized after his arrest.

It appears, from paragraph 3, that the court is taking the 'flawed' Hawser report conclusion that the case against Hanratty was 'overwhelming' at face value and does not confirm whether their lordships had carefully read it. It appears to ignore the wealth of other evidence that points to an alternative viewpoint and makes no mention of the fundamental issues of the Liverpool and Rhyl alibis. This makes it look like the court was not giving due attention to the evidence that stands in opposition to the DNA evidence. It appeared to be saying that the DNA evidence, simply by its existence, rendered all other evidence, no matter how compelling, null and void. In which case, what steps had it taken to ensure that the DNA evidence was scientifically sound?

It also highlighted the respondent's contention that the combination of the two sets of DNA evidence proved Hanratty was guilty, and the appellant's contention that the presence of this evidence was due to contamination and was not proof of guilt. Paragraph 8 states:

The DNA evidence does not 'stand alone' and the Court refers to some of the more striking coincidences in the light of the DNA evidence if James Hanratty was not guilty. He would have been wrongly identified by three witnesses at identification parades; first as the person at the scene of the crime and secondly, (by two witnesses) driving a vehicle close to where the vehicle in which the murder was committed was found. He had the same identifying manner of speech as the killer. He stayed in a room the night before the crime from which bullets that had been fired from the murder weapon were recovered. The murder weapon was recovered from a place on a bus which he regarded as a hiding place and the bus followed a route he could well have used. His DNA was found on a piece of material from Valerie Storie's knickers where it would be expected to be if he was guilty; it was also found on the handkerchief found with the gun. The Court concludes that this number of alleged coincidences mean that they are not coincidences but provide overwhelming proof of the safety of the conviction from an evidential perspective.

Here we have the criteria used by the court to claim that Hanratty's guilt was assured. Taking each of these in turn I make the following observations. There is no mention of the contentious nature of Miss Storie's selection of Hanratty at the identification parade (she failed to pick him out of a first identity parade). Then, regarding the other two witness identifications, it takes no account of the fact that DSU Acott's notebook throws considerable doubt upon their statements anyway, as was mentioned in *Horizon*. Nor does it mention that for the London identifications, one had a timing discrepancy, and there were two cars, each with two passengers, who were eyewitnesses to a car being driven erratically, yet only one person in each car identified Hanratty. As for the point that Hanratty had the same identifying speech as the killer (Miss Storie picked him out of a second identity parade when everyone was asked to speak and Hanratty said 'fink' for 'think'), well so would half of the population of the East End of London, making this contention sufficiently tenuous as to be worthless.

As for the court's claim that 'He stayed in a room the night before the crime from which bullets that had been fired from the murder weapon were recovered', I would point out that the bullet cartridge cases were not found by the cleaner the day after Hanratty vacated that room, but only turned up some three weeks later under extremely dubious circumstances, as this judgment itself explicitly confirms in paragraph 36. This is yet another link to Hanratty that could only be said to be highly tenuous, at best, and far from conclusive. Also, the claim that the hiding place for the murder weapon was one that Hanratty knew first came from the statement of Dixie France, whose unexplained suicide, just prior to Hanratty's execution, is highly suspicious in this context.[2] There is no indication anywhere that the court even knew of the suspicious nature of France's suicide. Nevertheless, the evidence of that discussion, which Hanratty did not dispute, in no way stands as proof that Hanratty did hide this weapon there. It could equally point to France having hidden it. Finally, there is the apparent presence of Hanratty's DNA on Miss Storie's knickers, as well as on the handkerchief in which the murder weapon was wrapped.

Therefore, out of these items cited by the court as being too suggestive of Hanratty's guilt to be accepted as coincidence, it transpires that the only items which link Hanratty to the crime are the identification by Miss Storie and the DNA evidence. The other items are of such a questionable nature as to be virtually worthless. It should also be noted that this list merely cites evidence supportive of the DNA findings; it contains none of the wealth of evidence standing against those findings. To try and understand what their lordships made of that other evidence and how they assessed the DNA evidence placed before them, I must turn to the judgment in full and highlight its important issues. For brevity I shall only deal with what I consider to be the key concerns. Nevertheless, I would recommend that the interested reader peruse the full judgment in addition to following my discussion, as this will highlight how confusingly it has been documented.

The Full Judgment

The first point I wish to consider is the following from paragraph 10:

> The referral has been followed by Perfected Grounds of Appeal which rely on 17 grounds. These grounds overlap. Eleven are based on failures by the prosecution to disclose material to the defence, one

concerns the conduct of the identification parade at which Valerie Storie identified James Hanratty, one relates to the interviews (and is supported by ESDA. testing of interview notes) and four deal with directions given during of the course of the summing up (all but one based on stricter standards introduced since 1962).

There were seventeen grounds for appeal brought by the CCRC, of which eleven relate to failures by the prosecution to disclose materials to the defence. These eleven failures to disclose evidence, on their own and without any other matter taken into consideration, show this was a flawed and prejudicial case against Hanratty, despite the conclusion of this court. The very fact that the CCRC felt the need to bring seventeen grounds for appeal highlights one of the arcane strictures of English criminal law about which I have serious concerns. The stricture is that an appeal can only be brought based on new evidence, which may sound fine in principle but means that cases, such as Hanratty's, where the previously considered evidence was extremely problematic and clearly misunderstood, cannot be rectified until new evidence is unearthed. More concerning is that it also means the appeal will not revisit the previously considered evidence, however clearly it might require reappraisal. How can this way of considering such important issues be helpful to the cause of criminal justice?

I am not criticising the CCRC, or those working on behalf of the Hanratty family, who must work within this legal framework. However, in this court, when the focus should have been on assessing the likelihood of the DNA evidence versus the large amount of evidence that supported Hanratty – such as the Liverpool alibi – it clearly failed to do this. I therefore contend, no doubt controversially, that this component of our criminal justice system needs to be removed.

Paragraph 25 briefly covers Miss Storie's account of her shooting, which raises a severe, and currently unresolved, issue with the supposed murder weapon:

> The man asked her to start the car and show him where the gears were; this she did and she also showed him how the lights worked.

She left the car running. It stopped; she re-started it and again showed him how the gears worked. He got in the car and she went over and sat down on the ground beside Michael Gregsten. The man then got out and went over to her. He threatened to hit her and she gave him a pound and asked him to go. He started to walk away and when about 6-10 feet away suddenly turned round and started to shoot. Miss Storie felt one bullet hit her; when the second bullet hit her she fell over and was hit by two or three more bullets while lying on the ground. She heard a clicking sound as if he was re-loading the gun, and then he fired another 3 shots which she thought did not hit her. (She was in fact hit by 5 bullets and, as we have recorded, was paralysed from the waist down in consequence.) He came over and touched her; she pretended to be dead. He then drove off in the direction of Luton.

Having shot Gregsten twice, Miss Storie said the killer fired five shots at her, before reloading and firing a further three shots, which she thought all missed her. Her account was pretty much confirmed by the pathologist Dr, later Professor, Keith Simpson who believed all five of the first volley hit her, as well as the two shots to Gregsten's head. He initially believed that the murder weapon must have been a .32 calibre gun to allow for the seven shots. However, ballistic tests indicated that the weapon was a .38 Enfield, known as an Enfield No.2 Mk1. Now, although this name was given to three different pistols, (Mk1, Mk1* and Mk1**), it is important to note that they each had 'six-round' cylinders only.[3] This anomaly does not appear to have been resolved anywhere to date. How the weapon found by police – at the prompting of France – under the back seat of the bus was modified to fire seven shots, when it was built for six, was never explained, as far as I have been able to find. Were these two key prosecution witnesses, Dr Simpson, and Miss Storie, mistaken in believing seven shots were fired before the weapon needed reloading? If not, how was the weapon confirmed to have been involved?

Valerie Storie was the prosecution's star witness; the only source of evidence for what happened in the car, and she said that having shot her five times, the assailant reloaded and fired three further shots, all of which missed her. I have struggled to envisage a rationale to explain this rather bizarre act, as she has described it, and I am afraid I have been unsuccessful. Not that this seems to have bothered our courts at all.

The judgment then discusses the first of three examples of evidence disagreement between witnesses at the trial. In its verdict this court chose to highlight the evidence supposedly supporting Hanratty's guilt and ignored the evidence standing in opposition.

Paragraph 27 states that the issue of the discrepancies between Miss Storie's later testimony regarding the assailant, and that which John Kerr – a student conducting a traffic census nearby, who was the first on the scene and raised the alarm – says she said to him, and which he wrote down and gave to a policeman at the time, were fully investigated at the trial. This is highly questionable since Kerr stuck to his story throughout the trial and its aftermath, and has never wavered, while Miss Storie claimed she never made the statements attributed to her by Kerr. The unfortunate but 'convenient' loss by the police of the contemporaneous notes written by John Kerr has never been explained. Therefore, to claim that this was fully investigated at the trial is something of an overstatement. Whatever investigation took place, this obvious issue remains outstanding, and the police have still not produced the missing note.

Paragraph 31 contains a similarly dubious claim regarding another evidential disagreement between two further witnesses, James Trower, and Paddy Hogan (friends who gave conflicting evidence about the sighting of Gregsten's car, near to where it was subsequently abandoned in Redbridge): Trower identified Hanratty, Hogan did not. Again, both men kept to their accounts, with no conclusive evidence being provided to show which witness was in error. To me, it is again questionable that, in its conclusion, the court chose to highlight only Trower's evidence and made no mention of Hogan's evidence, which contradicted him, and which did not support the claim of Hanratty's guilt.

In the case of a second supposed sighting of the murder vehicle in East London, where for a third time there was a disagreement between the two witnesses, John Skillett, who identified Hanratty and Edward

Blackhall, who was closer and did not identify Hanratty, the court again chose to discard the evidence of the witness casting doubt about the sighting.

Horizon highlighted the mileage discrepancy, from DSU Acott's own notebook, that called both these sightings into severe question (Acott calculated that Gregsten's car had driven more than 200 miles before being abandoned, but if all the different sightings of the car, in various parts of the country were true, the mileage would have been far higher). So, the BBC had access to this information, but the court was either not aware of the fact or chose to ignore it. Again, one must ask why this happened, and why the court chose to consider Trower's and Skillett's evidence only, when claiming the case against Hanratty was strong. It is also notable that, unlike these two conflicting witness sightings, there is no doubt that Harold Hirons, a petrol station attendant, saw the car and its passengers when it was on his forecourt. Tellingly, he did not pick out either Hanratty or Peter Alphon, the other main suspect, yet the judgment again ignores his eyewitness evidence. At the very least, this whole sequence of actions could be seen as evidence of this court's bias against Hanratty, in contravention of its duty of impartiality.

Paragraph 34 notes that the location of the murder weapon was provided to police by France, whose subsequent highly suspicious suicide just before Hanratty's execution still needs explaining. I contend that France, himself a criminal, was perfectly capable of taking a handkerchief, used by Hanratty, wrapping the weapon in it and hiding it in a place then revealed to the police to frame Hanratty; though what had happened to sour their earlier cordial friendship remains unconfirmed. It is not clear whether this court was ever informed of France's suicide, which is certainly one of the strangest and most compelling elements of this whole sorry saga. The court makes no mention of this clearly important and unresolved event, which is concerning to say the least. On to paragraph 36:

> On 11 September 1961 (some twenty days after the killing), two cartridge cases were found in room 24 at the Vienna Hotel, Sutherland Avenue, Maida Vale; it was later established

scientifically that they had been fired from the murder weapon. The circumstances in which they came to be found and the evidence given by four witnesses associated with the hotel (together with other material relating to them which was not disclosed) are the subject of a number of criticisms (Grounds 8-10), ... [it] is also important to underline that the spent cartridges were discovered before James Hanratty had featured in the investigation: it was their presence in room 24 that caused the police to seek to identify the 'J Ryan'. He had been one of only two people who had spent a night in that room (which had four beds) in the period between the week of the murder and the recovery of the cartridges.

As I highlighted earlier, the court points out that the spent cartridge cases were only found in the room at the Vienna Hotel nearly three weeks after Hanratty's stay, and that he had been one of only two people in the room in the period between the murder and their recovery. His stay had been on the night prior to the murder, Monday 21 August. It seems strange that the court was aware of this delay in the discovery, and yet still chose to consider this as important evidence against Hanratty, apparently without considering the implications of this timing issue. The fact that the cartridge cases were not discovered by the cleaner on the following day, when she cleaned the room, or on any subsequent day for the next three weeks, by cleaner or guest, was the subject of contention at the trial. I would also point out that, in yet another explanation that stretches credulity, the prosecution at the trial claimed that Hanratty had been performing target practice in the room.[4] Again, the absurdity of this claim, for which no evidence was ever produced, should not need clarification.

Discussing the Liverpool alibi, the court states in paragraphs 69, 70 and 71:

A number of witnesses were called to support different parts of this account. First, Mrs Olive Dinwoodie, an assistant in the sweet shop at 408 Scotland Road, Liverpool, said that a man who looked like James Hanratty did call at the sweet shop (of which she was temporarily in charge), in the afternoon and asked for Tarleton Road: but she was certain that the incident occurred on Monday 21 August 1961. Mrs Dinwoodie was in the sweet shop with her granddaughter Barbara Ford, aged 13.

This evidence was similar to that given by Albert Harding, a long-distance lorry driver. He had been called by the prosecution to support their contention that 21 August was the date that Mrs Dinwoodie was at the shop; he had visited both on Monday 21 and Tuesday 22 August and said that Mrs Dinwoodie was only present at the same time as he was there on Monday. Bearing in mind that 21 August was the date that James Hanratty had stayed at the Vienna Hotel, it was the case for the prosecution that he had not been in Liverpool that day and that he had found out about someone else who had made the enquiry when he went to Liverpool to purchase an alibi.

Robert Kempt, the Manager of a billiard hall in Liverpool, confirmed his recollection of an occasion when he was standing at the bottom of the steps near Lime Street Station when a man approached and asked him to buy a watch. He gave evidence of a conversation in similar terms to that recounted by James Hanratty: he said it could have happened at any time between June and September.

Here, the court gives only the most cursory account of this key element of Hanratty's case. To begin with the Lime Street Station eyewitness evidence is not even discussed. Then, regarding the evidence of Olive Dinwoodie and Barbara Ford, no mention is made of their contention that the conversation could have taken place on the Tuesday. When discussing Albert Harding's evidence, the court fails to mention that, as I noted earlier, even his own work logs contradicted his account, thereby making it extremely dubious. Also, the fact that the court merely recounts the prosecution's implausible claim that Hanratty subsequently bought the sweet shop alibi for the wrong day, and then accepts this claim without question is, I contend, astonishing. How and why did they miss this?

Finally, great credence is placed on Robert Kempt's apparent lack of certainty concerning the date that the conversation took place, again without mention of the fact that he said it must have taken place before 26 August when he went on holiday.

Paragraph 77, which highlights the points raised by Hanratty's counsel in his submission, states:

> James Hanratty was the man in the sweet shop incident which could only have occurred on the Monday 21 or Tuesday 22 August; as there was evidence, both from prosecution and defence, that he was in London on the Monday it could only have happened on Tuesday 22 August 1961 which, by itself, demonstrated that he was not the gunman.

This shows that not only was Hanratty's counsel aware of the significance of this alibi, but by documenting this, the Court of Appeal was duty bound to give this clearly pivotal point due consideration, not that it did.

In the next two paragraphs, the court considers its duties in this regard. In my opinion these are the most important paragraphs in the whole judgment as they explain why the court failed in its duty to justice:

> From the account of the facts which we have set out, coupled with the summary of the submissions of counsel at the trial, it is apparent, that the only issue with which the jury was concerned at the trial was the identity of the person who was guilty of murdering Michael Gregsten and raping Valerie Storie. By finding James Hanratty guilty the jury resolved that issue. That on the evidence which they heard, the jury were entitled to come to this conclusion was made clear by the previous decision of

this Court and the conclusion of Mr Hawser to which we have already referred ... . Mr Mansfield does not suggest otherwise. In addition, he accepts that judged by the standards of 1962 the summing up of Gorman J, except in one respect, was extremely fair and beyond criticism.

With this background the onus must be squarely on the appellant to establish that the appeal should succeed. Why then is it said that an appeal which has previously failed should now after all these years succeed? The complaints which are made are based on non-disclosure for the purposes of the trial by the prosecution, fresh evidence which was not available at the trial and, with one addition, omissions from the summing up of directions which by present day standards, as opposed to those which existed in 1962, should have been included in the summing up.

The court is saying that, based on the evidence presented to it, the jury was entitled to arrive at its decision, which was supported by the first Court of Appeal hearing and by the Hawser report. Again, this court is significantly bypassing the questions surrounding the Hawser report, and the validity, or otherwise, of the summing up and the police and prosecution tactics during the trial. It also appears to be saying that because the jury did not understand the pivotal nature of the Liverpool alibi, or of defence counsel Michael Sherrard's highlighting of that alibi in his submission, it is not within the remit of this court to consider it. Seemingly Mr Mansfield, the QC representing the Hanratty family, agreed with this contention. This seems to be a permanent block on previously submitted evidence being reconsidered. I believe that this is distinctly prejudicial when endeavouring to arrive at a truth, as shown by this case. How can this way of treating contentious evidence be considered fair or just? This only adds weight to my concern that the English judicial system seems less interested in providing justice for all those affected by its deliberations than in following its own arbitrary and frequently unfair strictures.

Then, in paragraph 80:

> The prosecution do not dispute there was non-disclosure as alleged and have not relied on the substantial difference between the duties of disclosure on the prosecution today as compared with 1962. Furthermore, it is not suggested that the appellant's additional evidence is not admissible.

This paragraph seems to downplay the importance of the whole extraordinary catalogue of police misbehaviour, which was severely prejudicial to the chances of a fair trial, merely saying that the prosecution agrees there was some non-disclosure. The importance of this misconduct is therefore being grossly underestimated.

Next, in paragraph 106, the court considers the critical DNA evidence put before it:

> We turn to the DNA evidence. As already noted seminal fluid was found on Valerie Storie's knickers and one of her slips. At the time all that could be shown was that the rapist's and hence the murderer's blood group was O secretor. So was James Hanratty's and Peter Alphon's together with 40% of the male population. The handkerchief found with the murder weapon bore traces of nasal mucus. Mucus was not capable of being analysed for blood type. Evidence based upon the comparison of hairs and fibres was inconclusive. Apart from some seminal staining on James Hanratty's striped trousers, said to be part of the Hepworth suit, that was the extent of the scientific evidence at trial.

This highlights the point raised earlier, that group O secretors constitute a large proportion of the population. Its only value to the court would be exculpatory: by excluding a non-group-O secretor as the attacker. It has extremely limited affirmative capability and I find it odd that this wasn't mentioned alongside the earlier statement. However, as noted, there was also group AB semen present, which raises questions about why the rapist was deemed to be a group-O secretor and not group AB. The staining on the handkerchief was attributed to nasal mucus, which was a critical point as will soon be apparent.

Then, in paragraph 109:

> Following the order of the court on 17 October 2000, James Hanratty's body was exhumed and samples taken from which it has been possible for Dr Whitaker of the Forensic Science Laboratory **to state with what a non-scientist would regard as equivalent to absolute certainty (or almost absolute certainty as makes no difference) that the DNA profile recovered from the fragment of knickers and the DNA profile recovered from the mucus staining on the handkerchief have come from James Hanratty.** That is not in dispute and, indeed, it is conceded by Mr Mansfield on behalf of the appellant that, should it transpire that all possibility of contamination can be excluded, the DNA evidence points conclusively to James Hanratty having been both the murderer and the rapist.

The court quotes Dr Whitaker as affirming, with 'almost absolute certainty', that these profiles from the mucus stain on the handkerchief and the fragment of knickers were both from Hanratty. For reasons I explain in the next chapter, I believe this was in contravention of his strict responsibilities to the court. I should point out that the slight element of doubt, implicit within this statement, does not appear within his oral testimony given in court, in which he frequently says the DNA *is* Hanratty's. I can only surmise that it arose in his written testimony, although, in my view, it still stands as a gross misrepresentation of the real situation, as will become clear. The statement that this claim is accepted by Mr Mansfield and is not disputed, shows a woeful lack of understanding of the reality of DNA profiling by this court in general. This also raises further questions about the evidence given and openness exhibited by the FSS witnesses, since it appears that none made the court aware of the issues inherent in such an attribution.

When discussing the possibility of contamination, the court makes the following astonishing, and critically important statements, in paragraphs 112 and 113:

> Quite clearly the knickers (exhibit 26 at trial) and later the fragment cut from the crotch area and the handkerchief (exhibit 35) are of first importance. So too, as possible contaminators, are James Hanratty's intimate samples and items of clothing which may have borne traces of his DNA.
>
> The knickers arrived at the Metropolitan Police Laboratory (MPL) on 23 August 1961 where they were examined by Dr Nickolls, the director and his assistant, Henry Howard. **They were found to be stained with seminal fluid in the area of the crotch and at the back for five inches upwards from the crotch. Vaginal fluid from Valerie Storie was also present. There were smaller quantities of seminal fluid of blood group AB assumed to have come at some earlier stage from Michael Gregsten**.

The bold text is crucial as it undermines, categorically, the FSS's central contention that only James Hanratty's DNA profile was found on the fragment of Miss Storie's knickers. However, there is another possible scenario here: that the seminal fluid assumed to belong to Gregsten did not actually come from him and could have been that of the assailant with a group AB blood. When the word 'assumed' is used, it means that this is not a definite attribution, and could therefore be wrong. It obviously means that it is far from confirmed. Gregsten's DNA has not been tested, although he was described as blood group AB by DSU Acott after initial testing in 1961 by Dr Nickolls. Whatever, the truth behind this statement, it clearly shows that, for the FSS scientists to be correct in their assertion that only one male profile occurred in their tests, an explanation for the absence of this other seminal fluid is required.

Next, when discussing the subject of the provenance of the samples used by the FSS, paragraphs 114 and 115 of the judgment state:

There is, of course, the possibility that all the exhibits were stored in the same place, albeit separately packaged, which, it is submitted, might have provided the opportunity for secondary contamination. Dr Nickolls is dead. Mr Howard is still alive though in poor health. His recollection is that the dangers of contamination were recognised even in 1961 and that the practice was to take elementary precautions such as making sure that clothing from victim and suspect were not examined on the same day.

All the exhibits, including those mentioned, were produced at the committal proceedings which took place between 22 November 1961 and 5 December 1961. If the usual procedures of the time were followed it would seem doubtful that any one of the exhibits, barring possibly the gun and certain of the cartridges, would ever have been removed from its packaging or container. Even so, as Mr Mansfield points out and the respondent concedes, the possibility that there was contact between the various exhibits cannot be excluded altogether.

As we will see, it was this issue of contamination that occupied the three days of the hearing involving the testimony of the expert witnesses, rather than what should have been a proper examination of the validity of these scientific tests and their conclusions. It is clearly stated that the possibility of contamination cannot be ruled out, despite this court doing just that. There is not a shred of evidence to confirm that contamination did not occur, nor indeed could there be, and yet the court, without any evidential justification whatsoever, discounts the possibility of contamination entirely. In fact, no one knows the actual provenance of the pieces of evidence, particularly that of the material sample from Miss Storie's knickers, and the unidentified items found placed in the evidence file with it. Mr Mansfield's perfectly valid contention was that in 1961 no one would have known about DNA, so the possibility of contamination, in the laboratory or in the subsequent committal and trial, or at any time in the following thirty years, cannot be discounted. Also, as you will see, in his testimony to this court, forensic anthropologist and scientist for the defence, Dr Martin Evison, pointed out that the process of washing forensic utensils in water, which was employed at the time, does not remove contaminated DNA. Yet the court ignores this evidence and considers contamination impossible. We will see the flawed reasoning for this later. Paragraph 121 states:

> That said we should also record that not one of the respondent's witnesses excluded the possibility of contamination.

This extraordinary assertion means that not one of the FSS witnesses excluded the possibility of contamination, which is a very questionable interpretation of the evidence from Mr Mann and Dr Whitaker, who both explicitly discounted it without any evidential basis in their testimony.

Then we have this troubling claim from paragraph 125:

> But that is to ignore the results of the DNA profiling. With regard to the knicker fragment we have what Dr Whitaker would describe as a typical distribution of male and female DNA following an act of sexual intercourse leading to the obvious inference that the male contribution came from James Hanratty. For that not to be the case we would have to suppose that the DNA of the rapist, also of blood group O, had either degraded so as to become undetectable or had been masked by James Hanratty's DNA during the course of a contaminating event. Moreover, we would also have to suppose that Valerie Storie's DNA had remained in its original state, or at least detectable, and had escaped being overridden by DNA from James Hanratty. The same would have to be true of the DNA attributed to Michael Gregsten. **Finally, we must visualise a pattern which is wholly consistent with sexual intercourse having taken**

place in which Valerie Storie and James Hanratty were the participants.

In view of the content of paragraph 113, which states that a DNA sample assumed to have come from Michael Gregsten was on the fragment of Miss Storie's knickers, paragraph 125 needs to be very carefully considered. The court claims that for the sexual intercourse scenario involving Hanratty not to be correct, the rapist's DNA would need to have broken down and Miss Storie's DNA to have remained in its original state, having escaped being overridden by Hanratty's DNA. This would imply that the court believed that Miss Storie's DNA was not in its original state and had been overridden by Hanratty's. We will see that this contradicts the presentation from Mr Sweeney QC for the respondent, of the DNA evidence, where epithelial samples from Miss Storie are found and discussed. So why did the court think this?

The court also says the same would have to be true of the DNA attributed to Gregsten, though it doesn't clarify what it means by this. Is it expecting Gregsten's DNA to have also broken down, or to have survived intact, having not been overridden by Hanratty's? What level of confusion in the court do these statements portray? Remember, their lordships apparently believed that Gregsten's DNA was on the knickers. Lastly, the final sentence in this paragraph is very strangely worded. Why must the court visualise a pattern wholly consistent with the rape of Miss Storie by Hanratty? If the court is saying that it is led to believe that Hanratty raped Miss Storie, because of the evidence, why does it use such strange language to report that belief? I am afraid that, for these reasons, I am struggling to understand just what the court is trying to say in this confusingly written paragraph. It is far from clear that their lordships themselves weren't confused.

Paragraph 126 of the judgment states:

Much the same reasoning would apply to the handkerchief. The only DNA extracted from the handkerchief came from James Hanratty. The only places on the handkerchief from which his DNA was extracted were the areas of mucus staining. …**In our**

The Court of Appeal Judgment   55

> view the notion that such a thing might have happened in either case is fanciful. The idea that it might have happened twice over is beyond belief.

Here the court is considering Hanratty's DNA in the nasal mucus stain – but only from the point of view of whether it was caused by contamination – and dismisses this possibility as 'beyond belief' because it would have been a second separate contamination event. However, as I shall now explain, the court in its entirety has critically overstated the significance of Hanratty's DNA in this mucus stain, always assuming that this was his DNA, and I shall explain later why such an attribution is not scientifically supportable.

I contend that rather than contamination being the cause, a much more likely explanation for the presence of Hanratty's DNA on the handkerchief, considering the involvement of France in its discovery, is that he used it to blow his nose. Remember that Hanratty had been at the France family home on the Monday before travelling to Liverpool, as they all confirmed, and that up until that day had maintained an apparently friendly relationship with France. Yet the court, as is shown by the verdict, has made the critically incorrect assumption that Hanratty's DNA in this mucus stain proves that he wrapped the murder weapon.

This is an extreme over statement of the FSS finding. There is absolutely no forensic testing available to show that he wrapped that gun, nor has there ever been. The DNA was in the mucus stain, which, at best, showed only that he had blown his nose on the handkerchief, at some point. Anything further regarding his connection to the gun is pure speculation. For the 'Hanratty was guilty' die-hards this assumption is easy to make, but it is without scientific confirmation, or justification. There is no established connection to the murder weapon. To make that connection requires the finding of Hanratty's DNA on the gun itself, and that is not the situation here. Therefore, the court was either misled as to the supposed significance of the handkerchief, or their lordships had managed to mislead themselves. This is the second outstanding area that requires further examination of the gun.

What is even worse is that this misunderstanding of the significance of the handkerchief was directly responsible for the appeal being turned down. Their lordships stated explicitly that the likelihood of two separate contamination events was so remote as to be discounted. If they had only been considering contamination as a possible cause for the supposed presence of Hanratty's DNA on just the knickers, might their verdict have been different? The other critical misunderstanding by this court was that even a full DNA match, which was not the case here, does not confirm the DNA is that of the accused, only that the accused might have been the donor. I shall explain why this is the case later.

As we have seen, this is not the first time the judiciary has spectacularly overstated the case against Hanratty and woefully misunderstood the significance of evidence supporting his case. Whatever the reason for this, it should be of concern, not just to the Hanratty family, but to the people who are subject to the deliberations of such a system and its practitioners.

Finally, in reaching its conclusion regarding this case, paragraphs 211 and 213 state:

> The DNA evidence made what was a strong case even stronger. Equally the strength of the evidence overall pointing to the guilt of the appellant supports our conclusion as to the DNA.
>
> On the appeal we focus on what are alleged to have been defects in the trial process. This is particularly true in relation to non-disclosure. ...In that context we are satisfied the procedural shortcomings fell far short of what is required to lead to the conclusion that the trial should be regarded as flawed and this conviction unsafe on procedural grounds. The trial still met the basic standards of fairness required. **We are satisfied that James Hanratty suffered no real prejudice.**

Conclusions

So, the court considered the case against Hanratty was already strong, and made even stronger by the DNA evidence, and that, although he was hanged, he suffered no real prejudice. I must disagree with these statements. There is a constant bias in the way the evidence is considered, and as already discussed, the supposed list of coincidences is tenuous, misleading, and quite clearly contradicted by evidence in the public domain, which appears not to have been properly considered. The lengthy list of police malpractice, such as withholding copious amounts of evidence from the defence, lying about tampering with Hanratty's statements, and failing to follow procedures when dealing with both witnesses and identity parades, has been ignored entirely.

The court failed to consider the validity of the FSS evidence presented, concentrating solely on the issue of possible contamination, which it discounted because it was being asked to consider that two contamination events had occurred. Critically, it also accepted that the DNA evidence in the mucus stain linked Hanratty to the murder weapon, which was a claim without forensic scientific foundation. The second contamination event was therefore unnecessary and completely misdirected the entire court, much to the Hanratty family's detriment.

Lastly, it is also clear that their lordships did not consider the evidence pointing to Hanratty's innocence, standing in opposition to the DNA finding, such as the Liverpool alibi. Instead, they merely rehashed a tired and flawed sequence of supposed coincidences, and an uncritical acceptance of the Hawser report, as supporting the forensic evidence. There was no consideration, let alone acceptance, of any evidence, except that which apparently pointed to his guilt. By deciding this, the court gave the green light to all lower courts to behave in the same way, and what is more, to adopt an uncritical approach to DNA evidence presented. How does this abject failure to be balanced when weighing contradictory evidence lead to fair justice, let alone a better justice system? What about the scales of justice? Equally, who polices the deliberations of the Court of Appeal? What can and should happen when, as here, the court fails spectacularly?

As an aside, I have recently been informed that the author of this judgment was the now Lord Justice Leveson. This came as a considerable surprise to me, as the much more critical and vocal interjections from the bench had mostly originated from his more senior colleagues, especially the Lord Chief Justice himself, as we will see when I discuss the trial transcripts. This had led me to assume that the latter had played the major role in the formulating of the judgment, in view of his seniority and expressed opinions. How much leeway Lord Leveson had while drafting this judgment – in other words how much was he the author and how much the scribe – remains unknown to me, but it would appear to have been more his own work than my perusal of the transcripts had previously led me to believe. However, of greater concern to me is that I have also been informed that Lord Leveson apparently doesn't believe the Liverpool alibi, although on what basis and what his alternative explanation for the multiple eyewitness accounts were not elaborated upon. I would love to know more.

Unfortunately, this was as far as I could get during my university project deliberations. I had so many more questions around the FSS testing and its conclusions, but most of all I wondered about that DNA on the handkerchief. The court had considered it was too fanciful to be explained by a second contamination event, and I was inclined to agree with it on this one point only. However, this led it to believe that Hanratty had been the person to wrap the gun, which, as I've explained is a dramatic over-statement of the evidence, and nothing more than pure speculation. Had the FSS witnesses explicitly stated this? If so, this is far beyond what the evidence could be said to have shown. All it shows, if it is his DNA, is that he blew his nose on the handkerchief. Most importantly, the court used the basis of the two supposed contamination events to find against Hanratty. Had it only been considering the possibility of one contamination event would the court have been so quick to dismiss it? As we will see, the provenance of the evidence file containing the fragment of Miss Storie's knickers is woefully inadequate, especially in terms of what would be required of a normal DNA sample today. And we know the burden of proof is supposed to be 'beyond reasonable doubt'.

This was how the situation remained until I was finally able to obtain a copy of the 2002 Appeal transcripts covering the FSS witness testimony and that of Dr Martin Evison.

Expert Witnesses in English Courts

Before reviewing these transcripts, it is important to spend some time providing the necessary background information, to enable the reader to fully understand the significance of what took place. Without this priming material, which is covered in the next three chapters, some of the issues discussed in court may lack sufficient clarity. I hope you will bear with me as I undertake these important digressions.

To begin with, these transcripts are dealing with the evidence from what are termed 'expert' witnesses. To properly understand their implications, the reader needs some knowledge of the roles and responsibilities of these experts, and of the courts.

The following principles, applicable to criminal cases, were approved by the Court of Appeal in 'Harris [2005] EWCA Crim 1980'[1]:

1. Expert evidence presented to the court should be and seen to be the independent product of the expert **uninfluenced as to form or content by the exigencies of litigation.**

2. An expert witness should provide independent assistance to the court by way of objective unbiased opinion in relation to matters within his expertise. An expert witness **should never assume the role of advocate.**

3. An expert witness should state the facts or assumptions on which his opinion is based. **He should not omit to consider material facts which detract from his concluded opinions.**

4. An expert should make it clear when a particular question or issue falls outside of his expertise.

5. If an expert's opinion is not properly researched because he considers that insufficient data is available then this must be stated with an indication that the opinion is no more than a provisional one.

It will become clear just how far short the testimonies of the FSS scientists were of meeting these principles (especially the ones I've stressed, in bold). When you understand just how contentious and cutting edge the forensic tests in this case were, you will recognise that the science employed was also at the frontier of knowledge. It remains so to this day and, as we will see, has been the subject of much debate, with at least one major revision since its use in this case.

The key point here is that an expert witness's duty is to the court, regardless of the side which engaged them. All experts should be impartial and highlight evidence that weakens or contradicts their case, which certainly didn't happen in this court. However, this judicial stipulation seems to me to be expecting the impossible when considering human nature. The expert witness will inevitably be minded to best represent the side by which they've been engaged which, by the way, is almost always the prosecution. The only potential counterbalance to this would be engaging an equivalent expert for the defence, which rarely happens. This is yet another weakness of our judicial system.

It is the court's responsibility to verify that the expert is sufficiently qualified to provide the evidence being proffered. This screening should take place before the evidence is given in court. It is a basic test to assure the court that the evidence is based on validated and verified science. In most jurisdictions in the USA, this is known as the 'Daubert standard', after the 1993 case 'Daubert v Merrell Dow Pharmaceuticals' (although some states still maintain the earlier Frye standard). In brief, Daubert states the following:

A witness who is qualified as an expert by knowledge, skill, experience, training, or education may testify in the form of an opinion or otherwise if:

(a) The expert's scientific, technical, or other specialized knowledge will help the trier of fact to understand the evidence or to determine a fact in issue;

(b) The testimony is based on sufficient facts or data;

(c) The testimony is the product of reliable principles and methods; and

(d) The expert has reliably applied the principles and methods to the facts of the case.

Unfortunately, for reasons best known to our judicial authorities, in English law the situation is much less clear and satisfactory.

As was set out by the South Australia Supreme Court following Bonython (1984) 38 SAAR 45, the admissibility of expert evidence was dependent on only two conditions. Firstly, whether the study or experience of an expert will give his or her opinion an authority that one not so qualified would lack, and secondly, whether the witness is qualified to express the opinion. In R v Clarke (1995) 2 Cr App R, the opinion was that there is no closed category where evidence cannot be placed before a jury. This was the woeful situation in the English courts regarding assessing the validity of expert evidence at the time of the Hanratty case.

Then, in R v Dallagher [2002] EWCA Crim 1903,[2] the court approved a passage from Daubert but chose not to consider the factors listed above which the American system requires to allow a piece of expert evidence. These include whether a given technique (in Hanratty, this would be the DNA LCN testing) can be independently tested, whether it has been published and peer reviewed in accredited journals and, crucially, whether it is generally accepted. Instead, it said that 'so long as the field is sufficiently well established to pass the ordinary tests of reliability and relevance, then no enhanced test of admissibility should be applied, but the weight of the evidence should be established by the same adversarial forensic techniques applicable elsewhere.' Remember that in many English courts very few cases have qualified experts appearing for the defence to counter invalid prosecution witness claims.

Later, in R v *Luttrell* [2004] EWCA Crim 1344,[3] the Court of Appeal established that, on some occasions, even the lack of reliability of expert evidence would not affect its admissibility. It would merely require the jury to be warned of its shortcomings and error rates during the summing up. I wonder if that has ever happened.

I am not alone in raising this as a concern. Interested readers might like to consider that in March 2005, even the House of Commons wrote a report outlining the troubled relationship the criminal justice system has with forensic science and its presentation in the courts. It is called the *House of Commons Science and Technology – Seventh Report*[4]

This situation has also been of sufficient concern to cause the Law Commission to publish a series of recommendations in February 2011 titled 'Expert Evidence In Criminal Proceedings'.[5]

It stated that:

> a jury, comprised as it is of lay persons, may not be properly equipped in terms of education or experience to be able to address the reliability of technical or complex expert opinion evidence, particularly evidence of a scientific nature. **This being the case, there is a real danger that juries may simply defer to the opinion of the specialist who has been called to provide expert evidence, or that juries may focus on perceived pointers to reliability (such as the expert's demeanour or professional status).**

In view of the way the Court of Appeal accepted *all* the FSS contentions in Hanratty, I fear it is not just juries that are deferring to the opinion of specialists. The Law Commission also noted:

In a similar vein, Judge Andrew Gilbart QC, the Honorary Recorder of Manchester, told us that he is often struck by 'how poor some suggested scientific evidence is in criminal trials', adding that he is also frequently struck by 'how ill equipped advocates are to challenge it when they have no experts of their own to advise them.'

With all due respect to Dr Evison, I don't believe he was fully equipped to properly challenge the FSS evidence in the Hanratty case. This was because the FSS scientists did not explain the experimental nature of the science used, and it was not clear that they were not working to generally acceptable scientific tolerances, nor were they having their procedures and their outputs independently monitored and verified, as we will see.

As of 2020[6], the criminal procedures that now define the rules governing expert witnesses, include the following:

Expert's duty to the court

19.2. (1) An expert must help the court to achieve the overriding objective –
   a) by giving opinion which is –
      (i) objective and unbiased, and
      (ii) within the expert's area or areas of expertise;

(2) This duty overrides any obligation to the person from whom he receives instructions or by whom he is paid.

Content of expert's report

19.4. Where rule 19.3(3) applies, an expert's report must –

(a) give details of the expert's qualifications, relevant experience and accreditation;

(b) give details of any literature or other information which the expert has relied on in making the report;

(c) contain a statement setting out the substance of all facts given to the expert which are material to the opinions expressed in the report, or upon which those opinions are based;

(d) make clear which of the facts stated in the report are within the expert's own knowledge;

(e) where the expert has based an opinion or inference on a representation of fact or opinion made by another person for the purposes of criminal proceedings (for example, as to the outcome of an examination, measurement, test or experiment) (i) identify the person who made that representation to the expert,

(ii) give the qualifications, relevant experience and any accreditation of that person, and

(iii) certify that that person had personal knowledge of the matters stated in that representation;

(f) where there is a range of opinion on the matters dealt with in the report –

(i) summarise the range of opinion, and

(ii) give reasons for the expert's own opinion;

(g) if the expert is not able to give an opinion without qualification, state the qualification;

(h) include such information as the court may need to decide whether the expert's opinion is sufficiently reliable to be admissible as evidence;

(i) contain a summary of the conclusions reached;

(j) contain a statement that the expert understands an expert's duty to the court, and has complied and will continue to comply with that duty; and

(k) contain the same declaration of truth as a witness statement.

As can be seen, even today, within these proposals there is still nothing to assure the courts that experts have applied peer-reviewed, independently verifiable, and generally accepted methods to their work. There is also nothing to ensure that their claims are not contentious, or, when they are, that the court is made aware of the contentious nature of the evidence proffered, with suitable caveats thus applied. Consider this in the light of the FSS claims that will be discussed.

This is the sorry situation when it comes to dealing with potentially contentious, cutting-edge forensic evidence, such as LCN DNA profiling. It is clear, that in the Hanratty case, the Court of Appeal had no legal requirement to properly verify the validity of the evidence being placed before it. This was hardly beneficial to the cause of justice. It appears that the situation has barely improved to date, despite the concerns of parliament, among others.

Finally, I shall draw your attention to this extraordinary and unfortunate, irony, again involving Lord Justice Leveson. In a speech to the Forensic Science Society and Kings College London, on 16 November 2010, he said:[7]

> It is, in my opinion, perfectly clear that expert evidence of doubtful reliability may be admitted too freely with insufficient explanation of the basis for reaching specific conclusions, be challenged too weakly by the opposing advocate, and be accepted too readily by the judge or jury at the end of the trial. In that regard, therefore, the law of England and Wales is not satisfactory, and reform is undoubtedly required.

I wonder if he had the Hanratty case in mind when he uttered these words.

Statistics and DNA

The material in the next two chapters is necessary to understand how badly I feel the Court of Appeal dealt with DNA science, but it also covers some technical areas and will therefore require some effort on behalf of the reader. I have done my best to make it comprehensible to the layperson, but if I have failed in this endeavour I can only apologise in advance.

The second area that should be considered when regarding the conclusion in the Hanratty case is the dubious use of statistical probabilities by the FSS experts. This is an area mired in controversy. It is unclear if the figures quoted by them have any sensible rationale at all, and, as we will see, the method applied to arrive at them is never explained.

To begin to assess the statistical evidence one must pay close attention to the question the statistics are trying to address. Usually, what is the chance that a randomly chosen and unrelated individual would have the DNA profile observed in a crime scene sample? Obviously, the calculation should vary, whether there is a single DNA source or a mixture of sources.

As my contention is that Hanratty could not have been in Dorney Reach, any occurrence of his DNA, if it is indeed his, on Miss Storie's underwear, cannot be from him raping her, regardless of any statistical probabilities quoted by the FSS. What are the odds that the Liverpool alibi is false compared to the interpretation of the DNA evidence? Which is the more likely? I also contend that the likelihood of contamination causing the DNA result on the knickers is not only potentially far greater than the FSS scientists acknowledged, but also that it cannot be proven *not* to have happened, especially in the light of the unknown provenance of the pieces of evidence involved.

The key thing to remember about any statistical claim, however it has been derived, is that it remains nothing more than guesswork, unless subsequently corroborated by empirically proven and separate evidence. Regardless of the veracity of any mathematical arguments employed by statisticians, the material I am about to discuss will demonstrate that the real world and that of advanced mathematics are not the same. Empirical evidence that refutes the basis for the statistical probability calculations used by DNA forensics has been in the public domain for the last twenty years yet is still being ignored by our political and judicial authorities. Even more unfortunately, that is only one of the issues with this science.

Bayes' Theorem

When it comes to the use of statistics by DNA scientists in our courts, you must also understand that there is usually more evidence for and against a defendant than just the results of any DNA profiling. A method for calculating probabilities in these circumstances is Bayes' theorem, which was developed by the Reverend Thomas Bayes in the eighteenth century. This requires that the probabilities suggested by each new piece of evidence must be combined with the 'prior odds' of guilt or innocence – as suggested by the other evidence or statistics – to establish the likelihood of the defendant's guilt. However, professional statisticians are still divided as to whether it is a valid method when considering DNA evidence in the courts, with those against its use favouring Classical or Frequentist analysis instead. The critics cite its computational complexity and potential to confuse juries, while its supporters claim it is the best method for attempting to integrate DNA match evidence with other evidence.

To outline its complexity, basic Bayesian notation, which is aimed at ensuring that any evidence, including that of a DNA match, is not considered in isolation, can be expressed as follows:

$$\text{Prior Odds} * \text{Likelihood Ratio (LR)} = \text{Posterior Odds}$$

Here the prior odds of a suspect's guilt are multiplied by the LR to give the posterior odds of the suspect's guilt, after the piece of evidence involved has been considered. When the LR is the DNA probability calculation figure, it is strongly supportive of the prosecution case, and thus considerably impacts the posterior odds. There is a further problem in that the prior odds calculation tends to be subjective, even though it should normally be based on observations. Nevertheless, the LR calculation should cover every possible outcome, from the suspect is guilty to the suspect is innocent and consider the 'probability of the evidence' given both the prosecution and defence hypotheses. This can be calculated as:

$$P(E/Hp) / P(E/Hd)$$

As we can see, this is hardly a simple calculation, and goodness knows how one is supposed to assess the validity of any such calculations, so courts need to examine the rationale behind these assessments with great care, to ensure fairness, and this is rarely, if ever, done. There is also no indication that the FSS presented any form of Bayes' calculation to the court in the Hanratty case.

It is worth bearing in mind that the Royal Statistical Society says statistics remains a specialised area, even though scientists from different fields will have some familiarity with its methods. It also says that our courts should ensure such evidence is only presented by appropriately qualified experts.[1] However, in most criminal cases the probability claims are made by the forensic scientists called by the Crown, and there is no guarantee that they have undergone sufficient statistical training to be able to properly support their calculations. Unfortunately, our courts tend to let these unverified claims continue to be made and accepted almost always without question.

When it comes to DNA profiling of crime scene evidence, forensic scientists do not use Bayes' theorem if there is only a single DNA profile in the evidence sample. Instead, they use a calculation called random match probability (RMP), which is a DNA focused calculation only, and takes no account of any of the other evidence. The result is that

Statistics and DNA 69

the courts hear astronomically high probability figures being claimed, as I shall explain shortly. Somewhat confusingly, they only consider it necessary to perform a Bayesian calculation if they are dealing with a mixed DNA sample, such as from a rape victim and, as we will see, it is extremely debatable as to whether any non-DNA evidence has been considered when this DNA evidence is presented to court. I consider it is a court's duty to ensure there is an understanding of what such claims really mean, by undertaking a proper examination of the assumptions and data involved in these calculations. Yet I have failed to find any evidence of such a duty being performed properly. It certainly wasn't in Hanratty. Unfortunately, this is just another example of the weakness of our judicial system. Why forensic scientists are allowed to present evidence in this isolated and very dubious fashion is another question I have been unable to answer.

However, things are even more askew here, since it is the duty of our courts to weigh up all the evidence, both for and against, when considering the defendant's guilt. This is essentially what Bayes' theorem is trying to do, yet no court is ever expected to grapple with its complexities. In addition, the DNA scientist is supposed to consider his or her evidence in isolation, to avoid bias when assessing and presenting it. In that situation, how can a valid Bayes calculation possibly be performed if it only considers the DNA evidence? How this clearly incorrect situation has been arrived at remains a mystery to me, and even more mysterious is that it continues to this day.

Random Match Probability

As I hope to show, the supposed power of DNA evidence, which most people believe must prove guilt when a match is proclaimed, is distinctly questionable when examined properly. People have been persuaded of its power due to the astronomical figures quoted when discussing the probabilities of guilt associated with such scientific testing. For example, since the late 1990s, with the advent of the Second Generation Multiplex Plus (SGM Plus®) DNA test which looks at ten chromosomal loci along with the Amelogenin gender identifier, the claim has been that the RMP for a full profile match is more than one in a billion. Tests introduced in the last decade now look at sixteen chromosomal loci, so the RMP numbers are now even larger. (A locus is a specific area within a chromosome that can be readily identified.)

To show why I doubt this evidence we need to go back to basics.

Logic will tell you that the more biological loci that are matched between two DNA profiles, the greater the likelihood of a DNA match being genuine. The probability that someone would match a random DNA sample at any one site is supposedly roughly one in ten (1/10). So, the probability that someone would match a random sample at three sites would be about one in a thousand:

$$1/10 \times 1/10 \times 1/10 = 1/1{,}000.$$

Applying the same probability calculation to all ten sites used in SGM Plus® would mean the chances of matching a given DNA sample at random in the population are about one in ten thousand million (ten billion):

$$(1/10)^{10} = 1/10{,}000{,}000{,}000.$$

This figure does not appear, on its own, to be the origin of the often quoted one-in-a-billion odds. It should be noted that it is being calculated using the product rule for multiplying probabilities, which assumes that the patterns found in two distinct sites are independent. However, this is an assumption only, and it would seem to be unjustified when compared against reality.

Probabilities are supposedly calculated by considering how many ways there are for an event to occur divided by the total number of outcomes. Consider the famous birthday problem, stated as follows:

What are the odds of two people in a room sharing the same birthday?

To calculate this, statisticians consider the converse, i.e., what is the probability of not sharing a birthday, which they work out in the following manner, assuming no leap years.

Two people: (365/365) * (364/365) = 0.997
Three people: (365/365) * (364/365) * (363/365) = 0.992
Four people: (365/365) * (364/365) * (363/365) * (362/365) = 0.984
and so on.

Therefore, for ten people the odds are 0.883 and for twenty people the odds are 0.589. When you come to twenty-three people the odds are 0.493. At fifty people the odds are 0.03. What this means is, if twenty-three people are in a room, it is more likely than not that at least two share the same birthday. If there are fifty people in the room, then there is a 99.7% chance that two will share the same birthday. By the time you get to 100 people in the room these odds are well over 99.99%.

How does this apply to DNA databases? If you look at it in terms of a given frequency estimate, e.g., one in a billion, rather than a given number of loci, this equates to the one in 365 frequency estimates for the birthday example. So, this is not starting with a specific profile or 'birthday' in mind, just a frequency of occurrence. Logic dictates that the more people there are in the database the more likely it is that two people will have matching profiles, where the RMP is the predetermined frequency. It turns out that for a frequency of one in a million, you only need 1,178 people in the database for the probability of two matching profiles to exceed 50%. For a frequency of one in a billion, the database need only contain 37,234 entries for the probability of a match to exceed 50%. The next question is how does this compare with reality? The answer is badly, as the following evidence shows.

In 2001, Katherine Troyer took the Arizona State database of 65,493 felons and analysed the DNA profiles it contained. She found that there were 122 profile matches on nine loci out of the thirteen loci in the CODIS test used in the United States – rather than the eleven loci covered by our SGM Plus® test – and twenty matches on ten loci out of thirteen. There was also one match each for eleven and twelve loci, although these were down to the presence of siblings in the database.[2] Some statisticians claim that these findings are not surprising given the potential number of pairwise comparisons that a database of more than 65,000 would contain, which is over two billion.

They also argue that the probability of a random match for the pair of profiles in question is not the relevant probability, and that this deeply worrying evidence is, in fact, what their models predict.[3] Not being a professional statistician I can make no assessment of the validity of these obtuse arguments, although since DNA profile matches are often proclaimed on partial profiles, I remain dubious. Nonetheless, Troyer's findings blew a hole in the claims for RMP being a valid calculation as currently calculated. Remember, all statistics remains guesswork until confirmed by external evidence.

One can obviously argue about the conclusions that could be drawn from comparing a database of 65,000 profiles in Arizona with the makeup of the UK National DNA database, which in 2012 contained over seven million profiles. By rights, this evidence should have led to similar analyses being done for all other DNA databases, especially our much larger UK National database, and a review of the assumptions involved in the RMP calculation. After all, basic logic would indicate that there would be a greater number of matches the larger the database. I am not aware of either having taken place in the intervening twenty years.

The reason this is concerning is because what is called 'a DNA match' is not the same thing as confirming the DNA belongs to the suspect, as I shall now explain:

DNA Match Definition

DNA in the cell nucleus is made up of twenty-three pairs of chromosomes, of which twenty-two pairs are autosomes, and one pair is the chromosome defining gender. The nuclear DNA in each human cell contains some six billion nucleotides (building blocks), each made up of a combination of four nucleic acid bases: adenine (A), thymine (T), cytosine (C), and guanine (G). We share 99% of our DNA with chimpanzees, and even 96% with mice, so only a small part of our total DNA results in our human characteristics. Nevertheless, even one percent of six billion is still sixty million nucleotides.

In the case of the pairs of autosomes, each human child receives one autosome from each parent. In the case of the gender chromosome, mothers are designated XX, and fathers are designated XY. Their children will each receive the mother's X chromosome and, either the X chromosome from the father if they are female, or the Y chromosome if they are male. At various points in the DNA strand there will be what is known as a short tandem repeat (STR), such as AGCTAGCTAGCT, which is AGCT repeated twice again, and these are the loci that DNA profiling targets. These repeats are supposedly polymorphic, that is highly variable in number, and that is why they are useful indicators. The number of times the repeat occurs at each locus is designated as its allele (variant). At each locus there are, apparently, up to forty possibilities per STR. It is also claimed that each STR occurs roughly the same number of times across the whole population, although I don't know whether either of these claims has been confirmed experimentally. Nevertheless, at each of these loci a child receives an allele from each of its parents. These can be the same but usually differ between parents.

So, in the UK National DNA database, based on the ten autosome loci used in the SGM Plus® test, the value of the alleles is noted, and recorded as a pair of numbers. Importantly, the convention is that the smaller value of the allele is noted before the larger value, such as 4-6, which would be known as a heterozygote, because the numbers differ, or a homozygote if the numbers are the same, such as 4-4. Crucially, this means that the donating parent is never identified or displayed, from which it follows that the same result cannot be assumed to confirm the same DNA, as the alleles could have come from either parent. No part of this test method ever identifies the donating parent involved in the allele results. The only way to determine this is to perform DNA profile testing on both parents, which very rarely happens. This is the vital, and generally completely misunderstood, explanation for why the calling of a match, unless confirmed by other evidence, does not prove that the DNA belongs to the suspect.

Therefore, the supposed strength of the DNA profiling tests stems from statistical assumptions that have been shown by clear empirical evidence to be false, and a widespread misunderstanding of what the calling of a profile match means. Critically, it is also an unfortunate fact that most match calls by DNA profilers are only based on partial, rather than full, profile matches, as happened in Hanratty. This raises huge questions as to the scientific basis for any such calls, but seems to be accepted unquestioningly in courts, unless the defence can call upon other forensic scientists to challenge these claims. This rarely happens because the profiling laboratories, where most such scientists work, almost always represent the prosecution side. This is another fundamental issue with our judicial system that desperately needs addressing. It needs to be understood that any one of the missing alleles in a partial match could exonerate the suspect if they did not match his or her DNA, even if the calculated odds of a match were still astronomic.

This is the Kafkaesque situation we are in before we even come to consider Bayes' theorem, and as noted above, there are fundamental disagreements between forensic statisticians as to whether Bayes' theorem is even the correct way of looking at things. So how do the laboratories make their statistical probability calculations?

Calculating RMP

In an American document from 2003, *'Evaluating Forensic DNA Evidence: Essential Elements of a Competent Defense Review'*, Dr, now Professor Dan Krane and others state that:

> Lab reports generally also contain estimates of the statistical frequency of the matching profiles in various reference populations (which are intended to represent major racial and ethnic groups). Crime labs compute these estimates by determining the frequency of each allele in a sample population, and then compounding the individual frequencies by multiplying them together. If 10% (1 in 10) of Caucasian Americans are known to exhibit the 14 allele at the first locus (D3S1358) and 20% (1 in 5) are known to have the 15 allele, then the frequency of the pair of alleles would be estimated as $2 \times 0.10 \times 0.20 = 0.04$, or 4% among Caucasian Americans. The frequencies at each locus are simply multiplied together (sometimes with a minor modification meant to take

into account the possibility of under-represented ethnic groups), producing frequency estimates for the overall profile that can be staggeringly small: often on the order of 1 in a billion to 1 in a quintillion, or even less. Needless to say, such evidence can be very impressive.[4]

I would again point out that, although the statistical calculations employed have a consensus of forensic scientific support, it does not follow that the underlying assumptions, upon which they are based, have the necessary empirical evidence to remove the potential for sampling errors, or worse. I suspect the courts are simply accepting the generalisation that if a DNA 'match' is claimed, it must represent an overwhelming probability of the defendant's guilt, regardless of the circumstances, or the calculations involved.

If the science is performed properly, which as I shall explain is far from a given, once the DNA profiling equipment has analysed its sample, it produces a graphical readout for the scientist to interpret. Note the use of the word 'interpret' here; it is a highly skilled and contentious process that is involved before the evidence can be presented in court – which I shall examine in more detail later. Anyway, this graphical readout is called an electropherogram. It has peak values relating to the previously discussed alleles, which are then noted by the scientist for each locus.

The standard method for calculating the RMP for a single source is that which is outlined by Krane above. However, I would point out that in view of the FSS propensity for deviating from standard practices, as is being shown in this case, there is no guarantee that this is the method employed by Dr Whitaker to arrive at his various probability pronouncements. Unfortunately, his methods were never examined or explained, which is yet another of my reasons for doubting them.

To calculate the RMP for a single source electropherogram the formulae used will differ between a heterozygote and a homozygote result at each locus. For heterozygote results, the formula is '2pq', and for homozygote results, the formula is 'p^2'. These are derived from the Hardy-Weinberg equilibrium equation, which dates from 1908, and which states that the amount of genetic variation in a population will remain constant from one generation to the next in the absence of disturbing factors. This is expressed as:

$$p^2 + 2pq + q^2 = 1$$

Bearing in mind that this equation was developed more than seventy years before DNA profiling was developed, and over forty years before Franklin, Crick and Watson mapped the structure of DNA, it concerns me that these formulae are accepted as being inviolate. I have been unable to find any evidence that they have been empirically proven to be valid in the specific circumstances in which they are being used here.

The laboratories usually reference tables that detail the number of observed occurrences of allele numbers at each locus by population type (Caucasian, Indo-Pakistani etc.). Taking Krane's figures, at locus D3S1358 there was an allele result of 14-15. This is a heterozygote, and so is subject to the 2pq formula. On his hypothetical laboratory table for this locus, 10% of Caucasians exhibit allele 14, and 20% of Caucasians exhibit allele 15. For this result the following calculation is performed: '2*0.10*0.20', which gives the answer 0.04, or, in other words, 4% of Caucasians would exhibit this allele result in this hypothetical scenario.

In turn, the same calculation would then be done for each of the allele results displayed by the electropherogram, i.e., 2pq or p^2 at each locus, and then all would be multiplied together to give the figure for the whole electropherogram. As Krane highlights, this can be an astronomically high figure, which is then arbitrarily reported as 'more than one in a billion'. Bearing in mind that the actual figure arrived at, using this method, is often potentially much greater, one might reasonably ask why is it reported to the court as 'more than one in a billion'? A cynic might suggest that this is simply to divert attention away from a full understanding of the process involved, and to avoid awkward questions concerning its validity. I wonder how many courts are going to accept a scientist claiming the odds to be one in more than the current human population. Obviously, valid questions can also be asked about the contents, and suitability, of the ethnic databases thus employed. For example, how genetically different are the various populations that make up these categories (Caucasian, Indo-Pakistani etc.)? Have any such findings resulted in changes to the tables being used? Let alone how the laboratories decide which ethnicity is relevant to their crime scene profile. After all, just looking at the ethnicity of the defendant precludes much of the population wherever you are, and therefore severely impacts the validity of the statistical claims.

As mentioned above, I have been unable to confirm what method of statistical calculation the FSS scientists employed when presenting their evidence to the courts in the Hanratty case, as it appears to have been a closely guarded secret. Remember, this is before the issues of mixed sample calculations are even involved. There was certainly no examination of how Dr Whitaker produced his figures in this case, nor any other until the pivotal Sean Hoey case in 2007. (Hoey was cleared of murdering twenty-nine people in the Omagh bombings in Northern Ireland in 1998. Prosecutors had attempted to implicate Hoey with LCN DNA evidence presented by Dr Whitaker, but the defence argued that it was unreliable. The subsequent verdict was extremely critical of his expertise and performance in court, leading to all such cases being put on hold and the Caddy review of the science.)

By rights this calculation should always be carefully examined by all courts to ensure it has some scientific basis and isn't just an assumption, but I am not aware of this regularly happening.

This is all before the additional complexity of mixed profiles and Bayesian analysis is even considered, and the evidence for how this is managed is, frustratingly, not in the public domain, so I cannot delve further into this critical area. Nevertheless, I hope this material has been sufficient to give you some idea as to why I have cause to doubt the statistical probabilities being claimed in this and all other criminal cases involving DNA evidence.

In conclusion, whichever approach is favoured, all courts should undertake a proper examination of the basis for any statistical probability claims. Rather than relying upon the RMP number alone, they should consider the inherent weaknesses with the RMP and understand the method of its calculation, as well as the fact that even a full DNA match does not mean it belongs to the accused, and what such statements, as 'more than one in a billion' can be said to mean. Unfortunately, in the Hanratty case, and many cases since, nothing of the sort was done. Had it been, especially in view of the powerful evidence pointing to his innocence, such as the Liverpool alibi, would the court have been so certain of Hanratty's guilt? And who can say how many other verdicts might have been fundamentally different?

Further Potential Issues

Before I bring this chapter to a close, I would like to make the reader aware of some further points that are relevant to the Hanratty case, yet which were not examined during the 2002 hearing.

Firstly, DNA degrades over time, as explained in a 2006 paper by Yang and Speller: 'Technical tips for obtaining reliable DNA identification of historic human remains'. It says:

> Unlike modern forensic DNA analysis that can use multiple nuclear DNA markers for identification, historic DNA cases are usually restricted to analyzing mitochondrial DNA, which is more likely to survive degradation over time due to its high copy number per cell (O'Rourke et al. 2000; Kaestle and Horsburgh 2002). Since mtDNA serves as a single DNA marker, it has limited discrimination power.[5]

This paper is discussing archaeological specimen DNA and, unfortunately, I have been unable to find any estimates, authoritative or otherwise, of the expected levels of nuclear DNA decay from a body buried for forty years. It is, however, known that the rate of DNA decay speeds up in conditions that are warm and wet, as opposed to those that are cold and dry. This obviously raises many questions regarding what kind of DNA was obtained from Hanratty's body after exhumation, why it needed to be a composite, and what level of discriminatory power it really possessed?

Also, according to a 2011 article in *Environmental Science and Technology*, we all shed between 0.03g and 0.09g of skin every hour.[6]

This might not sound like much, but at a conservative estimate this gives an average of half a kilogram of skin cells per annum. As a gram is equivalent to a million million (one trillion) pg, therefore, 0.5 kilogram equals 500 trillion pg, which is a monumental number when you consider that the DNA LCN test claims to be able to develop a DNA profile from just less than 100 pg of nuclear DNA material.

As it happens, skin cells are one of the primary sources of nuclear DNA; others include white blood cells and sperm, as well as oral and vaginal cavity cells. However, nuclear DNA is only one component of skin cells, so I am not saying that for every pg of skin you will have a pg of DNA. Again, I have been unable to uncover an estimate of the proportion of skin that DNA accounts for, although it seems that forensic scientists expect there to be approximately 5 pg of nuclear DNA per individual human cell, as will be documented in the Hanratty hearing transcript. I hope that this has given you a feel for the truly microscopic quantities involved when the DNA evidence is being discussed in the Court of Appeal, and how these numbers are well below the capacity of the human eye to differentiate when dealing with crime scene evidence.

It is no wonder then that even the FSS website highlighted the potential for contamination at these levels. The opportunity for cross-contamination in the Hanratty case certainly existed at several stages and should have been properly considered in a Bayesian assessment of the DNA evidence. For example, the whereabouts of the piece of fabric from Miss Storie's knickers has been mostly unknown for the previous forty years, and likewise its method of storage. In this light, the FSS certainty in disregarding contamination is, in my view, wilfully perverse. Even the little that is known about its provenance shows that this garment was certainly exhibited at the committal hearing and was worked on in the Metropolitan Police laboratory in 1961, while Hanratty's clothing was also present and unwrapped on both occasions.

Section 2 of the first official external review of the FSS laboratory's work by Professor Brian Caddy and his team,[7] which only took place in 2008, several years after the work with which this book is concerned was performed, highlights the extreme care with which such low template level crime scene evidence must be handled and stored. (Low template DNA profiling, such as LCN, refers to any evidence which has a minute amount of DNA present.) None of this was done with the evidence that was collected in 1961 – long before DNA profiling was even thought of – and stored in unknown conditions for the next forty years. This weakens the FSS reasons to discount the risk of contamination in the Hanratty case even further.

Yet another issue which should be of concern to the authorities, is the prevalence of profiling errors within the laboratories. As I have already stated, at the time of the Hanratty appeal, and for several years afterwards, the FSS was not subject to any sort of review to assess the validity of its work. However, in 2004, the *International Journal of Legal Medicine* published the results of German DNA Profiling Group (GEDNAP) blind trials of testing samples, at 136 labs in thirty European countries. These are reproduced here:[8]

Figure 1: GEDNAP Trial

Table 1 Details of the participation of laboratories and results in the trials GEDNAP 6/7 (1993) through GEDNAP 26/27 (2003)

GEDNAP (year)	Number of laboratories	Number of countries	Number of STRs tested	Size of stains tested (µl)	Number of tests	Error rate (%)
6 and 7 (1993)	29	4	1	5–300	104	0
8 and 9 (1994)	38	7	3	200	811	1.2
10 and 11 (1995)	48	9	5	20–200	2,550	2.1
12 and 13 (1996)	59	10	8	10–100	4,448	1.2
14 and 15 (1997)	72	11	8	5–50	5,184	1.6
16 and 17 (1998)	75	12	10	20–50	7,468	0.7
18 and 19 (1999)	78	12	21	5–50	11,409	0.5
20 and 21 (2000)	85	12	15	25	13,868	0.7
22 and 23 (2001)	122	28	17	10–25	21,743	0.5
24 and 25 (2002)	136	30	17	5–25	30,479	0.4
26 and 27 (2003)	160	31	30	5–25	n.a	n.a.

n.a. not available

This found that the actual error rate in 2002 was 0.4%, which means that four tests in 1,000 were wrong.

This error rate occurred even though all the participating laboratories knew of the test in advance. They would have had time to ensure that both their processes and equipment were satisfactory to remove any associated issues, and yet the errors still occurred.

A further piece of information, which is also worth bearing in mind, is the possibility of human error in such interpretive activity is more likely than may be acknowledged. This is shown in the fingerprint recognition study by Dror and Charlton. They comment that:

> If the nature of mind and cognitive processing can give rise to error in fingerprint individualization, then these errors are inherent in the domain. Nevertheless, they do not reflect a basic ontological scientific flaw in the domain nor are they the fault of a specific practitioner. They are, in essence, epistemological problems that derive from the mechanisms of human cognition and the workings of the mind.[9]

One final point to consider is the following paragraph from the 2003 document by Professor Dan Krane and others, referred to earlier:

> It is well known that people tend to see what they expect (and desire) to see when they evaluate ambiguous data. This tendency can cause analysts to unintentionally slant their interpretations in a manner consistent with prosecution theories of the case. Furthermore, some analysts appear to rely on non-genetic evidence to help them interpret DNA test results. When one of us questioned an analyst's interpretation of a problematic case, the analyst defended her position by saying: 'I know I am right – they found the victim's purse in [the defendant's] apartment.' Backwards reasoning of this type (i.e., 'we know the defendant is guilty, so the DNA evidence must be incriminating') is another factor that can cause analysts to slant their reports in a manner that supports police theories of the case. Hence, it is vital that defense counsel look behind the laboratory report to determine whether the lab's conclusions are well supported, and whether there is more to the story than the report tells.

At this point I would like to return to the wise aphorism from Robert Anton Wilson, with which I began this work: 'What the thinker thinks the prover proves.' Obviously, I include myself as being subject to this failing. However, since I have it in mind, I hope that I am alert enough to ameliorate its worst effects upon my arguments.

How much relevance any of these factors has to the Hanratty case is, unfortunately, still a matter of conjecture. But from the evidence in the judgment, the FSS experts and the Court of Appeal would appear to have grossly understated the probability of contamination, and interpretation error, when using a technique that is far more subjective, risky, and misunderstood than has been credited. I would also point out that LCN DNA analysis has been and remains extremely controversial among the international forensic science community.

However, before, I finally move on to consider the content of the transcripts, it is worth understanding just what is involved in the DNA testing process, and the ramifications of the numerous issues associated with it. I would remind you, once again, that forensic DNA evidence requires correct interpretation by the scientist before presentation to a court. As we are about to see, this involves so much more than just reading numbers. It is fraught with difficulties and open to expert disagreement, even if the science has been performed properly, which unfortunately is not always the case. Scientific results are only valid if the science has been performed correctly, and this requires regular external oversight to confirm and maintain scientific standards. Unfortunately, this cannot be said for all the evidence presented to courts by the FSS before mid- 2009 when it finally implemented the key finding of the Caddy review, relating to quantification, documented in its section 3.2 as follows.

> The first question that must be resolved is whether or not the isolated DNA (assumed to be <200pg) should be quantified. Because the amount of DNA is so small the FSS take the view that it is unnecessary to quantify because it uses up too much DNA in the process thereby reducing the chances of producing a successful profile. Other forensic science providers routinely quantify the DNA extract believing that in so doing it reduces the chances of generating over amplification of the PCR products, something the review has observed with some

FSS analyses. Additionally these providers believe that this enables a better estimate of potential inhibition. Unless there is a recognised method for addressing problems relating to over amplification, the reviewers would favour this second approach. The availability of real time PCR quantification makes this not only feasible but uses acceptable levels of DNA product leaving sufficient to carry out a full analysis in duplicate with sufficient material being left over for a third analysis should it become necessary. Further research into the best ways of quantifying very small DNA samples (for example using a repetitive DNA target) may be indicated. The Forensic Science Regulator should monitor the use of DNA quantification procedures.

Then in Section 3.5 Caddy explicitly states:

The Forensic Science Regulator should insist that as a matter of best practice a DNA quantification step is implemented for all DNA analyses submitted to the CJS and should monitor its implementation.

Clearly, although Caddy considered that so-called low template science, including LCN, was valid, it could only be considered valid if quantification was always initially performed. The Caddy review is also highly critical of the FSS performance standards in other key respects such as validation, anti-contamination and performance standards and subsequently documents twenty-one recommended changes to the way the science was being performed in the UK.

I wonder how vigilant our forensic authorities have been in monitoring the work of the private laboratories that replaced the FSS after it was disbanded. Correctly handling issues such as these is vital to most people's notion of justice. After all, when one is dealing with science such as this, which is routinely used to take away citizens' liberty, or, as in Hanratty's case, their lives, one would hope the laboratories were operating to collectively agreed performance standards. Unfortunately, as you are about to discover, such hope is severely misplaced.

DNA Profiling Issues

Such has been the enthusiasm with which the police, the courts, our political authorities, and the media have greeted the development of DNA profiling as a tool to 'solve' crime, most people seem persuaded that the proclamation of a DNA match is a cast-iron guarantee of guilt. I have already pointed out that there are serious reasons for concern when considering the use of statistical probabilities with this evidence, and the fact that even a full match is not a confirmation that the DNA is that of the suspect. In addition, there is the unfortunate fact that many of the matches proclaimed are only partial, which raises huge doubts concerning their scientific basis. However, equally concerning are the potential issues around the reliability of the testing involved. It is to this area I shall now turn.

It is important to understand that when the Court of Appeal in Hanratty was presented with DNA evidence by the FSS scientists, the standard accepted test was SGM Plus®, which had only been introduced a couple of years before. The use of LCN with the thirty-four cycles of PCR, as detailed in *Horizon* had, as far as I can tell, never been considered by the courts before and as will be shown, it is debatable whether the court in Hanratty's case was even informed that such cutting-edge science was involved. However, it will become clear that many of the issues about to be discussed apply equally to the SGM Plus® technique. As was explained earlier, LCN extends the standard SGM Plus® testing from twenty-eight to thirty-four cycles of PCR amplification, and has been, and remains, controversial for reasons that should become clear.

To begin to outline the issues I would refer you again to the American document by Professor Dan Krane and others.[1] It was written in 2003 to provide defence teams with a sufficient understanding of the science of nuclear DNA profiling, to ensure that any such evidence had been produced by rigorous scientific work and was not making invalid claims. Had it been published before the Hanratty Appeal in 2002, that verdict could have been very different.

The authors point out that, even if the reliability and admissibility of the underlying tests is well established, there is no guarantee that the test will produce valid results each time. Remember that valid scientific results require proper set up and performance and regular external oversight. The authors also reiterate my earlier point, that even when the suspect has the same alleles at every locus, or in other words is a full match, this only means the suspect is a *possible* donor, and it is not a confirmation that it is the suspect's DNA. This document also states that the tests are powerless to provide any insight into how the sample was deposited, and often even the type of tissue that was involved. The Caddy review confirms this, as follows:

> It is our opinion that any LTDNA profile should always be reported to the jury with the caveats: that the nature of the original starting material is unknown; that the time at which the DNA was transferred cannot be inferred; and that the opportunity for secondary transfer is increased in comparison to standard DNA profiling.

In addition, this document cites many reasons for warning against accepting, uncritically, any DNA laboratory report, let alone any interpretation put on it, such as inconsistencies between purportedly matching profiles, evidence of additional unreported contributors in DNA samples, errors in statistical calculations and unreported problems with experimental controls. There is also the potential for unconscious, or even conscious, bias in evidence interpretation, with labs treating peak heights (explained below) as a reliable indicator of DNA quantity when it supports the prosecution, and as unreliable when it doesn't.

86　Executed: But was James Hanratty Innocent?

In a mixed DNA sample, the complications soon multiply exponentially. To clarify, the paper states:

> Some laboratories try to determine which alleles go with which contributor based on peak heights. They assume that the taller peaks (which generally indicate larger quantities of DNA at the start of the analysis) are associated with a 'primary' contributor and the shorter peaks with a 'secondary' contributor. …But these inferences are often problematic because a variety of factors, other than the quantity of DNA present, can affect peak height.
>
> In mixed samples, it may be impossible to determine whether the alleles of one or more contributors have become undetectable at some loci. Often analysts simply guess whether all alleles have been detected or not, which renders their conclusions speculative and leaves the results open to a variety of alternative interpretations. Further, the two or more biological samples that make up a mixture may show different levels of degradation, perhaps due to their having been deposited at different times or due to differences in the protection offered by different cell types. Such possibilities make the interpretation of degraded mixed samples particularly prone to subjective (unscientific) interpretation.

Stochastic Threshold Issues

As if all of this was not bad enough, the paper also details several issues associated with what is known as the 'stochastic threshold', which complicates the interpretation further. Stochastic means random or unreliable. This is the minimum level of DNA material in a sample, below which the testing equipment cannot be relied upon to produce a reliable result. Twenty years ago, this would have been a little below 1 ng (1 billion ng = 1 gram), as documented in the user guide for the kit used at the time.[2]

Technology has moved on, and today kits claim reliability down to 250 pg (1,000 pg = 1 ng). These sorts of microscopic dimensions are obviously well below the ability of the human eye to discern. However, the key issue is that this threshold is not a fixed value, despite its name. Instead, it is highly variable depending upon a variety of environmental factors, and so great care needs to be taken to confirm these have been eliminated in the test results. Some examples of these issues are:

Allelic Drop-out or Drop-in

Drop-out is where an allele that is expected to appear at a locus does not. This is wholly dependent on the proposed profile – usually that of the defendant – and is, therefore, critically affected by bias. Usually, laboratories will not report alleles that are observed only once, although they sometimes refer to them as unconfirmed alleles. What the courts then make of these 'unconfirmed alleles' is a moot question. Anyway, allelic drop-out is either due to sample degradation or the test approaching the threshold of its reliability. Analysts then need to decide whether the mismatch reflects a true genetic difference or the failure to detect the missing allele. Because of this, laboratories often ignore these loci results with missing alleles, claiming that this is a conservative procedure that favours the defendant, despite the fact this ignores the potentially exculpatory nature of these loci results. This is the reason why the calling of a DNA match by an expert on a partial profile is contentious; because if one of the missing alleles is not a match, it means the sample cannot belong to the suspect regardless of the number of alleles that do match. In turn, allelic drop-in is when the sample is impacted by the presence of contaminating DNA alleles.

Spurious Peaks

These can be produced by unavoidable imperfections in the DNA analysis process. The most common are 'stutter', 'noise' and 'pull-up'. 'Stutter peaks' are small peaks occurring immediately before, or after, a real peak. These are difficult to distinguish if mixed DNA samples are involved. 'Noise peaks' are small background peaks occurring along the baseline of all samples. Occasionally, due to factors such as air bubbles, urea crystals and contamination, these can become random flashes that are large enough to be confused with, or even mask, actual peaks. 'Pull-up', sometimes called 'bleed-through', is where the analysis software cannot discriminate between the different dye colours used to generate the test results, thereby creating false peaks. It can be identified by a careful analysis of the peaks across the colour spectrum but may be unrecognised, especially if the result is consistent with what the analyst expected or wanted to find. Though these artefacts can be identified, standards can be subjective, leading to expert disagreement, and analysts can also be inconsistent in their approach across cases. This is the reason why the lack of agreed international scientific interpretation standards was, and possibly remains, so critical.

Additionally, when the quantity of DNA being examined is very low, the equipment may fail to detect the entire profile of a contributor, or it may be difficult to distinguish true low-level peaks from an artefact. As a result, laboratories tend to have established peak height thresholds expressed in relative fluorescence units (RFU), below which an allele will not be counted. However, this threshold can vary between laboratories and equipment, and even within laboratories in different cases. Professor Krane has informed me that in the USA, the Scientific Working Group on DNA Analysis Methods (SWGDAM) has set the accepted RFU threshold for confidently calling alleles to be 150 RFU.[3] Great care must be taken when making allele calls below the standard threshold, as peak height imbalance ratios are not reliable. Allelic drop-in, allelic drop-out, and pronounced baseline stutter can occur randomly. There is also an issue if the laboratories err too much in the other direction, and apply RFU scales that are too big, as they then run the risk of ignoring genuine low-level peaks. Unfortunately, no such threshold standard is applied in the UK; again, this is an entirely unsatisfactory situation that should not be allowed to continue.

It is also an unfortunate fact that the DNA testing technology can be responsible, on its own, for spurious profiling results, even when no human error is apparently involved in the running of the test. This is mostly, but not always, due to the extreme sensitivity involved and microscopic nature of the DNA being tested. A worthwhile paper on this subject was published in 2001 by Jennifer N. Mellon.[4]

She argues that it is in the interests of justice to ensure that the manufacturers of the equipment used in DNA analysis provide access to the scientific data that supports the testing method employed – both to the courts and to the wider scientific community. The data at issue is twofold: firstly, the overall developmental validation studies, and secondly, the primer sequences used to amplify the DNA via PCR before it is typed.

Developmental Validation Studies

These should determine the limitations of the new technology, such as whether it is prone to errors, and what kind of precautions should be taken to prevent these. Access to this data is required to ensure that, at the basic level, such testing was performed. It must be extensively performed before the equipment can be routinely employed, to show whether the method and/or the kit produce regular, accurate and reliable results. The FSS did not publish any such results for its LCN test method before it was shut down in 2012. As we'll see, it later admitted to reliability issues with this test – not that it informed the Hanratty hearing of this – and my strong suspicion is that the lack of validation testing played a considerable part in these reliability issues.

Primer Sequences

These primers are used in PCR, which is the amplification step of DNA testing. In PCR, the technician extracts the DNA from the cells and divides the strands from each other. The technician then adds a primer, which is a short piece of DNA, to the single strands, which marks the section of the DNA to be amplified. The polymerase enzyme is then added to the primer DNA mixture. Like other naturally occurring enzymes, this creates a new complementary strand of DNA to bond with each of the original strands. This is the process that is repeated twenty-eight times in SGM Plus® testing to create sufficient DNA for testing.

The primary issue here is the risk of contamination due to the extraordinary sensitivity of the PCR process. It may occur from several sources, such as handling in the field during collection, cross-contamination of samples in the laboratory, carry-over contamination from PCR products from prior amplifications, or even from the kits themselves. Without knowing the primer sequence involved, it is impossible to determine if this has also contributed in any way to the results produced.

This paper then highlights that at the time two separate manufacturer's kits were producing different results when reading the VWA locus of the DNA sequence. Obviously, potential issues like these can have catastrophic impacts on the accuracy of such tests, with associated deleterious effects on the criminal justice process, and the person in the dock. I am not aware whether the data discussed in this paper is now readily available; nevertheless, this paper was produced at about the time of the Hanratty appeal and reflects known concerns at that time.

The Reed Judgment

To continue this discussion, I shall refer to a later judgment from the Court of Appeal: R vs Reed, Reed and Garmson [2009] EWCA Crim 2698[5]. This is a critical judgment when considering how the English criminal courts deal with DNA evidence because it has been used by our courts as a reference case to determine how to approach such evidence. Unfortunately, it contains several factual and interpretation errors, which mean that our courts have been, and potentially still are being, misled regarding how to handle this critical evidence. Accordingly, the implications for our justice system are stark. Remember this is on top of the already mentioned issues regarding the lack of acceptable validation of 'expert' evidence by our courts. The judgment dates from 2009, which is some seven years after the Hanratty appeal, but my reasons for discussing it should become clear as my argument progresses.

The Quantification Process

The quantification process is essential to the correct performance of the science of DNA profiling. It is required to correctly calibrate the testing equipment for the size of the DNA sample to be dealt with.

If the ultra-sensitive machine is not properly calibrated it will not produce valid results. Quantification means correctly measuring the size of the sample before the performance of any testing method such as SGM Plus® or LCN.

The Reed judgment states:

> The DNA is then extracted from the cells by chemical treatment and can be measured. The process of measurement is known as quantification (or quantitation), but the process of quantification consumes part of the amount of the available DNA. For that reason, it was not at the time of the trials of the appellants the practice of the FSS for that reason to quantify the amount of DNA. Professor Caddy recommended in his review that quantification should take place. It now is standard practice in the FSS to quantify, **as it can be helpful to take into account the quantity in determining the subsequent process and the interpretation of the result.** The DNA obtained is generally divided into three parts (aliquots). Two are used in the tests carried out immediately and one retained for use in a further test or by the defence.

Please note that the phrase in bold, stating that this step can be helpful, is not what the Caddy report said. Caddy said that although the basic science of LCN was valid, the technique was only valid if the quantification step was done. To be clear, this step does not just apply when running LCN, it applies to all DNA profiling test machinery and always has done. The FSS totally ignored this requirement, for the reason given in the judgment here, until Caddy's review forced it to begin to implement the step of routine quantification, and presumably correct calibration, in the summer of 2009. By rights this should have led to a review of all earlier cases in which FSS results were key, or at the very least all those that involved LCN test results, but to my knowledge this has not been done. So, here is yet another problem with the DNA evidence relied upon in Hanratty, and potentially many other cases as well.

This is crucial, because the smaller the sample of DNA used to generate the profile, the greater the risk of stochastic effects, and contamination, corrupting the profile results. Remember, this is on top of issues associated with incorrect calibration that will occur without quantification. The FSS reason for this practice was that using up some of what is, in fact, a very small starting template was seen as a waste of the total available DNA. This means that it remains unclear whether the quantity of DNA being tested was below the stochastic threshold in all cases, including Hanratty, prior to this time, regardless of any certainty ascribed by the FSS witnesses. I wonder how many convictions have resulted from all these years of unverified and potentially invalid science; not that the authorities have shown any inclination to try and answer this critical question. This, I believe, is yet another example of the FSS laboratory not adhering to proper scientific procedures.

The additional point, that the DNA collected is divided into three separate aliquots, including one for the defence, should be viewed against what happened in the Hanratty case. There, the defence scientist, Dr Evison, was not provided with DNA material to perform his own testing and had to rely solely upon a review of the documentation. Again, this is another failing in the way the case was handled, much to Hanratty's disadvantage.

Stochastic Threshold Issues

As already noted, this threshold refers to the equipment being at the limits of its capabilities and thus producing unreliable results when dealing with samples smaller than those it is designed to test. The equipment should be subject to rigorous validation testing by the manufacturer, before being taken to market, to identify the reliable limits of its capabilities. This means that whenever the test is run at lower than the manufacturer's minimum recommended sample level, there is no guarantee that unreliable results won't occur.

From Reed again:

> The standard profiling test involves copying using 28 cycles. Originally 2 nanograms of DNA were required. In 1999, the

SGM+ test permitted 1 nanogram (one billionth of a gram (10^{-9})) of DNA to be used as the standard starting template. The standard kit used is designed optimally to produce a full profile on 1 nanogram.

This is confirmation that the standard SGM Plus® test uses twenty-eight cycles of PCR copying, and that it required DNA samples of 1 ng or more to provide a full profile. The earlier SGM test required 2 ng. As already noted, one gram is equivalent to a billion ng, so 1 ng is a vanishingly small quantity of material anyway, well beyond the capabilities of the human eye to discern. This raises major questions as to why the FSS felt the need to try, and felt justified in arbitrarily, going to even smaller levels where stochastic effects would occur even more frequently.

Back to Reed:

Two runs of the test are carried out; the runs are often conducted simultaneously in crime investigations as there is normally urgency to obtain the result. Sequential runs have the advantage of enabling the scientist to consider and evaluate the results of the first run to see whether any adjustments to the process are needed.

As we will see in the Hanratty transcripts, it is not entirely clear whether two runs of the tests were carried out, whether they were run simultaneously or sequentially and, even if they were, whether the correct interpretation of the results was applied. To reiterate, it is better to run the tests sequentially, for the reason noted here, but due to urgency this is often dispensed with, and the tests are run simultaneously. I contend that the implications of this fact upon overall test reliability need to be carefully researched and much more clearly understood, as they could be considerable. However, it seems that the forensic regulator does not agree, since no such research appears to have been carried out.

Reed continues:

> The results of each test run are produced in graphical form known as an electrophoretogram. [sic] The electrophoretogram requires expert interpretation, as, for example, the different loci can react differently on amplification. The process can generate results, known as 'artefacts', which are the consequence of the process and which are not an analysis of the DNA itself.

Here the judgment confirms my earlier point, that the electropherogram (not electrophoretogram, as it is called here) requires expert interpretation to be correctly attributed, which is often a far from straightforward task. This involves the scientist very carefully evaluating the peaks recorded to ensure they are valid. Also highlighted is the fact the SGM Plus® test, by itself, can generate artefacts that do not belong to the DNA sample, as explained earlier in this chapter. That is even before the involvement of the much more contentious low template testing. I wonder how often our courts have been told this inconvenient fact when dealing what is a generally accepted and uncontroversial scientific test procedure.

Back to Reed:

> The standard SGM+ test is designed to produce a full profile with 1 nanogram of DNA. **It can be employed for smaller quantities....** Where a sample is measured to be less than what is required to generate a profile using the standard SGM+ test, then Low Template DNA analysis is often undertaken. ...It is important to note, **that the FSS at the time of the testing did not quantify the DNA,** but acted on the judgment of the forensic science officer as to whether it was appropriate to use the LCN process based on that officer's judgment of the quantity of DNA.

This judgment, like Hanratty's, was concerned specifically with the contentious form of low template DNA profiling known as LCN, developed by the FSS. When the FSS scientists presented LCN evidence to the Hanratty appeal, they did not quantify the amount of DNA present in the sample, for the reason given here. This is crucially important for two reasons: firstly, because the smaller the sample of DNA used to generate the profile, the greater the risk of stochastic effects and contamination corrupting the profile results. Secondly, because they were relying on human judgments as to the potential sample sizes, which inevitably moves the results beyond rigorous scientific boundaries. Caddy quite specifically stated that this was not an acceptable practice, yet it had been going on for at least eight years to the potential detriment of many criminal cases.

The Reed judgment also states that reliable samples can be produced from lower than the manufacturer's recommendation but note the use of the word 'can' here. It does not mean it is guaranteed to occur. To be sure of success the minimum recommended sample size is required, as well as the correct performance of the scientific processes involved, and even then, this is no guarantee against the test producing an occasional invalid result.

Reed adds:

> As we explain at paragraph 74. ii) **the threshold below which stochastic effects can be produced is at present accepted to be between 100 and 200 picograms...** . Above that threshold (often called the stochastic threshold), the stochastic effect should not affect the reliability of the DNA profile obtained. **Below that stochastic threshold the electrophoretograms [*sic*] may be capable of producing a reliable profile, if for example there is reproducibility between the two runs.**

This claims that the threshold for stochastic effects is now generally accepted as between 100 pg and 200 pg. Firstly, as already noted, it is important to understand there is no single threshold value where stochastic effects will begin to occur; it is very variable and depends upon a great many environmental factors. You cannot just assume that above a certain minimum number you will not run into stochastic effects. The only way to confidently remove the potential for stochastic effects is to ensure you have at least 1 ng of DNA to sample, as per the test kit manufacturers' instructions. However, here the court is implying that any level above 200 pg is considered reliable without having to reproduce the result with a second run of the test. As such rulings are usually extremely carefully worded, the last sentence above allows any court to accept another claim for reliability that does not involve reproducibility. This is an extremely dangerous misrepresentation of the real situation. There are some serious issues here that do not appear to have been considered by the Court of Appeal in this case.

To begin with, it appears that the first mention of the 200 pg level was from the terms of reference for the Caddy Review in 2008.[6] In addition, I surmise that the 100 pg threshold may have arisen because that was the target level used by the FSS, below which they were aiming LCN. These numbers are extremely questionable since, as already noted, the SGM Plus® testing kit user guide, in use at the time, sets the lowest threshold value for producing a reliable profile at 1 ng. The manufacturer stipulates that the testing kit requires at least 1 ng of DNA material to function correctly. So, the key question is, at what level should laboratories start using low template technologies? The user guide makes no guarantees below the 1 ng level and does not make any recommendations accordingly. Therefore, this court is dangerously misrepresenting the reliability of the standard test, between the 200 pg and 1 ng levels, even before one involves the contentious LCN test. Current kits claim to be able to function reliably down to 250 pg, which shows that the technology has significantly improved, but still not to the sort of levels the FSS were targeting twenty years ago, or that this court is implying does not require to be reproduced.

Mixed Samples

Another issue at these low levels occurs when there is a mix of DNA donors in an evidence sample, such as in a rape, which will contain both rapist and victim DNA. In the Hanratty case, there was DNA material on the knickers from Valerie Storie, as well as at least one semen sample, supposedly from Hanratty. In addition, the court was under the impression that there was a group AB semen sample on the knickers that was assumed to have come from Michael Gregsten.

When considering a mixed profile DNA sample that only contains a little more than 200 pg, the amount of material from each of the donors will be considerably less than the supposedly acceptable 200 pg threshold. Therefore, how do you scientifically identify that the donor material involved can be reliably interpreted, and has not been subjected to stochastic effects, without at least having been reproduced?

In the later, critically important, Sean Hoey[7] case, which predated this Reed judgment, it was shown that because of such stochastic effects, a minimum of three runs is needed, and even then, there is no guaranteed certainty. I shall discuss further the importance of the Hoey case and its relationship to Hanratty when we come to the court transcripts. We will also see what was said about the number of profiling tests performed by Dr Whitaker.

Lack of Interpretation Standards

Another issue at these low levels is the fact that there are no internationally agreed interpretation standards. This is a fundamental problem with all such evidence, as without a reliable and agreed scientific basis for any interpretation, how can it be demonstrated objectively to be anything more than just an opinion? This is so much more than an argument about semantics. Unfortunately, the FSS refused to engage with the international forensic community, but instead supposedly created its own standards, which it never published to allow independent experts to assess their validity.

LCN Test Reliability

Another key concern with the scientific accuracy of the DNA profiling done in the Hanratty case concerns the actual reliability of the test method itself. The Reed judgment states:

'The FSS had found that in a very high proportion of profiles obtained using the LCN process the profiles were not capable of robust and reliable interpretation because of stochastic variations.'

This confirms that even the FSS itself has admitted to considerable stochastic problems with LCN profiles, which is hardly indicative of a reliable technology despite the authorities' claims to the contrary. This is another reason why this science is so controversial among international forensic experts. You should note that the Hanratty hearing was never informed of any doubts concerning the reliability of this testing. This could be related to the fact that the FSS never published the results of any validation tests of its LCN equipment and technique before using it in Hanratty, and in subsequent cases. Yet Jennifer Mellon's paper discussed the importance of such testing being performed to assess the reliability of the method. I strongly suspect that the FSS relied solely upon the manufacturer's validation testing of the kit and made no attempt to assess the impact of introducing thirty-four PCR cycles into the reliability of the test before bringing it into our courts. The manufacturer authorised the kit to be used if performing twenty-eight cycles only, so if my suspicion is correct this, in my view, would have been wilfully unethical, unscientific, and arguably criminal.

Statistical Probabilities

The Reed judgment makes the following comment about the vexed area of statistical probabilities:

> If the profile is full, it is possible to express the match probability as a billion to one. If the unknown person is a close relative or the profile is incomplete, then the match probability will be higher, for example 1 in 10,000. Where there is a mixture, then this has to be taken into account in the evaluation of the match probability.

This seems to be an example of how easy it is to make errors when discussing statistical probabilities with DNA evidence. As I stated earlier it is not possible to do the RMP calculation in mixed samples, only in those where there is a single identifiable major contributor. For mixed samples in the UK a Bayesian Likelihood Ratio is the most common statistical approach, whereas the Americans may use a Combined Probability of Inclusion (CPI) or a Random Man Not Excluded (RMNE) approach. However, these should never be expressed as a billion to one; it should be a one in a billion chance of coming from someone other than the suspect, and even then, only in the case of a full profile match. In the light of this judgment, it seems that the Court of Appeal was not fully aware of the seriousness of these issues. I would ask the reader to imagine that they are a juror hearing a figure such as 'one in a billion' being quoted, and to consider how they might respond to such a claim.

Partial Profile Matches

Where only a partial profile is capable of being produced, Reed further states, in my view misguidedly:

> However, the fact that there exists in the case of all partial profile evidence the possibility that a 'missing' allele might exculpate the accused altogether does not provide sufficient grounds for rejecting such evidence. In many cases there is a possibility (at least in theory) that evidence exists which would assist the accused and perhaps even exculpate him altogether, but that does not provide grounds for excluding relevant evidence that is available and otherwise admissible, though it does make it important to ensure that the jury are given sufficient information to enable them to evaluate that evidence properly.

I have already pointed out that calling a match on a partial profile raises all sorts of issues, especially regarding the objectivity and bias of the scientist. To allow a partial profile, without guidance as to how many alleles can be missing before it is discounted, is entering even more dangerous territory. I contend that the calling of a match in anything other than a full match circumstance is unscientific and should not be allowed, as it involves the introduction of personal judgments and other random variables that cannot be scientifically verified. Unfortunately, the judiciary don't agree. This greatly overstates the value of the evidence and biases courts unfairly against the defendant.

Reed continues:

> The probative value of evidence relating to match probabilities will depend upon all the circumstances. For example, the mere possibility that a missing allele might not match the profile of the accused is not of itself a sufficient ground for excluding the evidence. However, where it is not accepted that the DNA is that of the defendant, then if evidence as to match probability is to be placed before the jury so they can evaluate the probabilities in the context of all the other evidence in the case, then the judge must explain its relevance, the other evidence which provides the context which gives the match probability its significance.

This means that trial judges must draw attention to evidence that exculpates the defendant, which, yet again, the Court of Appeal failed to do in its Hanratty judgment. You should also note that from the content of the third and final sentence, the court appears to be under the impression that a DNA match confirms the DNA as belonging to the suspect, which, as has already been explained, is factually incorrect. It is a blatant overstatement of the value of the evidence and has misdirected the entire UK judiciary.

DNA Transferral

Finally, when considering the mechanisms of contamination, Reed notes:

> DNA can be transferred in many ways, of which the following are of particular significance:
>
> i) Primary transfer by a person directly to the object from which the sample was taken.

ii) Secondary transfer by a person to another person and by that other person to the object from which the sample was taken.

iii) Tertiary transfer by a person to an object and from that object to another person and by that person to the object from which the sample was taken.

This was a key area of dispute at the 2002 hearing. According to Dr Whitaker from the FSS, the profile characteristics were indicative of Hanratty being the rapist, but what evidence exists through prior testing to support this contentious claim? In other words, how different are the profiles from rape to those from secondary or tertiary contamination, and how can we be sure that his conclusion was justified? In addition, there was also DNA present which was supposed to have originated two days earlier from Gregsten. No research has been published regarding how one might differentiate between these two specific circumstances. A 2013 paper by Dr Georgina Meakin and Professor Allan Jamieson, from The Forensic Institute, concludes:

> The experimental data reviewed ... **shows that neither the quantity of DNA recovered nor the quality of the DNA profile obtained can be used to reliably infer the mode of transfer by which the DNA came to be on the surface of interest**. From our court experience, some forensic practitioners assert that an opinion can be given, whilst others do not ... forensic practitioners should resist pressure from the police, lawyers, or even the Court, and only provide an opinion that is scientifically supported.[8]

It is therefore clear that the FSS position in the Hanratty case, over a decade later, lacked a sufficient evidential basis to be acceptable to other forensic practitioners. Importantly, in addition to this finding that no mode of transfer, contamination, rape or otherwise, can be reliably inferred, the Caddy review stated that the DNA source material, such as sperm, mucus, saliva etc. cannot be inferred either. This flatly contradicts the FSS case that Hanratty raped Storie.

Unfortunately, the status of the FSS equipment regarding this lengthy list of potential concerns remains unknown. To ensure that the Hanratty evidence is supportable, these issues would need to be satisfactorily explained, which now seems to be extremely unlikely, again much to the Hanratty family's detriment.

Analysing DNA Profiles

In this final section I shall demonstrate just how complex and open to dispute the interpretation of DNA test results can be – and this is even after all potential issues with the tests, which have already been discussed, have been recognised and eliminated. Again, it will require some effort on the reader's behalf. This evidence needs to be assessed carefully, on the grounds of possible contamination or incorrect attribution, especially in the light of the myriad issues that can affect such testing, of which you will now be aware.

What cannot be avoided here is this. If the FSS interpretation of events is correct, all the Liverpool alibi witnesses were either lying, or mistaken. I, for one, cannot begin to calculate the odds of that being the case.

What did the FSS testing show?

From a document presented to the Court of Appeal during an earlier hearing to request the exhumation of Hanratty's body, and kindly provided to me by the law firm, Bindmans LLP, the following nuclear DNA tests were performed, prior to the testing done on his remains.

Figure 2: FSS results prior to exhumation

ITEM	Am	TH01	D21	D18	D8	VWA	FGA	Source	Tester
Valerie S / BS	XX	7, 9.3	59, 65	15, 19	8, 12	18,19	20, 20	VS	RF
Mary H / BS	XX	6,6	63,65	13, 15	8, 13	15, 17	19, 20	Mary H	RF
Michael H / BS	XY	6, 9	61, 65	13, 14	13, 15	15, 18	19, 25	Michael H	RF
Petticoat	XX	7, 9.3	59,65	15, 19	8, 12	18, 19	20, 20	VS	RF
Knickers Seminal	XY	6, 7, 9	NR	13, 14, 16, 18	13,	16, 17, 18	19, 21 ,25	Unknown 1&2	RF

DNA Profiling Issues 103

ITEM	Am	TH01	D21	D18	D8	VWA	FGA	Source	Tester
Knickers Epithelial	XY	6,7,9,9.3	59,65	13, 14, 15, 19	8, 12, 13	17, 18, 19	19,20,25	VS & Unknown	RF
Hankie Stain 1	XY	6, 9	63, 70	13, 14	13, 13	17, 18	19, 25	Unknown 1	JB
Hankie Stain 2	XY	6, 9	NR	13, 14	NR	17, 18	19, 25	Unknown 1	JB
Hankie Yellow Stn1	XY	6, 9	NR	13, 14	13, 13	17, 18	19, 25	Unknown 1	JB
Hankie Yellow Stn2	Poor partial profile obtained – no reproducible results								JB
Postcard RH stamp	NR	NR	NR	NR	NR	NR	NR		JB
Postcard LH stamp	XY	6	NR	NR	NR	17, 18	NR	Unk 1&2 or JB	JB
RH side of stamp	XY	6, 9.3	65	NR	13	17, 18	24, 25	Unknown	JB
LH side of stamp	XY	6	NR	NR	NR	17, 18	NR	Unk 1&2 or JB	JB
John Bark for ref	XY	6	63, 65	14, 18	13	17, 18	22, 22.2	JB	JB
Knicker pellet	XY	6	NR	NR	13	17, 18	NR	Unknown 1	MG
Knicker supernatant	XY	6, 9	NR	13, 14	13	16, 17, 18	19	Unknown 1 & 2	MG
Knicker spinaroo	XY	6, 7, 9	N	13	13	16, 17, 18	19, 25	Unknown 1 & 2	MG
Knicker blue liquid	XY	6, 7, 9, 9.3	63, 70	13, 14	13	16, 17, 18, 19	19, 20, 21, 25	VS + Unknown 1 & 2	MG
Mary H	XX	6, 6	29, 30	13, 15	8, 13	15, 17	19, 20	Mary H	JW
Mary H / BS	XX	6,6	63,65	13,15	8,13	15, 17	19, 20	Mary H	RF
Michael H / BS	XY	6, 9	61, 65	13, 14	13, 15	15, 18	19, 25	Michael H	RF
Michael H	XY	6, 9	28, 30	13, 14	13,15	15, 18	19, 25	Michael H	JW
James H (Snr)	XY	9, ?	28, ?	14, ?	15, ?	18, ?	25, ?	Inferred	
Knickers	XX	6, 9	29, 32.2	13, 14	13, 13	17, 18	19, 25	Unknown	JW
ITEM		D3	D16	D2	D19				
Mary H		15, 15	11, 11	18, 20	14, 14.2			Mary H	JW
Michael H		15, 16	10, 11	18, 20	14, 14			Michael H	JW
James H (Snr)		16, ?	10, ?	18 or 20, ?	14, ?			Inferred	
Knickers		15, 16	10, 11	20, 20	14, 14			Unknown	JW

The testing here was performed by three FSS scientists: Rachel Frazier (RF), John Bark (JB) and Dr Jonathan Whitaker (JW) and as far as I am aware by Matthew Greenhalgh (MG) from the Metropolitan Police Laboratory. The Am column designates the gender Amelogenin finding – where xx is female and xy is male. In addition, TH01, D21, D18, D8, VWA and FGA represent the chromosome areas targeted by the SGM testing (remember 6 autosome loci plus the gender marker). The four additional targets D3, D16, D2 and D19 were added by the SGM Plus® or LCN testing (10 loci plus gender), whichever it was that was done by Dr Whitaker. BS stands for buccal swab, which is a DNA sample taken from the inside of the mouth. In addition to the testing results reported for Mary and Michael Hanratty, the accused's mother, and brother, I have added a row showing what can be inferred regarding the accused's father on this basis. Remember that a child receives two alleles at each location, one from each parent. It does not follow that James would receive the same alleles as his brother Michael. Remember also that these figures have been transcribed by the scientists from the actual electropherograms produced by their equipment and could thus be in error. I have not seen the associated electropherograms so cannot confirm if they contain any transcription errors.

The testing by Mr Greenhalgh was STR/Quad, which he ran in 1995 on material from Valerie Storie's knickers, and from which the pellet fragment would be expected to contain sperm. As the more critical testing results for this garment were produced by the FSS scientists, I shall not be discussing his testing further, except where testimony from the latter refers to his results. In addition, I should point out that Mr Bark also ran Mitochondrial DNA tests against hair samples, supposedly from Hanratty, which are not reproduced in this table. These are separate from, and irrelevant to the thrust of my arguments, which relate to the veracity of the Nuclear DNA testing, so for brevity will not be discussed further.

This table immediately raises several important questions and issues. Firstly, Dr Whitaker does not say what biological source he is using for his testing of Mary and Michael Hanratty, unlike Frazier who used buccal swabs. If you look in the D21 column you will see that he reports Mary as having alleles 29, 30, whereas Frazier reports alleles 63, 65. Also, he reports Michael as having alleles 28, 30, whereas she reports alleles 61, 65. I have repeated her findings for both Mary and Michael next to those from Dr Whitaker for ease of comprehension. Their figures for the other alleles for Mary and Michael agree. So, who is right?

In the documentation presented to the pre-exhumation court hearing to accompany these results, Frazier stated that the version of the SGM test she ran was 'experimental' and that her results should be treated with caution. However, no mention of the experimental nature of her test occurred in her court testimony in 2002. For his part, Dr Whitaker confirms that the protocol he used in July 2000 increases the amplification cycle number over the standard test to increase the potential of detecting very small amounts in the sample – I believe he is referring to LCN testing. He issues a sort of caveat that 'such profiles must be interpreted with reference to the circumstances of the case and in particular the possibility of detecting trace amounts of DNA from unknown sources.' He also states that all preparations have been profiled in duplicate, though whether this was performed simultaneously or contiguously, and what they showed, is not detailed. He is nowhere nearly as explicit as Frazier in stating the experimental nature of his testing. In court he only refers to it as SGM Plus®. In both cases, no description of the validation of these non-standard test mechanisms before their use is forthcoming. Both these instances raise some very concerning questions. For example, why did the FSS keep altering the standard tests? What changes were made? How were they validated? When did the FSS start doing it? And were the judiciary and political authorities made aware? The implications of these questionable practices go far beyond the Hanratty case.

If we then look at the SGM test figures for the handkerchief stain1, we see that again at D21, John Bark reports alleles 63, 70. Mary was reported as 63, 65 and Michael was 61, 65. So, if this figure is correct, it would mean that James Hanratty Senior would be 61, 70 at D21. On this basis, it would mean Hanratty himself must have had any combination of two of the following – 61, 63, 65 and 70 at D21.

Confusingly, I would point out that in the transcripts John Bark was not questioned regarding the tests on the handkerchief, though Rachel Frazier was. She said that he prepared the handkerchief tests, whatever that might have involved, so I am afraid I cannot be 100% certain as to which of them produced the reported figures, even though the documents provided to me indicate that it was Mr Bark.

Dr Whitaker did not report any testing done on the handkerchief in these results, although again confusingly, handkerchief test evidence not documented before the exhumation was discussed during his testimony in court, as we'll see. However, in these results he reports the D21 alleles for Mary of 29, 30 and for Michael of 28, 30, which would infer that he did separate tests to Frazier on both and that Hanratty's father therefore had alleles 28, ? at D21. So, Hanratty himself would have had any combination of two of the following: 28, 29, 30, ? at D21. The rest of the reported figures can be explained as coming from Hanratty, although scientifically it can only be said he might have been the donor. Nevertheless, I am inclined to believe it was his DNA in the handkerchief stain, since I've already explained that blowing his nose is almost certainly the most plausible explanation, and it in no way links him to the murder weapon. Therefore, the case for saying Hanratty matches this stain, despite the D21 figures, is stronger, although it is still not definitive since the actual electropherogram results are unknown, and even a full match is only scientifically saying that he could have been the source.

I am not going to discuss the very disappointing results relating to the postcard stamps, performed by John Bark. These were the only known source of Hanratty's DNA prior to his exhumation. It is clear from the lack of firm results that the samples involved were at the limits of what the SGM test could cope with. Nevertheless, his SGM test also reported the D21 alleles to be 63, 65, in agreement with Frazier's testing. This greatly diminishes the likelihood of these figures being a transcription error but does not confirm which of these or Dr Whitaker's numbers is correct. At least Mr Bark provided his own DNA profile for reference, unlike his colleagues, although why he only reported one figure at TH01, and D8 is unknown.

DNA Profiling Issues

So far, based on the testing done by Frazier and Whitaker on Mary and Michael Hanratty, each would infer that James Hanratty's own DNA profile would contain any two of the following:

Figure 3: James Hanratty's inferred profile

Tester	TH01	D21	D18	D8	VWA	FGA	D3	D16	D2	D19
RF	6, 9, ?	61, 63, 65, ?	13, 14, 15, ?	8, 13, 15, ?	15, 17, 18, ?	19, 20, 25, ?				
JW	6, 9, ?	28, 29,30, ?	13, 14, 15, ?	8, 13, 15, ?	15, 17, 18, ?	19, 20, 25, ?	15, 16, ?	10, 11, ?	18, 20, ?	14, 14.2, ?

So how does this tie in with any findings related to Valerie Storie's knickers?

Figure 4: Frazier's test results taken from Figure 2

ITEM	Am	TH01	D21	D18	D8	VWA	FGA	Tester
Valerie S / BS	XX	7, 9.3	59, 65	15, 19	8, 12	18, 19	20, 20	RF
Knickers Epithelial	XY	6, 7, 9, 9.3	59,65	13, 14, 15, 19	8, 12, 13	17, 18, 19	19, 20, 25	RF
JH Inferred	XY	6, 9, ?	61, 63, 65, ?	13, 14, 15, ?	8, 13, 15,, ?	15, 17, 18, ?	19, 20, 25, ?	
Knickers Seminal	XY	6, 7, 9	NR	13, 14, 16, 18	13,	16, 17, 18	19, 21, 25	RF

In Frazier's testing of the seminal material on the knickers, she reports alleles 13, 14, 16, 18 at D18. As James Hanratty could only possibly have one of either 16 or 18 this is evidence of a second male DNA being present. This is vitally important because it immediately invalidates Dr Whitaker's claim, made both in *Horizon* and in the Hanratty hearing, that Hanratty's was the only male DNA found on Miss Storie's knickers.

At D21, she doesn't get a valid result, and at D8 she only reports one valid allele of 13. In the case of TH01, VWA and FGA, there are no results to discount Hanratty, but remember that a second male profile is present. This in no way confirms any sort of match to Hanratty, especially as Michael Gregsten's DNA has not been profiled. This second male is assumed to be Gregsten, but this not confirmed. It could easily be that Hanratty, and the rapist share multiple alleles. It might also indicate testing reliability issues due to the failed alleles.

In Frazier's testing of the epithelial sample from the knickers, it seems to contain matches to Valerie Storie's reported profile in all 6 loci – as expected – but when it comes to other material contained here the situation is unclear. In TH01, D18 and FGA there were two alleles not matching Storie. Then in D8 and VWA, there was only one allele not matching Storie, and in D21 there were none. In both the seminal and epithelial results, the gender was XY and therefore male. This obviously would apply to the seminal result, but in the case of the epithelial result I am not clear if this is a transcription error as again it appears that Storie's DNA was most likely present. This is discussed during her evidence to the court in 2002, but raises a further question, as we will see.

Again, apart from at D21, there is nothing here to discount Hanratty as being a possible donor, but equally there is nothing here to confirm it is his profile, let alone that he was the rapist. The situation with D21 remains unclear and depending upon whether Frazier's or Dr Whitaker's figures are correct, could exculpate him. This is the reason why this is such an important outstanding area of disagreement between these scientists' results, which unfortunately was not examined in the 2002 hearing.

Moving on to Dr Whitaker's SGM Plus®, or LCN testing, on the knicker sample, we see the following:

Figure 5: Whitaker's test results taken from Figure 2

ITEM	Am	TH01	D21	D18	D8	VWA	FGA	D3	D16	D2	D19
Knickers	XX	6, 9	29, 32.2	13, 14	13, 13	17, 18	19, 25	15, 16	10, 11	20, 20	14, 14
JH Inferred	XY	6, 9, ?	28, 29, 30, ?	13, 14, 15, ?	8, 13, 15, ?	15, 17, 18, ?	19, 20, 25, ?	15, 16, ?	10, 11, ?	18, 20, ?	14, 14.2, ?
Mary H	XX	6, 6	29, 30	13, 15	8, 13	15, 17	19, 20	15, 15	11, 11	18, 20	14, 14.2
Michael H	XY	6, 9	28, 30	13, 14	13, 15	15, 18	19, 25	15, 16	10, 11	18, 20	14, 14

Firstly, he reports the gender as being XX (female) and not XY (male). My strong suspicion is that this is a typing error and indicative of a lack of care and attention. We will see that several other examples of such documentation errors were picked up in the Court of Appeal hearing. Looking at each reported locus we can only say the following:

TH01 – On the knickers it's 6, 9. James Hanratty could be 6, ? or 9, ? and no match.

D21 – On the knickers it's 29, 32.2. Hanratty could be any of 28, ? or 30, ? and no match. Remember this is the locus where the two scientists reported different values.

D18 – On the knickers it's 13, 14. Hanratty could be 13, ? or 14, ? or 15, ? and no match.

D8 – On the knickers it's 13, 13. Hanratty could be 8, ? or 13, ? or 8, 15 or 13, 15 and no match.

VWA – On the knickers it's 17, 18. Hanratty could be 15, ? or 17, ? or 18, ? or 15, 18 and no match.

FGA – On the knickers it's 19, 25. Hanratty could be 19, ? or 20, ? or 20, 25 and no match.

D3 – On the knickers it's 15, 16. Hanratty could be 15, ? or 16, ? and no match.

D16 – On the knickers it's 10, 11. Hanratty could be 11, ? or 10, ? and no match.

D2 – On the knickers it's 20, 20. Hanratty could be 18, ? or 20, ? and no match.

D19 – On the knickers it's 14, 14. Hanratty could be 14, ? or 14.2, ? and no match.

As we can see, he is only reporting two alleles found at each target loci on the knickers in contrast to Frazier. Why is there a difference? He would obviously be using a different piece of knicker fabric to perform his test, which could explain it. However, it is possible that the other male profile was present but not clearly identifiable in the electropherogram, or that it was deliberately not reported, being seen as a potential stochastic threshold effect, or even that the single alleles being reported could have come from separate donors. Only access to the original electropherograms from which these figures derive could answer this definitively. Nevertheless, Frazier's find of a second male profile demolishes his claim that Hanratty's supposed DNA was the only male DNA in contact with these knickers.

This evidence can in no way be said to provide a definitive link between Hanratty and the knicker stain. Remember, even a full match makes Hanratty no more than a potential source. This is obviously the reason for the subsequent exhumation request.

There is one final, crucial point about this evidence as it stands:

If you also consider that Dr Whitaker claimed in the Court of Appeal that this material could only have come from Hanratty being the rapist, where is the basis for this in Figure 5? These are just numbers and there is nothing in them to identify how they were deposited on the knickers or even what type of biological sample was involved. As has already been highlighted nothing can be inferred about the biological source of a sample at these levels, nor how it might have arrived. It required the most sensitive test in existence at the time to produce Dr Whitaker's findings and would have represented something invisible to the naked eye to require this test, so there is no scientifically supported basis for considering rape rather than contamination as the source. This is very strong evidence for Wilson's aphorism in action. We will see how he tries to justify this in court when we come to consider his evidence in detail in the transcript.

The material in this chapter should have shown, once and for all, just how complicated and serious the interpretation process can be. There is so much more involved than just taking figures off a graph created by a machine. The reader will, I hope, now be aware just how far from clear-cut the process is, just how important the correct interpretation of the DNA test results is, and how open to contention these results can be. This information needs to be borne in mind when assessing any certainty ascribed by the FSS to the Hanratty case, or any other. All interpretations need to be examined with great care, by both sides in a case. Again, this is the reason that both the lack of agreed international interpretation standards, and the lack of sufficient DNA experts to represent the defendant in all cases, is so critical.

Most people, alongside the highest legal office holders in the land, may have been convinced that the DNA data cannot lie. However, I hope that you will now understand why I have serious reasons to doubt the certainty of the DNA scientists in this case.

Anyway, after this lengthy, but I hope that you'll agree necessary, digression, it is time to consider the material in the Hanratty appeal transcripts, to see if, and how, these issues were handled.

Introducing the Transcripts

Having formulated my arguments thus far, especially when considering the strength of the evidence that proclaimed Hanratty's innocence versus the Court of Appeal's claim that the DNA evidence proved his guilt, I was even more minded to consider that there was either something wrong with the attribution of the crime scene DNA to Hanratty, or the interpretation of it that discounted contamination.

The court claimed it was extremely unlikely both occurrences of Hanratty's DNA – on the handkerchief and on Valerie Storie's knickers – had come from contamination. However, it had completely misunderstood the significance of the DNA in the mucus stain on the handkerchief, and believed it proved that Hanratty handled the gun, whereas absolutely no connection to the gun is established by this find. If it was Hanratty's DNA in the mucus stain, then all it showed was that he blew his nose with it, nothing more. Additionally, when one is dealing with low template amounts of DNA in evidence from a crime scene, nothing can be confirmed about the source of the DNA (semen, skin, mucus etc.), or how it might have been deposited. Therefore, the court's claim that the DNA found on the sample of Miss Storie's knickers proved Hanratty was the rapist, and thus the murderer of Gregsten, had, and still has, no scientific validity whatsoever. How had this court peopled by very senior judges, including the then Lord Chief Justice, come to such a perversely woeful verdict? Had they been misled by the FSS witnesses, or had they managed to mislead themselves?

I would again point out that Dr Jonathan Whitaker, the FSS scientist who discussed the DNA evidence in *Horizon*, was the main prosecution expert witness in the previously mentioned and critically important

Sean Hoey trial. His evidence in that trial was savaged by the DNA scientists for the defence. As a result, the judge dismissed that case and was extremely critical of Dr Whitaker's work and performance in the court, especially regarding the use of LCN. As a result of the judge's criticisms, all British cases based on such evidence were put on hold, as the authorities commissioned the Caddy review to investigate so-called low template profiling and, particularly, the validity of the LCN modification to the standard SGM Plus® test, being performed by the FSS. As noted, Caddy made twenty-one recommended changes to the way the science was performed in Britain. These were aimed at the laboratories, the police force Scenes of Crime Officers (SOCOs) as well as regulatory authorities in forensic science. Always bear in mind that valid scientific testing requires proper procedures and performance and independent verification. Therefore, the lack of any independent assessment of the work of the FSS for so long was critical to, and potentially disastrous for, the British judicial system. Worryingly, the forensic regulator reinstated low template evidence, including LCN, in our courts, within one month of the publication of the Caddy report, without actioning any of the twenty-one recommendations.[1] How many have been implemented in the interim is for the regulator to answer.

If this was the sorry state of the FSS scientific performance in 2008, how could one have faith that everything was as it should have been during the testing for the Hanratty case up to eight years earlier? If, as I strongly suspected, Dr Whitaker's evidence was central to any justification for the court's opinions, to be able to reach a firm conclusion regarding the veracity of the respondent's case, I needed to somehow gain access to the transcript for, and the evidence presented to, the 2002 Court of Appeal hearing.

By dint of an extremely fortuitous set of circumstances, I was put in touch with a fellow researcher who sent me a copy of the Hanratty hearing transcripts for the days in which the DNA evidence was considered, which was provided to him by Paul Foot. Since Paul Foot is no longer alive, it is not possible to confirm whether he produced the record of the transcript himself or received it from a third party. As a result, I cannot verify the provenance of these transcripts, or whether they are 100% accurate. Nevertheless, I have no reason to assume anything other than they are what they purport to be. The chance of them being an invention, in whole or in part, seems to me to be off the scale as far as improbability is concerned. Due to the number of minor errors that they contain, I believe that they were transcribed by a non-technical observer, such as a journalist, either in the court via shorthand or from audio recordings of the events at some later stage. Nevertheless, I see no valid reason not to take the transcripts at face value for the purposes of this work. I have confirmed with Paul Foot's estate that they have no issue with this work being reproduced here. However, if the transcriber was a person other than Paul, and they wish to make themselves known to me, I shall be more than happy to make any necessary amendments, and to credit them accordingly. To request a copy of these hearing transcripts please email enquiries@pen-and-sword.co.uk. However, I shall make a couple of general observations about the transcripts as they stand, before considering them in more depth.

Firstly, a written transcript can only give part of the story, in so far as it gives no indication as to the tone of voice and body language employed by the protagonists. Secondly, the reader is reliant on the accuracy of the person who has written the transcript, whatever the official nature, or otherwise, of the source. It will also be clear that the transcript contains grammatical errors, which to the sceptic might be indicative of inaccuracy of transcription. Despite these caveats, I am still inclined to believe that these documents are a reasonable facsimile of the events in the Court of Appeal for the days in question. If any alternative copy of this transcript surfaces that materially raises doubts about this version, I shall be happy to consider it, although based on what I've already uncovered, I remain doubtful that it would lessen my concerns with this case.

As I write this, I am mindful that Wilson's aphorism – 'What the thinker thinks, the prover proves' – could equally apply to my interpretation of these events. Nonetheless, I have attempted to apply scientific rigour to my research and make my sources clear and available to all, and I have so far failed to find any evidence to persuade me

James Hanratty - The defendant

Murder victim, Michael Gregsten, with his wife Janet

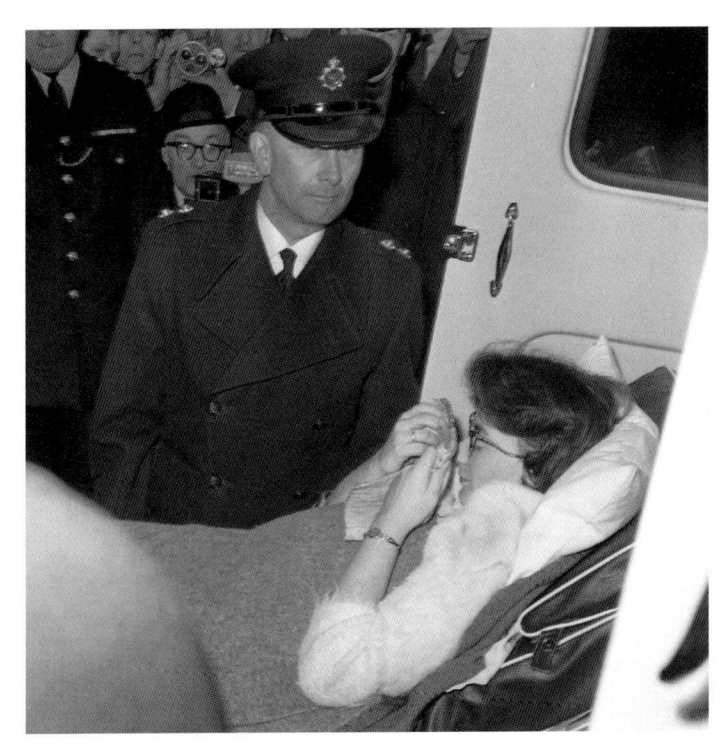

Gregsten's lover, Valerie Storie, on a stretcher at the Committal Hearing at Ampthill

Peter Alphon – The initial suspect

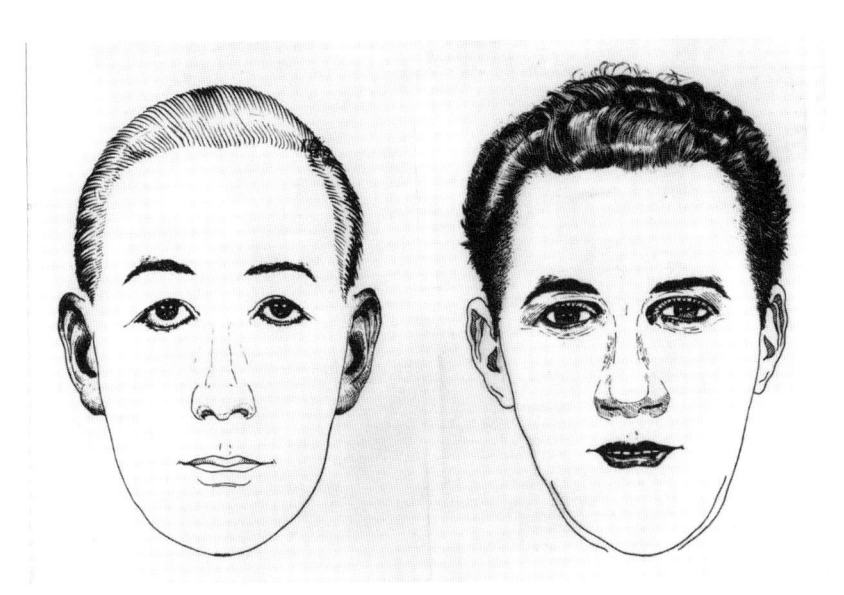

Identikit images of suspect based on Miss Storie's description

Senior Investigating Officer, DSU Acott, at the murder scene lay-by at Deadman's Hill

Mr Justice Gorman – The trial Judge

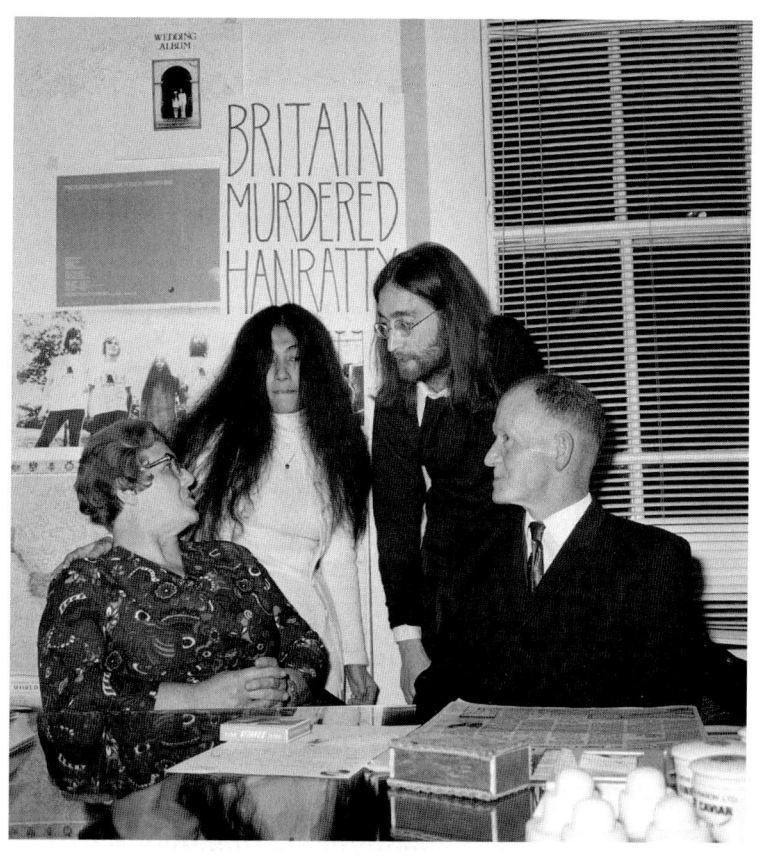

Hanratty's parents with John and Yoko Lennon who believed Hanratty innocent

Lewis Hawser QC - Author of questionable report into the case for the Home Secretary

Paul Foot - Journalist and tireless campaigner for Hanratty's innocence

Bob Woffinden - Journalist and equally convinced of Hanratty's innocence

Sir Geoffrey Bindman QC (Hon) - Founder of Bindmans LLP who co-authored the submission for a second appeal with Woffinden

Members of the Hanratty family pictured at the cemetery after James' exhumation

Lord Chief Justice Harry Woolf – The senior justice overseeing the 2002 Appeal Court hearing

Mr Justice Brian Leveson – Author of the Appeal Court's verdict. Later chair of the 'News of the World' phone-hacking enquiry

Michael Mansfield QC - Represented Hanratty (the appellant) at the 2002 hearing

Nigel Sweeney QC - Represented the Crown (the respondent) at the 2002 hearing

Dr Jonathan Whitaker - Senior FSS witness at the 2002 hearing, whose evidence was discredited in the later Sean Hoey trial.

that my doubts are without foundation. If others can unearth such evidence, that can always change, but it would have to be spectacular to undermine what is now apparent.

It becomes clear, almost immediately, that the protagonists in the court refer frequently to external documents, the contents of which I am not privy to and can only infer from the discussions that take place. This obviously makes following their arguments much more complicated, for which I must beg your indulgence. The good news is the most obtuse elements of these often-arcane discussions are not relevant to this work and will not need to be discussed here.

Initially I wanted to understand whether the overstatement of the significance of the handkerchief DNA was explained through the statements of the witnesses, or those of the various counsels. Why had the court assumed that the presence of Hanratty's supposed DNA on the handkerchief, linked him to the murder weapon? Unfortunately, although these documents shed much light, they do not provide a definitive answer. I can see no explicit statement anywhere to this effect, so I can only speculate that this was either stated at some point within the remainder of the hearing, or within the documentation provided to the court. The only alternative is that their lordships surmised this for themselves unbidden. However, it is worth noting how many times Mr Nigel Sweeney, QC for the respondent, took the opportunity to discuss the DNA on the handkerchief throughout these three days of the hearing, thus reinforcing the message that this was a significant finding, without once explaining its true level of significance to the court. Whether this was because the FSS had not highlighted this important fact to him remains unclear.

Mr Michael Mansfield QC and Dr Evison, for Hanratty, seemed solely concerned with positing their theory of contamination, and unfortunately missed the crucial fact that, even if Hanratty had blown his nose on the handkerchief, it provided no evidence of a connection to the gun. Equally, I find it worthy of note that not one of the FSS witnesses brought out the true level of significance of the mucus DNA finding. Remember, their duty was to the court and not the respondent. Is this down to incompetence, or something else? Either way, it does little to establish confidence that the FSS DNA case is solid. In addition, you should consider the statement, made in *Horizon*, that this established a link between the rapist and the murder weapon, which is obviously in error. As the FSS must have collaborated fully with the BBC in making that programme, I contend that this is unlikely to have been the musing of a BBC producer, but more likely to have been pointed out by the FSS experts while not on camera. This is not the only questionable element around the evidence of these 'expert' witnesses.

A second general area of concern is the fact that the respondent's legal team, and the FSS witnesses, make no mention throughout the transcripts that at least some of the testing used the contentious LCN method – according to *Horizon*. Instead, they referred to Dr Whitaker's testing being SGM Plus®. They could counter that the LCN test is in fact a version of the SGM Plus® test that has been extended by an additional six cycles of PCR amplification, so therefore they were not telling an untruth. However, the reader will by now be aware of the significance and contentious nature of the LCN testing, so for them not to make this distinction clear to the court during witness testimony is certainly dubious.

This is especially so as this hearing was apparently the first time such evidence had ever been presented in any court. From the evidence in the transcripts, Dr Whitaker and Mr Sweeney appear to have been hiding behind the generally accepted nature of the standard SGM Plus® test, rather than acknowledge that this cutting-edge science, with its associated risks, was employed to make a connection to Hanratty.

A couple of scenarios might have explained this. Perhaps *Horizon* was incorrect in stating that the testing involved thirty-four cycles of PCR amplification – which again would seem to be improbable. Alternatively, the respondent, and the FSS, might have mentioned it in the written evidence submissions, to which I am not privy; though whether they also highlighted the contentious nature of the science is unclear. I would say that had their lordships been aware of this, for them not to refer to it during the judgment document is questionable. Taken with the unfounded connection between Hanratty's DNA on the handkerchief and the murder weapon, these actions do not give me any assurance that the FSS is being open with the evidence to the court, but rather that it is acting solely as an agent of the respondent.

There seems to be no understanding on the part of their lordships of just how risky and contentious this actual science was, or the fact that it was a new technique, so I must question whether they had been informed of this fact in any of the documentation.

I would at this point note that Professor Krane shares my understanding that the Hanratty case was the first case before the English courts to have LCN evidence presented by the FSS. Therefore, the onus on the team for the respondent to make this point understood by the judges is clear and fundamental. To me, a failure to do so is yet more evidence of the prejudicial nature of the case against Hanratty.

Another point that applies throughout the transcripts is the issue of the court assuring itself that the findings of the FSS expert witnesses are scientifically valid, and that they are qualified to support them. A perusal of the transcripts will show that this consisted primarily of the witnesses merely stating how long they had been employed by the FSS, or other companies. To illustrate this point, consider the following section from the transcript for 23 April:

MR SWEENEY: Could you tell us your full names, please?

DR WHITAKER: My name is Jonathan Paul Whitaker.

SWEENEY: What is your occupation?

WHITAKER: I am a Senior Forensic Scientist, working at the research laboratories in Birmingham.

SWEENEY: How long have you been a practising scientist?

WHITAKER: 13 years.

SWEENEY: What is your particular area of expertise?

WHITAKER: It is in the interpretation of DNA profiling results and the research into forensic DNA profiling tests.

SWEENEY: For how long have you been specialising in that field?

WHITAKER: For the whole of my career.

SWEENEY: Are you the scientist who has been responsible for the SGM Plus testing in this case from 2000 onwards?

WHITAKER: Yes.

This is the respondent's key forensic witness, the scientist responsible for pronouncing Hanratty to have been the rapist in this case, and the scientist whose evidence was criticised by other forensic experts in the subsequent Sean Hoey case, which led to the Caddy report with its fundamental criticisms of the FSS culture and performance. How much that report contributed to the eventual decision to disband the FSS in 2012 is moot, though the official reason given was ostensibly financial.

The lack of questioning about Dr Whitaker's qualifications and training to suit him to this critical role should be seen as particularly egregious. Seemingly, based on his statements above, the court accepted his expertise and everything he subsequently said about the evidence, unquestioningly. Despite these comments, I am aware that expert witnesses should provide a statement of their relevant experience to the court as part of any evidential report that they produce. Nevertheless, it is still noticeable how little focus on the actual experience of the FSS experts took place, especially when compared to the focus that was given to the experience of Dr Evison, as we will see.

I shall now finally move on to discuss the contents of the transcripts and I shall concentrate predominantly on three key elements: firstly, the introduction by Mr Sweeney, the QC for the respondent, of the DNA evidence at the start of the first transcript on Monday, 22 April;

secondly, the testimony of Dr Whitaker on Tuesday, 23 April, and thirdly, the testimony of Dr Evison on Wednesday, 24 April. I shall refer occasionally to the testimony of other witnesses, but only where this is relevant to the issue of the fragments of Miss Storie's knickers, and the testing performed on these.

I shall, mostly, refrain from discussing the issue of the handkerchief from now on. As the presence of Hanratty's DNA – if indeed it was his – in no way constitutes a connection to the murder weapon, I shall not waste time detailing the copious arguments as to whether that DNA 'match' was due to contamination. Instead, I shall endeavour to elucidate the testing on the key piece of evidence – Valerie Storie's knickers – as this is the crux of the remaining case against Hanratty and stands in direct opposition to the Liverpool alibi.

I am aware that these three days of testimony, and my attempted analysis, will prove complex, and potentially difficult to follow. At times, it may feel akin to wading through treacle. I can only apologise again. Unfortunately, it is brought about by the peculiar, and frequently contradictory, way that the evidence was presented by Mr Sweeney and the FSS.

On occasions, despite my best endeavours, parts of these transcripts will defy satisfactory comprehension. Nevertheless, I hope that my concerns about these deliberations will become clear. In fairness to the protagonists, just because I have been unable to elucidate certain points does not mean that a rational explanation for some of these confusing elements is not possible. Clarification of these points might have existed in the documents presented to the court, of which I have not had sight. I reiterate that my observations are based upon these transcripts only, and thus must remain provisional. Nevertheless, my concerns over what I am about to document are real and would require dramatic information to be substantially altered.

Lastly, I would ask you to ask yourself when considering the contents of the next three chapters, how easy would you have found it to understand the complicated case put before the court, and to see the wood for the trees?

To sum up, based on everything I have documented so far, I believe the following critical points of what is essentially a relatively simple case:

1. The overwhelmingly likely fact that Hanratty was in Liverpool just two and a half hours before the start of the attack in Dorney Reach means that he cannot be the attacker, regardless of any DNA finding linking him to Miss Storie's underwear. I believe that the court was led, by an unjustifiable legal principle, to discount this compelling evidence of his innocence. In view of Lord Leveson's subsequent comment, that he does not believe the Liverpool alibi, the role of bias in the invoking of this reasoning is hard to discount.
2. While it cannot be said with scientific certainty, the most likely explanation for the purported finding of his DNA in the mucus stain is that Hanratty would have blown his nose on the handkerchief, which was later found wrapped around the murder weapon. Even so this does not prove a link to the gun, despite the respondent's implicit case to that effect. The involvement of Charles 'Dixie' France in the finding of both the gun and handkerchief, and his subsequent suicide just before Hanratty's execution are the major reasons for my line of thought. I feel this to be more likely than an unexplained contamination event being responsible, although no one can be 100% certain in this instance.
3. The only mechanism for his DNA being associated with the knicker evidence – if it is his DNA – is therefore contamination, and as the provenance of this evidence is unproven, this mechanism cannot be discounted, despite the respondent's and the verdict's claims. Remember for the DNA evidence interpretation to be correct means that Hanratty must have had access to a helicopter to be in Dorney Reach when the attack started.

It is with these thoughts uppermost that I shall now review what was said in court.

Monday, 22 April 2002

Mr Sweeney's DNA Case Presentation

For the purposes of doing my best to try and elucidate what is about to be discussed I have extracted the following information from Figure 2, and it now becomes Figure 6.

Figure 6: Key evidence

ITEM	Am	TH01	D21	D18	D8	VWA	FGA	D3	D16	D2	D19	Tester
Knickers Seminal	XY	6, 7, 9	NR	13, 14, 16, 18	13,	16, 17, 18	19, 21, 25					RF
Knickers Epithelial	XY	6, 7, 9, 9.3	59, 65	13, 14, 15, 19	8, 12, 13	17, 18, 19	19, 20, 25					RF
Valerie S / BS	XX	7, 9.3	59, 65	15, 19	8, 12	18, 19	20, 20					RF
Knickers	XX	6, 9	29, 32.2	13, 14	13, 13	17, 18	19, 25	15, 16	10, 11	20, 20	14, 14	JW
Hankie Stain 1	XY	6, 9	63, 70	13, 14	13, 13	17, 18	19, 25					JB
Hankie Stain 2	XY	6, 9	NR	13, 14	NR	17, 18	19, 25					JB
Hankie Yellow Stn1	XY	6, 9	NR	13, 14	13, 13	17, 18	19, 25					JB
Hankie Yellow Stn2	Poor partial profile obtained - No reproducible results											JB

There are a few things in here that I would like to point out:

1. As noted earlier, since we all have only two alleles at each of these locations, the seminal test from Rachel Frazier shows

clear evidence at 4 of the 6 loci of at least one other male profile. Hanratty could only have one of either 16 or 18. Note that Dr Whitaker said only one male profile was found in his test. Even if Dr Whitaker was unaware of Frazier's findings, Mr Sweeney certainly was aware of this finding, yet this mixed message was presented to court without clarification.

2. Considering the failure at D21 and the partial failure at D8 in the seminal test, alongside the experimental nature of this test, how much faith can we put in Frazier's results, especially considering the earlier additional disparity at D21? It should be remembered that John Bark's testing on the postcards matched her result at D21, thereby strengthening the possibility that her figure, and not Dr Whitaker's, was correct at D21. In addition, the failures in the handkerchief testing could also be due to either lack of material or test unreliability.

3. There is no indication of the type of test performed by Dr Whitaker on the knickers, but I must assume it was a form of seminal test, even though the gender was wrong.

4. Was his lack of an additional profile found on the knickers due to a different sample, profile interpretation issues, or something else?

5. Apart from at D21 the handkerchief shows potentially consistent but not conclusive evidence of one male profile, but as this does not constitute a link to the gun, its only possible relevance is if Hanratty's exhumed DNA is different. However please note that during Dr Whitaker's testimony he will discuss test results for this item, which were not reported in the pre-exhumation test documentation.

For brevity, I am only incorporating Mr Sweeney's presentation of what he calls the 'respondent's DNA evidential reports' to the court, and not the several additional pages that try to refute contamination. These are the tests summarised in Figure 6, in addition to any testing performed after Hanratty's exhumation. I had, incorrectly, assumed the latter would merely have consisted of establishing his profile, rather than revisiting any of the evidence samples, but it appears to have included further tests on Miss Storie, and on the initial suspect, Peter Alphon, at the very least. This just goes to show that assumptions are never without risk. Unfortunately, without access to this remaining material some doubt must remain, despite my efforts to bring some clarity to this strangely cursory and frequently incomprehensible presentation of what is claimed to be proof of Hanratty's guilt.

As Alphon is irrelevant when considering Hanratty's guilt, or innocence, he is not part of my argument here, and is being ignored accordingly. I am not going to discuss the references to the handkerchief here for reasons already stated, but I would point out that over the three days of proceedings documented in the transcripts Mr Sweeney frequently implies that this is very important evidence, without ever properly explaining its significance, or lack of, to the court. I shall expand a little on the more noteworthy statements in this presentation at its end. Nevertheless, I would ask you to consider, in the light of how confusing and incomprehensible this initial presentation is, how difficult it must have been for the court to have followed anything Mr Sweeney was saying, even with the benefit of access to the copious documents to which he refers. Here is how he presents the supposedly conclusive DNA evidence to the court:

Monday, 22 April 2002 – 10.30am

MR SWEENEY: We are extremely grateful for the time your Lordships have afforded us. The court has, I hope, now received some graphic representations of the eventual DNA findings in colour.

LORD CHIEF JUSTICE WOOLF: I am not conscious of having done so.

SWEENEY: Yes. Thank you. The first sheet that I held up sets out in colour co-ordinated fashion the DNA findings using the SGM system.

WOOLF: Yes.

SWEENEY: Your Lordships will notice from that that at the top of the page are set out the results of the SGM work, insofar as the profiles obtained from swabs or remains respectively are concerned of Valerie Storie, who is set out in blue, of Mr Hanratty's remains, set out in yellow and Mr Alphon's sample, set out in green.

From that your Lordships will see that the SGM test includes, firstly, a sex test and, secondly, six areas of the DNA in which, in each case, there are two results; one inherited from the father, one inherited from the mother. So that there is an immediate cross-check to the results set out below, which are a colour representation of the various findings of which your Lordships are going to hear.

The results, insofar as they took place in chronological order are concerned, in fact start about two thirds of the way down the page where your Lordships see knicker fragment which fell on a rack during the 1995 extraction.

WOOLF: Yes.

SWEENEY: Your Lordships will see that the first finding recorded under that relates to the seminal, where major and minor profiles are set out, and beneath that the epithelial fraction, where again the major and minor profiles are set out.

As your Lordships may recall from our DNA document, the purpose of extracting two different fractions, the epithelial fraction and the seminal fraction, is because, although the result is not absolute, dealing with intimate samples from a rape victim, the epithelial fraction is designed to catch principally the relevant woman's DNA but can also get the rapist's DNA, the seminal fraction is designed to catch, as its name implies, the male DNA from the rapist.

Your Lordships, therefore, see that, insofar as the epithelial fraction is concerned, the lower of the two, as would be expected, produced in the blue line an almost complete profile, unsurprisingly, of a female which matches Valerie Storie.

Insofar as the epithelial fraction is concerned, it also revealed a minor profile, which as your Lordships can see, being Y in the sex column for male, and matches where it has, as it were, developed, the appellant's DNA profile.

In the seminal fraction, there are a major profile and some minor pieces. The major profile, again in yellow, matching the appellant's DNA profile. The seminal fraction, minor profile, having a small number of readings in red and one in blue, as your Lordships can see. Insofar as the blue one is concerned, that is a match with Miss Storie. Insofar as the red one is concerned, that is another person, neither the appellant, nor Miss Storie, which, as it happens would be consistent with finding Mr Gregsten's DNA, there having been intercourse between him and Miss Storie some two days before the fatal event.

Also, insofar as the first work at the Birmingham laboratory is concerned, the next item down is handkerchief, as your Lordships can see, examined in 1997. On the handkerchief, four particular stained areas were looked at. We will come to the detail of the stains and what their significance is in due course. Your Lordships can see that, in each instance where there is a result in stains 1, 2 and 3, it is the appellant's profile alone which was found in those areas.

The petticoat slip, at the bottom of the various columns, your Lordships will remember was blood stained, Valerie Storie of course having bled, and it was her blood, as the blue representation shows.

The next work that was done at the Birmingham laboratory was a re-examination of what had produced no result in 1995 – your Lordships see knickers, re extraction of 1995 tubes, and then again a predominance of the appellant's profile in yellow, as there set out.

The SGM Plus work, which was done subsequent to the 1995/1997 and 1998 work set out on that schedule, is represented in the other graphic which your Lordships now have, which is set out in a slightly different way.

WOOLF: Which one are you referring to?

SWEENEY: That one.

WOOLF: The green, the 2000?

SWEENEY: That is right. The SGM Plus work looks at a sex test. The same six areas as SGM but another four in addition; so that there are 11 boxes of findings, therefore, sex and the 10 areas. Again, set out across the top of the page, the appellant in yellow, Mr Alphon in green, and Miss Storie in a bluey green.

Insofar as the knickers are concerned, your Lordships see the result described as the major component profile in yellow, as your Lordships will see, a male profile, of which there were results in 17 of the 20 possible results, the F in three places indicating where the test failed to produce a result, as sometimes happens in those particular areas there recorded.

WOOLF: Yes, the three situations.

SWEENEY: It is that profile which gave rise to the random chance ratio of 1 in 500 million.

Your Lordships see that the minor bands are seen in red, consistent with the red in the first schedule, and in the bluey green to show consistency with Miss Storie's profile.

In the epithelial fraction, which is beneath, your Lordships see that the major profile is plainly consistent with Miss Storie and the minor profile again matches the appellant.

I will come back to the no results recorded in a moment. If one turns over to the second page, as to the handkerchief, the two principal stains, stain 1 and 2, are dealt with in the first box, and again it is all the appellant, and top line of the two is the one which gave the random chance ratio of 1 in 250 million. Your Lordships can see the reason for the difference being that, on the handkerchief, in the top profile, there were four areas where no result was obtained, as opposed to the three in the previous example.

Insofar as yellow stain 1 on the handkerchief is concerned, which is the top line in the box with colourations in it below, again, as your Lordships can see from the yellow findings, all consistent with the appellant.

Then, in yellow stain 2, your Lordships can see some minor findings, as it happens, the first of which, 16 could be consistent with the appellant, and insofar as the findings in the D19 box are concerned, again, one of those could be consistent with the appellant, although it has not been coloured in as such.

This SGM Plus schedule includes – because of some factual disagreement with Dr Everson, which I suspect will soon disappear – details of controls and other tests that were done using the SGM Plus system, where no result was obtained, but I need not take your Lordships' time with that at the moment.

Your Lordships will, therefore, have seen from our DNA document the position, therefore, being that, in respect of the seminal fraction profiles and in respect of the epithelial fraction profiles, one finds the appellant's DNA in precisely the sort of major profile role which is to be expected if he was the donor of the semen which the murderer left at the scene, as it were.

Equally, in so far as the handkerchief is concerned, stains 1, 2 and yellow stain 1 are all the appellant and the appellant alone. Insofar as non-stained areas of the handkerchief were concerned, two areas were tested, and there was no DNA found on either of the unstained areas.

WOOLF: I notice on the handkerchief and the sex test that X and Y is both shown; that surprised me.

SWEENEY: My Lord, that is because XY is a male profile.

WOOLF: XY is a male profile?

SWEENEY: Yes.

WOOLF: I had assumed that where I saw XY in the original document you showed us, that was a combined male/female, but I am wrong on that, XX is a female, but XY does not indicate that there is a mixture.

SWEENEY: XY is indicating a male. XX would indicate a female.

WOOLF: Why on the knickers minor is it just Y as opposed to XY? That is what has led me

SWEENEY: I am sure that there will be a technical answer to that, which I cannot off the top of my head give, other than to indicate that it is intended to reflect a male profile.

LORD JUSTICE MANTELL: Why is Peter Alphon shown as XX on that one?

SWEENEY: I hear the word 'mistake': it is coming from the author, so I think I can take it that that is right.

In what is, or can soon become, an extremely complicated area, it may be somewhat to the court's relief that the work which we were able to do last week and the discussions that we were able to have between the parties last week have, I believe, narrowed the scope of the material which it will be necessary to place before the court.

Your Lordships will recall from our DNA submissions that we made the point, the issue of possible contamination within the laboratory examinations having been raised, that the testing at stage 2 in 1998, re extracting the work that had been done in 1995, and getting the same result in effect as the work done on the knickers in 1997, was itself indicative that the positive results in 1997 on both items were not as a result of contamination in the laboratory.

I think the force of that is seen and accepted. In those circumstances, the issue before your Lordships is not whether the appellants DNA is there, because those findings are accepted; it is not whether Mr Alphon's DNA is or is not excluded, because it is accepted, as Mr Mansfield indicated the other day, that it is; and it is not whether contamination occurred in the work in either 1995, 1997 or thereafter; but is limited to an exploration of whether contamination may have occurred prior to the start of the scientific examination.

End of transcript.

It is clear, from even a cursory review of the above, that Mr Sweeney's presentation is impossible to follow without full access to the extra documentation to which he frequently refers, and even then, quite possibly not.

The brief discussion of the supposedly compelling case for it being a match to Hanratty's DNA is confusingly presented, jumping around all over the place, with the nub of this claim supposedly shown by a full match with Hanratty's exhumed DNA, however that might have been arrived at. As we will see in his evidence given the next day, Dr Whitaker stated that Hanratty's profile produced after the exhumation was a composite – whatever that meant. He never explained it although I assume he produced the result from more than one sample of Hanratty's DNA material, which, to me, raises huge questions about its reliability and the conclusions drawn from it. I've already explained that even a full match only means Hanratty might have been the donor, not that it is his DNA. Mr Sweeney didn't make the court aware of this here. His presentation also doesn't agree with the information in Figure 6 in several respects. He seems to refer to later testing on the knickers, not documented in Figure 6, that is in addition to obtaining a full profile of Hanratty. Without access to what these showed it is impossible to confirm his arguments.

Then he spends some time discussing the handkerchief evidence without explaining its actual significance to the court. This is just the first of many times throughout these days that he implied it was a significant finding, as the judgment made woefully clear. Why he did this remains an open question that should by rights be addressed.

I would make the following points about some of Mr Sweeney's statements, which I have highlighted in bold text:

- Mr Sweeney presents SGM profiles to the court for Valerie Storie, Peter Alphon and Hanratty, yet Hanratty's remains were profiled using SGM Plus® or LCN, and we've already seen the disparity between results from this and from SGM. I must assume later testing was also performed for Alphon and Storie.

- 'and matches where it has, as it were, developed, the appellant's DNA profile' is a very strange choice of phrase. Figure 6 shows D21 failed and did not match Whitaker's SGM Plus®/LCN knicker test and would not have matched his full profile, whatever it was. I would remind the reader of the statement in paragraph 125 of the judgment from this hearing, which implied that Miss Storie's DNA had been overridden by Hanratty's seminal DNA. Not so, according to Mr Sweeney here, so why did the judgment include it? Is this evidence of their lordships being confused, or have they been misinformed?
- **'Insofar as the red one is concerned, that is another person, neither the appellant, nor Miss Storie, which, as it happens would be consistent with finding Mr Gregsten's DNA, there having been intercourse between him and Miss Storie some two days before the fatal event.'** This confirms the presence of an additional male profile, assumed but not confirmed to have been Gregsten's. This is key in demolishing Dr Whitaker's claim for only one male profile.
- **'The next work that was done at the Birmingham laboratory was a re-examination of what had produced no result in 1995 – your Lordships see knickers, re extraction of 1995 tubes, and then again a predominance of the appellant's profile in yellow, as there set out.'** This testing appears to be separate from Frazier's already discussed tests. If so, then was it SGM, when was it done and by whom? Note use of the phrase 'predominance of appellant's profile', thus implying just a partial match.
- **The SGM Plus work looks at a sex test. The same six areas as SGM but another four in addition; so that there are 11 boxes of findings, therefore, sex and the 10 areas. Again, set out out across the top of the page, the appellant in yellow, Mr Alphon in green, and Miss Storie in a bluey green.'** This section suggests that Dr Whitaker did SGM Plus®/LCN tests of both Alphon and Storie, which were not among those provided for Figure 6.

- **'Insofar as the knickers are concerned, your Lordships see the result described as the major component profile in yellow, as your Lordships will see, a male profile, of which there were results in 17 of the 20 possible results, the F in three places indicating where the test failed to produce a result, as sometimes happens in those particular areas there recorded.'** No failures were recorded on the knicker test in Figure 6 by Dr Whitaker, yet here they are being discussed. This statement is also noteworthy in that multiple failures with this testing is being acknowledged as happening, yet providing no details, which raises severe questions as to the reliability of this FSS test method. I would love to know which loci and alleles failed and whether this was yet another later test. The claim that these three failures gave rise to what he erroneously calls a 'random chance ratio' of one in 500 million is highly dubious, and the method used to derive it never explained. Remember there was a male profile, assumed to be Gregsten, found in Frazier's testing, which by rights supposedly required a Bayesian likelihood ratio calculation. No satisfactory explanation for Dr Whitaker's test not finding that profile has been provided to date.
- **'In the epithelial fraction, which is beneath, your Lordships see that the major profile is plainly consistent with Miss Storie and the minor profile again matches the appellant.'** It is not clear to me if this is referring to Frazier's testing or Whitaker's as Mr Sweeney has not referenced a new report, having been discussing Dr Whitaker's testing. If it is the latter, something very strange is going on as Dr Whitaker has not reported any epithelial test results anywhere, and if it is the former, Frazier's test results from Figure 6 shows only a very partial match here.
- **'This SGM Plus schedule includes – because of some factual disagreement with Dr Everson [*sic*], which I suspect will soon disappear – details of controls and other tests that were done using the SGM Plus system, where no result was obtained, but I need not take your Lordships'**

time with that at the moment. As previously noted, this brief mention of control tests failing is potentially highly significant, or even critical, to assessing Dr Whitaker's test results, but it is brushed off as immaterial. What tests were these and what did they show? Mr Sweeney, and by inference the FSS, did not explain it at the time, or, as far as I can tell, at any later stage, yet the court allowed this to pass without comment.

- **'in respect of the seminal fraction profiles and in respect of the epithelial fraction profiles, one finds the appellant's DNA in precisely the sort of major profile role which is to be expected if he was the donor of the semen which the murderer left at the scene, as it were.'** The claim that Frazier's seminal and epithelial tests showed consistency with Hanratty being the rapist is one that I doubt would be supported by a great many objective DNA scientists. Frazier's testing was experimental, and had multiple failures, and didn't agree with Dr Whitaker's test results, plus the control tests performed also failed. Also, if the *Horizon* programme is to be believed, it appears that Dr Whitaker's testing was LCN and not SGM Plus® and was therefore highly questionable, so how much faith can be put in his reported numbers? In addition, no scientific testing has been done to establish how one differentiates between semen deposited through rape as opposed to contamination. Furthermore, the basis for Dr Whitaker's claim that Hanratty was the rapist was that no other male semen was found, which even this court has been told is untrue.

- **'I hear the word "mistake": it is coming from the author, so I think I can take it that that is right.'** This comment from Mr Sweeney is evidence of two further FSS documentation mistakes made, I suspect, by Dr Whitaker. His apparent propensity for errors in his documentation does nothing to bolster confidence in his claims. To me, this is indicative of an organisational culture that is not being subjected to diligent oversight at this time. As already noted, FSS performance standards and procedures were not independently reviewed until 2008 and were then found to

be wanting. This lack of demonstrable care from this scientist has implications for our criminal justice system that are potentially profound and currently unknown. What happened between this case and the Sean Hoey case? Sadly, this court accepted Dr Whitaker's and Mr Sweeney's claims without question.
- Finally, the phrase, **'the issue before your Lordships is not whether the appellants DNA is there, because those findings are accepted'**, is a woeful indictment of this court and most specifically of Hanratty's team, who seemingly accepted that it could be said to be his DNA. I think they were so focused upon contamination they allowed the court to be severely misled here.

Having produced this strangely cursory overview of the supposedly convincing evidence for saying it is Hanratty's DNA and that he was the rapist, Mr Sweeney spends over four times as many pages trying to dismiss the possibility of contamination (apart from a brief digression highlighting yet another example of the police's questionable actions). For brevity I have chosen not to do a line-by-line analysis of his arguments. I shall just say that for me there is nothing even remotely convincing and I wonder what the Court of Appeal justices could have made of it.

What is also not made clear, either here or throughout the whole three days of the hearing, is the provenance of Miss Storie's underwear and the handkerchief. How had they been stored, and where, for nearly forty years? Even if contamination could be proved to have *not* taken place – which it cannot – these garments would potentially be suffering from a level of DNA degradation due to age. This could be an explanation for at least some of the evidence testing failures. Mr Sweeney is reporting these results as though these were samples taken from a recent crime scene and stored in optimal conditions; none of which applies here. There are extreme sensitivity levels in play with this evidence. The court should have been made aware of these risks and sought explanations as to how they had been confirmed as not applying in this case.

I also contend that, had the respondent's team been more confident of the veracity of the FSS testing, Mr Sweeney would surely have spent more time detailing the firmness of the results instead of this brief and confusing presentation. The fact that this didn't happen may be seen as potentially significant. Even if the full Hanratty profile, which, as of writing, is still unknown, was a complete match to Dr Whitaker's LCN test, and therefore a strong but not proven pointer to it being his DNA on the knickers, it would not have matched Frazier and Bark's tests at D21, and there is nothing here to say he's a rapist or to discount contamination.

This brings my frustrating perusal of the limited useful information in this first day's transcript to a close. Fortunately, the following days' transcripts will prove a great deal more enlightening. I cannot help but wonder how enlightened their lordships will have been feeling at this stage.

Tuesday, 23 April 2002

The hearing for this day begins with this interjection from Mr Sweeney: 'I am sorry to interrupt Mr Mansfield. May I just correct some errors on our note, which I would have corrected with the witness yesterday; so that your Lordships are not misled?' The details of the documented errors are unknown and immaterial but, yet again, this shows the lack of proper care undertaken with such important documentation from the FSS and must raise doubts about the overall standard of work being undertaken here. Interestingly, or perhaps tellingly, the court makes no reference to this as a concern and accepts the documentation and the conclusions based on it, unquestioningly.

Mr Bark's Cross-examination

During the cross-examination of Mr Bark by Mr Mansfield, the following point arises:

> MR MANSFIELD: The levels of sensitivity of detection of the various tests, we had an example yesterday, that was the Quad test, the STR/QUAD, was 1-5 nanograms of sensitivity. Do you agree with that?
>
> MR BARK: I think that would be a reasonable range, yes.
>
> MANSFIELD: That was the one in 1995. What about the levels of sensitivity of the tests that were carried out in 1997 and 1998?

Tuesday, 23 April 2002   137

BARK: Can we start with the nuclear tests?

MANSFIELD: Certainly.

BARK: I do not know whether a particular figure was actually put on this test, but I would expect it to be able to detect something like 100 picograms or 1/10th of a nanogram as its lower limit. You could probably get less than that if we are going – in general terms we would expect it to work at that level.

MANSFIELD: So you are saying the sensitivity of the nuclear test is 100 picograms?

BARK: Yes, a good quality DNA, this would probably be correct.

This testimony says that the testing applied in 1997/1998 had an expected low threshold of about 100 pg to produce a viable DNA sample. Based on the fact the FSS website factsheet gave 1995 as the year the SGM test was introduced, and June 1999 for the introduction of SGM Plus®, with LCN being introduced at some unspecified time thereafter, I have assumed that this testing was SGM. However, the low threshold for SGM testing, according to the Reed judgment, is 2 ng, with a contentious value of possibly somewhere between 250 pg and 1 ng for SGM Plus®. It is only with LCN that the technology is supposed to be able to cope with a low threshold amount of DNA material of 100 pg. So, if it was SGM testing, or even SGM Plus® testing, Mr Bark is either completely confused, or there must be another reason. Alternatively, if it was LCN testing the FSS was publishing incorrect information on its website until 2007, at the very least. Again, this does nothing to support the veracity of the FSS claims in this case.

Rachel Frazier's Evidence

During the subsequent testimony of Rachel Frazier, we have these relevant exchanges. I have repeated Figure 4 here to aid comprehension:

138   Executed: But was James Hanratty Innocent?

Figure 4: RF's test results

ITEM	Am	TH01	D21	D18	D8	VWA	FGA	Tester
Valerie S / BS	XX	7, 9.3	59, 65	15, 19	8, 12	18, 19	20, 20	RF
Knickers Epithelial	XY	6, 7, 9, 9.3	59,65	13, 14, 15, 19	8, 12, 13	17, 18, 19	19, 20, 25	RF
Knickers Seminal	XY	6, 7, 9	NR	13, 14, 16, 18	13,	16, 17, 18	19, 21, 25	RF
JH Inferred	XY	6, 9, ?	61, 63, 65, ?	13, 14, 15, ?	8, 13, 15,, ?	15, 17, 18, ?	19, 20, 25, ?	

MR SWEENEY: Taking the work in the order in which it was done, we begin, I think, with the entry: 'Knickers fragment which fell on rack during 1995 extraction.'

MS FRAZIER: That is right, yes.

SWEENEY: In the seminal fraction, we can see a major profile consistent with the appellant in yellow and aspects of minor profile in red and blue, blue to indicate a compatibility with Miss Storie's profile?

FRAZIER: That is right, yes.

SWEENEY: In the epithelial fraction, we can see a major profile in blue of Miss Storie and a minor profile in yellow matching the appellant?

FRAZIER: That is right, yes.

LCJ WOOLF: Is there any significance to the fact that in the sex test it is Y as opposed to XY?

FRAZIER: That is because, as it was a mixture, you cannot necessarily say that X originated as a minor component.

The seminal fraction result obtained in Figure 4 was, at best, only a partial match. To claim that this is matching the appellant is an overstatement. No additional information is provided regarding the minor profile in red in the seminal fraction. I believe that this is the group AB profile, attributed to Gregsten. At the very least, this finding must be viewed against the FSS claim in *Horizon*, that they only found one male DNA profile on Valerie Storie's knickers. The question from the Lord Chief Justice raises an interesting point, in so far as the Amelogenin entry for both the seminal and epithelial tests was XY in the version that I received, as can be seen from Figure 4. I have no explanation for this, other than this could have been a transcription error that the witness spotted and amended before the 2002 hearing, though this is only an assumption on my part.

After yet another discussion of the handkerchief profiles, presumably again intended to reinforce their supposed significance in the mind of the court, we have this exchange.

> SWEENEY: Thank you. Insofar as these various results are concerned, are you able to judge from the readings that you obtain what sort of levels of DNA are giving rise to the results which you obtained?
>
> FRAZIER: Yes. We did not quantify the amount of DNA in the extractions. However, we can cross-reference with the PCR positive, which is a known concentration that we used in the tests.

This is significant, because it confirms that the amount of DNA was not quantified, as per Caddy's recommendation. In other words, the cross-referencing with PCR positive, whatever that might mean, was not a sufficient step to guarantee the validity of this DNA testing.

Next, we have this exchange:

> SWEENEY: It obviously gives a profile. The question really is – I am trying to do it briefly – is it a relatively low level of quantity that we are dealing with here, whether it is the knickers or the handkerchief?

FRAZIER: It is not a particularly low level, no, we are looking at between half a nanogram to almost a full nanogram for the handkerchief, which is a considerable amount of DNA for the test that we are using.

This is noteworthy because this is SGM testing which requires a minimum of 2 ng to guarantee results. Yet again the FSS is going way beyond the test boundaries, with unknown but potentially significant impacts on our justice system – as seems to have been its habit for some considerable time.

The next exchange was the subject of an attack the next day on Dr Evison, the defence DNA expert, and so needs to be considered carefully:

FRAZIER: That is for the knickers.

SWEENEY: Is that a total?

FRAZIER: In that particular sample that I amplified we are probably looking at about 400 cells, because it has been amplified four times, so we process that four times.

SWEENEY: So that we can see in the nanogram side of it the total concerned. Certainly as far as the knickers are concerned, the seminal gives the largest amount, 36 nanograms, then it says 1710. Are you aware of the amounts of DNA that are commonly supposed to be produced by blood, bloodstains, semen, hairs, saliva and so on?

FRAZIER: I know the amount of DNA that is expected to be in a cell, yes, that is right.

SWEENEY: How much DNA is there expected to be in a cell?

FRAZIER: **Between 3-6 picograms of DNA.**

This exchange contains some details that are confusing. Frazier says that they had about 400 cells on the knickers, which would equate to about 2 ng of DNA material, because the rule of thumb that a nuclear DNA cell contains approximately 5 pg of material, as noted in bold. Then Frazier makes the confusing statement that the knicker sample was amplified four times to produce that amount. Again, you need to remember that for amounts of less than 2 ng, the SGM test is not guaranteed to produce a result. I believe this is meant to be the starting amount of material before any amplification is performed, not the amount you finish with after amplification. Whatever it was, the reason for the four cycles of amplification is not explained here, or during the attack on Dr Evison the next day, which I shall discuss in the next chapter. I am assuming it was just to give them the 2 ng of material to then run the SGM test, which seems to be procedurally questionable on that basis. If this was the case, for four cycles to have produced 2 ng, Frazier was starting with 125 pg, as each step of PCR amplification doubles the amount of starting DNA. I have been unable to find how many cycles of PCR were normally performed when using an SGM test kit, as this is going back over twenty years. However, Mr Sweeney then says the seminal fraction on the knickers also gave 36 ng, presumably after an SGM PCR amplification process, although this is not confirmed. He then follows this with a mysterious number of 1710, the significance of which is unexplained. If you start with 0.125 ng, eight cycles give you 32 ng, nine cycles 64 ng, so where does 36 ng come from? If you consider an exchange like this, is it really any wonder that the court failed to understand the substance of the evidence presented?

Dr Jonathan Whitaker's Evidence

I shall now consider the testimony of the key witness for the respondent, Dr Whitaker, the scientist responsible for proclaiming that Hanratty was the rapist. Remember, his evidence was torn apart by scientists working for the defence in the later Sean Hoey case with dramatic ramifications for the whole of our criminal justice system.

MR SWEENEY: Are you the scientist who has been responsible for the SGM Plus testing in this case from 2000 onwards?

DR WHITAKER: Yes.

This confirms that he did testing after Hanratty's exhumation in 2001. The first question here, yet again is, was this SGM Plus® or LCN testing? It could be that the standard FSS testing after 1999 was, as a matter of course, at the SGM Plus® or LCN level or, alternatively, this could be related to the issue of DNA sample degradation, due to Hanratty's burial in unknown conditions for almost forty years. I shall look for clarification of this statement as this testimony progresses. As this testimony is critical, I intend to review it carefully, and in detail.

SWEENEY: Again, I am going to take your statements as read, if I may. Do you have available to you the graphic representation of your results?

WHITAKER: I do.

SWEENEY: Insofar as the first page is concerned, are there set out, subject to the correction in Mr Alphon's case, XY, the full profiles that you have obtained from the samples provided to you in relation to the appellant, Mr Alphon and Miss Storie?

WHITAKER: Yes.

This appears to confirm that the witness created profiles from samples provided to him from Peter Alphon, Valerie Storie and Hanratty. It does not say what those samples were, when they were created, or the method employed to create them. Nor does it say what process Dr Whitaker employed to obtain his reported profiles. These test results remain unknown, but here are his already discussed results, plus the earlier pellet profile, which will be mentioned during this testimony:

Figure 7: Whitaker pre-exhumation results including knicker pellet from Figure 2

ITEM	Am	TH01	D21	D18	D8	VWA	FGA	D3	D16	D2	D19
Knickers	XX	6, 9	29, 32.2	13, 14	13, 13	17, 18	19, 25	15, 16	10, 11	20, 20	14, 14
JH Inferred	XY	6, 9, ?	28, 29, 30, ?	13, 14, 15, ?	8, 13, 15, ?	15, 17, 18, ?	19, 20, 25, ?	15, 16, ?	10, 11, ?	18, 20, ?, ?	14, 14.2, ?
Mary H	XX	6, 6	29, 30	13, 15	8, 13	15, 17	19, 20	15, 15	11, 11	18, 20	14, 14.2
Michael H	XY	6, 9	28, 30	13, 14	13, 15	15, 18	19, 25	15, 16	10, 11	18, 20	14, 14
Knicker pellet	XY	6	NR	NR	13	17,18	NR				

The testimony continues:

> SWEENEY: Is there then set out beneath that your examination of the pellet fraction of Mr Bark's extraction from the knickers in 1997?
>
> WHITAKER: Correct.

Dr Whitaker appears to have examined a pellet fraction, apparently produced by Mr Bark, although why this was done is not examined further or explained. As I was under the impression that the pellet, supernatant, spinaroo, and blue liquid results in Figure 2, were from Mr Geenhalgh's STR/Quad test, I cannot explain Mr Sweeney's statement that this pellet fraction had been produced by Mr Bark. Was Mr Sweeney mistaken here, or were there further unknown STR tests run by Mr Bark? Whatever the truth, this is yet further evidence of the confusing and potentially erroneous way that the respondent's DNA evidence is being presented to this court.

Next, we come to the three failures, mentioned by Mr Sweeney in his initial presentation of the DNA evidence from the day before, none of which appear in the test results we have seen.

> SWEENEY: We can see, going across the page from left to right, readings matching the appellant. I wonder if our eyes could stop when we get to the D2 column, which reads '20F'. Can you just help us as to what 20F means and how it comes about?

WHITAKER: 20F is scientific nomenclature. The F indicates that. Where we might have expected to see two bands in the other DNA sites tested, at this particular site we only see one, which we have designated 20. The F just allows for the fact that another band may be present or may have been present, but we are not actually visualising it.

SWEENEY: If we then go up to the appellant's profile, we see that he is in fact 20-20?

WHITAKER: Yes.

I cannot confirm which result Mr Sweeney is discussing here. It doesn't match Bark's knicker pellet or Dr Whitaker's pre-exhumation knicker profile. This says that only one of the two alleles at locus D2 was measured as 20, whereas the other allele was not picked up, hence the F designation. Quite what the witness meant by the statement 'another band may be present or may have been present', is not clear to me. However, Mr Sweeney immediately states that Hanratty's own post-exhumation composite profile had two alleles present, both of which measured 20. Therefore, as it stands, this is not a match at this locus. Dr Whitaker tries to justify his claim that it is a match in the following exchange:

SWEENEY: In that area. What is the significance of that, on the one hand, set against your 20F on the other hand?

WHITAKER: The DNA profile from the appellant has been typed under different conditions really and duplicated from a number of different samples. So it is certain that, at this particular site, he has inherited two DNA bands of the same type from each of his parents, and both of those bands have been designated 20. In relation to the profile from the knickers, we are introducing a degree of conservatism and allowing for a fact that another band at that position may not have matched him. But the fact that we only observe one 20 band means that I can still report the DNA match between the profile from the knickers and from his sample.

Firstly, it should be remembered that Hanratty's DNA profile was a composite. The choice of language throughout the FSS evidence has been highly confusing so, again, I may be misinterpreting what was being said. However, we need to try and understand the logic Dr Whitaker uses to justify his calling of the DNA sample on the knickers as a match to Hanratty.

The logic seems to be this: 'I have also only found one allele at locus D2S1338, from Hanratty's exhumed DNA, but it is "certain" that he will have inherited the same allele from both parents, because this is a composite.' Where is the evidence for this statement? They only had DNA samples from his mother and brother, not from his father. Is this an example of 'What the thinker thinks, the prover proves'? This also appears to contradict Mr Sweeney's presentation of the evidence when he said that Hanratty's DNA profile at locus D2S1338 was 20-20. The only way I can explain this is that Mr Sweeney was previously reporting Hanratty's assumed profile – based on this thinking by Dr Whitaker – as his actual profile.

Then Dr Whitaker says that when matching with the profile recovered from the knickers, only observing one band 20 still means that he can report a match. Was it the profile from Hanratty himself that only had one allele of 20, or was it the profile from the knickers? Remember that Mr Sweeney was reporting the profile from the knickers as being 20-F. However, if Hanratty's own profile, from a composite, is only assumed to be 20-20, how much faith can one have in the interpretation given here? Whatever the situation that applies here, this must be a 'match' that is open to doubt. What another forensic scientist would have made of this evidence is a moot point, but I suggest that a different interpretation is quite possible.

Unfortunately, as will be seen from the following, the same situation also applied at two other loci, one of which is D19S433, while the other is not identified:

SWEENEY: As we can see, in fact, it is precisely the same situation in the next area, where he has two 13s and it is 13F, and precisely the same situation in the D19 area, where he has two 14s and it is 14F.

WHITAKER: Yes. This is a standard Forensic Science Service procedure when we are looking at DNA sites where potentially the individual has inherited the same DNA bands from their parents.

SWEENEY: Thank you. So your limitation in each of those areas, in accordance with standard practice, is designed, as it were, to protect who?

WHITAKER: Yes, we would say that, in terms of a statistical assessment, it would favour the appellant because, by reducing the number of bands we have scored, we have increased the chance that somebody else could have that profile in the population.

The similar logic being applied here is apparently in accordance with FSS standard procedure. The claim that this would favour Hanratty must be dubious, as he is including three unconfirmed matches. This should have required a retest to see whether the three failures would re-occur, or whether an actual reading could be obtained, rather than presuming a match. This is yet another example of the dubious nature of the FSS practices. We will see that there is a later claim of retesting, although what it showed, and whether it was related to this issue, is not clarified anywhere within the transcripts.

SWEENEY: In fact, insofar as this profile is concerned, even making those allowances in his favour, the match is complete in all other areas, and is it that one which led to the random chance statistic of 1 in 500 million?

WHITAKER: Yes.

Again, no explanation is forthcoming for how these 'apparently damning' statistics were calculated (remember that SGM Plus® and LCN has a 'supposed' RMP discriminatory power of one in more than a billion for a full profile match). Seemingly the court didn't require one. Additionally, with a mixed profile scenario, as applied here, it should have been expressed as a Bayesian likelihood ratio, according to common practice.

> SWEENEY: Then we see minor DNA bands observed beneath.
>
> WHITAKER: Yes.
>
> SWEENEY: Blue to indicate a match with Miss Storie?
>
> WHITAKER: Correct.
>
> SWEENEY: Red to indicate a match with neither, the appellant or Miss Storie?
>
> WHITAKER: Yes. These were much smaller bands, minor bands.

Once again, the red minor profile that seems to have been attributed to Gregsten, is mentioned by Mr Sweeney. Tellingly, Dr Whitaker makes no comment or explanation here, or anywhere else in his testimony regarding this profile. He was obviously aware of its presence, so how could he claim that the only male profile found was Hanratty's?

> SWEENEY: Then the epithelial fraction, insofar as the knickers are concerned, producing a detailed profile, insofar as Miss Storie is concerned, in blue. Then a male profile matching the appellant in the four areas that are there indicated.
>
> WHITAKER: Yes.
>
> SWEENEY: The negative control that is underneath is part of the safety procedures involved in the testing, is it not?

WHITAKER: It is.

SWEENEY: Although you have recorded it so that it is a full reflection of your results, does it otherwise have any significance insofar as any conclusions are concerned?

WHITAKER: None whatsoever.

No explanation is given as to why the control sample that showed negative is of no significance to the conclusions. It is doubtful, though again not impossible, that any reasoning for this will have been provided within the accompanying documentation, though the judgment makes no mention of it. The reluctance to proffer an explanation, in conjunction with the way the FSS evidence is being presented by the respondent, speaks volumes. I would point out that once again Mr Sweeney confirms that the epithelial fraction produced a detailed profile for Miss Storie. So, we are back again to the unanswered question of why did their lordships apparently believe her DNA had been swamped by Hanratty's, as per the judgment's paragraph 125?

SWEENEY: Then we can see no result in the buffer wash, no result in relation to an examination by you over the page of two aspects of Mr Greenhalgh's original work back in 1995.

WHITAKER: Correct.

This exchange is confusing in several respects. Why was the witness examining two aspects of the unsuccessful STR/QUAD test from 1995? Which were they? What is really being said here, and why is it being discussed? Again, no explanation is forthcoming.

For reasons that will become apparent, I am going to break my rule and discuss the next piece of evidence regarding the handkerchief, – see Figure 2 above – even though it does not provide a connection between Hanratty and the murder weapon.

SWEENEY: Then, insofar as the handkerchief is concerned, you have set out stain 1, as it has been called, which Mr Bark has dealt with as being apparent nasal mucus. We can see again, insofar as the Fs are concerned, arising – the first two in areas where he is 20-20 and 13-13 respectively?

WHITAKER: Yes.

SWEENEY: Can you just help us about the FF in the D19 column?

WHITAKER: In this particular case we have two designations of F, two fails. The reason for this was that the DNA band observed at that site was at such a high value that it was effectively distorting the result we obtained. Therefore, in my opinion, having looked at a lot of these profiles from experience, I was not happy at being able to designate that with the fullest confidence and, therefore, failed that result.

SWEENEY: Thank you. Whose benefit was that practice designed to work towards?

WHITAKER: That, again, would have favoured the defendant because, my leaving those DNA bands out of the profile, statistically the chance of somebody else having that profile would have increased.

SWEENEY: However, insofar as that profile is concerned, is that the one with the random chance of 1 in 250 million?

WHITAKER: It is, yes.

The day before, Mr Sweeney had said that there were four failures on the handkerchief, and three failures on the knickers; while earlier in Dr Whitaker's testimony, it wasn't clear whether Hanratty's profile entries were actual, or assumed by the witness. Either way, they both claimed that Hanratty had 20-20 at D2, 14-14 at D19 and 13-13 at one other unidentified locus, whereas the profile from the knickers was 20-F, 14-F and 13-F. In other words, this was not a match.

Now here, for the handkerchief, Mr Sweeney appears to be saying that the DNA from the mucus 'Stain 1' for D2 was, again, 20-F, and that the unknown locus was, again, 13-F. Yet for D19 the band was reported as F-F, seemingly because Dr Whitaker felt the band was too high to be trusted. These figures do not match the values reported in the testing by Frazier or Bark, whoever produced them, so it seems that Dr Whitaker did further non-reported tests on the handkerchief. I would remind the reader of the standardised notation system used for these results, whereby the lower value allele is always placed first and that, as a result, there is no confirmation of which parent produced the allele. In other words, there is no confirmed equivalence between these two results, even if they appear to be a match. The onus should be on the scientist interpreting such results to fully explain this to the court, and to provide supplementary evidence to back up any claim of equivalence. It is vital that the court fully understands this fact, and its implications. Yet I can see nothing within the testimony from these three days to have made the court aware of this critical fact and as we have seen in the judgments from both this case and Reed, many senior members of the judiciary were not aware of this. Whether this situation has improved since these judgments is for others to answer.

What is also not clarified is the actual value at D19, which Dr Whitaker considered was too high to be trusted. This is important because we have a difference between the reading for D19 on the knickers and on stain 1 on the handkerchief. Regardless of this, Dr Whitaker says that the profile readings have produced a match with Hanratty. I would dearly love to understand his rationale for this attribution, since, as it appears to stand, they are nothing of the sort. Again, no explanation of the statistical probability figure is provided. I can only wonder just what another potentially less biased analyst might have made of this evidence.

Moving on to a second mucus stain, we have the following exchange:

SWEENEY: Then you have also set out your findings as to stain 2 on the handkerchief, likewise yellow stain 1, in both instances where there is a result matching the appellant. Again, insofar as the Fs are concerned on those results?

WHITAKER: Fs indicate here that a DNA band was not visible at the site. We were just seeing single DNA bands. For example, in the first column, D3, only the 16 band was observed.

Mr Sweeney claims that the results from Stain 2, and from Yellow Stain 1, both match Hanratty. This is further proof that this is additional SGM Plus® /LCN testing because it includes loci D3. Whether this means a full match, or a partial match, such as on the knickers and stain 1, is not explained. Unfortunately, the only information provided is that D3 gives a reading of 16.

Regarding the final stain on the handkerchief, denoted as Yellow Stain 2, we have the following exchange:

SWEENEY: Then, finally, insofar as yellow stain 2 is concerned, you have readings in two areas: in the first area, F and 16, and in the other areas, 12, 13 and 14. As we can see, in fact, the appellant would match both the 16 and the 14. The reason why you have not coloured it in being?

WHITAKER: Because of the result at D19. The fact that we observed three DNA bands is indication that there is a mixture of DNA there. The maximum number of bands you would expect from one person is two. Because of the poor quality of the results, the fact the DNA bands were very small and were not particularly reproducible from a different test that I did, meant that I was not confident in appropriating any of these bands to any particular person.

SWEENEY: Did that in any way detract from the other results that you obtained in relation to the handkerchief?

WHITAKER: No. This was an independent sample taken from an independent area.

SWEENEY: Therefore, insofar as stain 1, stain 2 and yellow stain 1 are concerned, did you find any DNA other than that which can be attributed to the appellant?

WHITAKER: No.

It is not clear from the way Mr Sweeney phrases it, but Dr Whitaker seems to say that locus D19 produced a result of 12-13-14. Mr Sweeney also seems to be saying that a result of 16-F has occurred at another unidentified locus, although he says F-16, which does not accord with standard notation. He then says Hanratty would match both the 16 and 14 alleles. Whether this represents D3, where a band 16 is mentioned earlier, is not clarified.

The results for D2 and the unknown locus, where Hanratty's DNA reading was apparently 13-13, are not discussed, but because of the 12, 13 and 14 result on D19, Dr Whitaker correctly calls this a mixed DNA profile. Therefore, at least one other person had handled the handkerchief at some point. In view of my suspicions concerning Dixie France, I wonder if his DNA was involved, though I suspect that this will never be established this far after events.

If we now take stock of precisely what has been said so far, in this confusing and difficult to follow testimony, it can be represented graphically in the following fashion:

Figure 8: Dr Whitaker's testimony

Source	D3	Unknown	D2	D19
Hanratty	?	13, 13	20, 20	14, 14
Knickers	?	13, F	20, F	14, F
Hankie Stain1	?	13, F	20, F	F, F
Hankie Stain2	16, F	?	?	?
Yellow Stain 1	?	?	?	?
Yellow Stain 2	16, F	16, F	?	12, 13, 14

Although not mentioned in these exchanges, I believe the unknown column refers to D16, the fourth of the additional loci targeted by the SGM Plus® / LCN test. The reader should note that the figures for Hanratty himself are believed by Dr Whitaker to be full matches, which must be doubtful since only one allele at each locus was noted, even though this was his exhumed DNA. Remember also that the same figure is not indicative of equivalence, because the donating parent is not identified. I would again point out that Hanratty's father's DNA is unknown so there is even less certainty here. Based on these figures, and the others not discussed during his testimony, Dr Whitaker is claiming that Hanratty raped Miss Storie and, at least by inference, wrapped the gun with the handkerchief. The earlier material I have discussed, especially from Chapter 7, highlights just how tenuous I believe these claims are. It should also be pointed out, again, that Dr Whitaker does not explain the full significance of the handkerchief findings to the court, vis-a-vis the relationship to the gun.

On this highly unsatisfactory note we now move on to even stranger material.

> SWEENEY: If one proceeds upon the basis of a scenario of a rape with two days before consensual intercourse with a deposit by the rapist of his liquid semen on the victims knickers, are you able to help us, firstly, as to what major profile which matches the appellant is or is not consistent with, in your experience, that scenario?
>
> WHITAKER: That scenario is one which I personally have encountered quite a lot in forensic casework. We can make the pre-assessment of what we might expect to find under the circumstances that you have described. I have to say that the DNA profiling results which we observed are entirely in accordance with that scenario.

Dr Whitaker's claim to have encountered this scenario 'quite a lot' is extraordinary. To reiterate, the scenario was that the rape victim, from forty years earlier, had been wearing knickers with two-day-old semen stains (potentially through vaginal seepage) from apparently consensual intercourse, when she was attacked and raped. He claims that he had come across this scenario, not just this once, but on numerous earlier occasions. I've already indicated that it might have been that washing in 1961 didn't remove microscopic amounts of DNA; however, we will see that the FSS witnesses and the court discount this, though Dr Evison points to this as a potential cause of contamination.

If, instead, he is claiming that he's dealt with 'quite a lot' of modern cases where rape has occurred up to several days after consensual intercourse, which I also find at the very least questionable, it doesn't mean that the evidence will appear the same as forty-year-old evidence. Don't forget that there are three other factors to be considered. Firstly, Miss Storie was not wearing the knickers when she was raped, as was detailed in Lord Russell of Liverpool's book,[1] so the staining from the rape will have been due to vaginal seepage. Secondly, as this evidence was almost four decades old, and with an unknown provenance, when examined by this witness, with an unknown level of degradation, the strength of his conclusion is scientifically unjustified. Thirdly, the consensual intercourse was apparently from two days earlier. This evidence is not questioned by their lordships, even though they are perfectly at liberty to do so; another fact which I find extraordinary.

> SWEENEY: Equally, insofar as the epithelial fraction is concerned, where one is targeting obviously the female cells principally, again on the scenario I have described, can you help us with the result that was obtained in the epithelial fraction?
>
> WHITAKER: Again, the epithelial fraction is designed to concentrate the contribution of DNA from the female victim in these particular types of circumstance. **Therefore, the DNA profiling result I observed, again, is entirely in accordance with what we were trying to achieve.**

In view of the court's belief that Miss Storie's epithelial fraction had been swamped by Hanratty's DNA, which seems to run counter to the evidence given here, what might this say about the level of confusion experienced by their lordships? The resonance of the bold part of Dr Whitaker's answer, when considered against the propensity for bias in the reporting of such findings, is noteworthy.

> SWEENEY: Mr Mansfield mentioned a little earlier the maxim: every contact leaves a trace. Does your particular specialisation enable us to put that into context in the DNA field?
>
> WHITAKER: It is a phrase which I have heard an awful lot when I have been lecturing to police officers and talking about the subjective [should this be *subject of?*] DNA profiling. But we have to be very careful, I would suggest, using it in a particular context because we have to remember that, although we anticipate DNA as being all around us, it would not follow that we would be able to test and detect it. **We have to understand that the tests that we perform are really geared to detecting quite a lot of DNA because we are fully appreciative of the fact that contaminating DNA can give error in our results and interpretation.**

The reader might recall that the amount of DNA the LCN test is geared to find is something of the order of 100 pg. Here is Dr Whitaker claiming that this is quite a lot of nuclear DNA material. He also claims that the FSS scientists fully appreciate the risks of contamination influencing their results. Please note that on its now discontinued website, in Factsheet Number 6, the FSS stated: 'As with all forensic evidence, the context and interpretation need to be considered carefully. This is even more important with DNA LCN, due to its sensitivity and the possibility that the DNA detected is unconnected with the offence under investigation.'

However, I would also highlight the following part of the abstract from a further FSS document, which states explicitly that it is impossible to prevent contamination, even laboratory based, never mind all the other potential sources, from potentially affecting such testing:

> By increasing the PCR amplification regime to 34 cycles, we have demonstrated that it is possible routinely to analyse <100 pg DNA. ...The analysis of mixtures by peak area measurement becomes increasingly difficult as the sample size is reduced. **Laboratory-based contamination cannot be completely avoided, even when analysis is carried out under stringent conditions of cleanliness.** A set of guidelines that utilises duplication of results to interpret profiles originating from picogram levels of DNA is introduced. ...The method used is complex, yet can be converted into an expert system. We envisage this to be the next step... .[2]

This weakens his dismissal of contamination even further. We will see his reasoning shortly. Back to the transcript:

> SWEENEY: Thank you. Have you also been kind enough to do some calculations of the amount of DNA involved in the results of your test?
>
> WHITAKER: I have, yes.
>
> SWEENEY: I wonder if I could hand another document to the court. (Handed) As part of the testing, is a standard amount, as it were, run through the test to ensure its integrity?
>
> WHITAKER: Yes, and also to ensure that the DNA profiling process is working.
>
> Q. Thank you. Have you set out the figures from the standard on the left hand side?
>
> WHITAKER: I have, yes.

These calculations and their method were not valid, according to the subsequent Caddy report, although to be fair to the court it will not have known this. Also, in view of the minimal amount of DNA involved in this case, it would have been useful to know how much was used in this integrity testing.

> SWEENEY: Firstly, the significance of those sorts of amounts within the DNA field, large amounts, small amounts, what are they?
>
> WHITAKER: The DNA test we are using examines ten DNA sites, is a commercial kit. You can buy it and any forensic laboratory can use it. Manufacturers give a recommended scale for use with DNA samples, **and the lower end of that scale is approximately 200 picograms or 0.2 nanograms.** You have to remember that the test would be used routinely in forensic casework, and these amounts of DNA between 0.2 nanograms up to about 2 nanograms are what we routinely would be using in any DNA forensic test. Therefore, the amounts of DNA which I have calculated – and I have to stress these are estimates – fall within the range which we would normally expect to encounter in normal everyday forensic practice, although at the lower end of the scale.

Dr Whitaker is claiming that the SGM Plus® manufacturer's recommended lower end amount of DNA is 200 pg. This is counter to the other evidence cited: that a minimum of 1 ng is required to guarantee a reliable profile, or even the alternative 250 pg level, from which profiles may sometimes be obtainable. Any lower than 250 pg would have required the use of the contentious LCN process, which is not a manufacturer-approved use of the SGM Plus® technology.

> SWEENEY: Secondly, this: you will have understood the issue of contamination that is being suggested. Can you help us from your perspective, given that these principal results are your results, as

to your view of what they are consistent with or not consistent with, given the issues you have heard unfold in this court?

WHITAKER: In making any assessment of the evidence, what would go on in my mind and what we teach in forensic interpretation and practice, is to look at two different scenarios: to look at the probability of the evidence. If the DNA had arrived by a course which is described by the events in the case, by the rape and intercourse on Valerie Storie and the deposition of the semen, I would assess that against the probability of obtaining this evidence if it arrived by another route, for example, contamination. Really, to come to any sort of conclusion in my own mind, I would be weighing up pros and cons of each of those scenarios.

In terms of the knickers, we have gone through what might be considered in a pre-assessment of looking at those samples, given that intercourse had taken place, the sample was taken from the victim's knickers. We have targeted an area where we visualise sperm heads. We have chemically selected for those sperm heads in our DNA profiling tests. In that particular sample we have obtained a male profile, which we would expect to find had it originated from sperm.

Therefore, my interpretation of the DNA profiling on the knickers are that, as I have said before, they would be what I would expect to find had that DNA that we have tested originated from the semen which has been deposited, as described by the offence.

Here we have Dr Whitaker's explanation for why he discounted contamination as the reason for the presence of Hanratty's DNA on Miss Storie's knickers. In other words, this is the absolute crux of the whole case: was Hanratty a killer and a rapist, and in Dorney Reach that evening? Or was he in Liverpool and a victim of a misidentification, through contamination or some other factor? His reasoning therefore needs to be carefully assessed and verified to support his claim that Hanratty was the rapist.

Taking the first part of his answer, he says he would look for two different scenarios, and would look at the probability of the evidence. I would refer the reader to my earlier discussion of statistical probabilities, and specifically to the Bayesian likelihood ratio calculation. From the point of view of assessing whether the evidence more closely fits the prosecution hypothesis, or that of the defence, this statement would sound reasonable, if a little vague and open to interpretation.

He goes on to say that he is assessing the likelihood of the evidence being the result of rape, as opposed to contamination. This sounds fine in principle, although I believe there is no evidence that he assesses any such probabilities when you consider his next statements: 'we have gone through what might be considered in a pre-assessment of looking at those knickers, given that intercourse had taken place, the sample was taken from the victim's knickers.' What is meant by this? Remember, the knickers apparently had semen from at least two occurrences of intercourse, from two separate donors, from two separate events, two days apart from forty years ago. There is no mention of how he has pre-assessed things differently to separate out the two intercourse events. Then he has chemically selected for sperm heads in the DNA profiling test, and obtained a male profile, supposedly from Hanratty. No mention is made of the group AB semen result attributed to Gregsten. He then says that the interpretation is as expected, if the DNA had originated from semen deposited, as described, by the offence. This is a circular argument that takes no account of the semen possibly being deposited by contamination. How semen deposited by rape, as opposed to semen deposited during consensual intercourse or, more importantly, through contamination might appear in such a mixed test result is not made clear. There has been no published scientific research, even today, into how one might differentiate between these two methods of deposition. So, this central point rests purely upon how much credence one can place upon his interpretation. Remember also that the FSS did not quantify the amount of DNA present before running these tests, and that to require LCN testing, the evidence would have been invisible to the naked eye. In addition, the Caddy report stated explicitly that it is not possible to infer the source of the DNA, or how it was deposited when dealing with these low template amounts of DNA. Therefore, I believe Dr Whitaker's claim is without scientific justification.

Although he claims to have been adopting a Bayesian approach to this evidence there is, in my mind, no sign of a resulting likelihood ratio calculation in any of his pronouncements, in either this court or the *Horizon* programme. Again, it is not impossible that one was provided in the documentation presented to the court, but I doubt it. As with everything I am documenting in this work, should evidence come to light to change this, I remain willing to revisit my conclusions.

Dr Whitaker then goes on to state:

> It has to be said that, in every case in which we apply these DNA tests, I would like to say that the issues we have heard about in court today are in my experience not unique to it. The DNA profiling results really identify the source of the DNA, and how that DNA got there depends on other circumstances as well as the possibility of contamination. There seems to me to be so many geographical and temporal and spatial ifs and whys and buts and wherefores that it could have arrived through contamination that, if asked, I would also come down on the side that it has originated through the rape that we are discussing.

Here, yet again, he claims that a forty-year-old rape case with two separate instances of intercourse from two days apart on the same pair of knickers is not unique in his experience. He then talks about the many possible means for the DNA to have arrived because of contamination, but he ignores them all and says it could only have arrived due to Hanratty being a rapist. I shall leave it to the reader to decide how much credence they wish to give statements like these, although I remain to be convinced.

A little later we have this exchange:

> LCJ WOOLF: Does it provide any assistance, if so what, in relation to the source of the possible contamination of the type that we have heard of in this case?

> WHITAKER: Taking the two items as a whole, the suggestion of contamination would have to then follow that on the knickers contamination, in my opinion, would have to be semen. We have looked for semen, we have seen sperm, we have chemically targeted for semen and we have a profile from that sample.

Dr Whitaker seems to say that because they chemically targeted for semen when examining the knickers, the source of any sample found must be spermatozoa. Therefore, if the reason was contamination, it must have come from spermatozoa from Hanratty. Don't forget that both Caddy and Krane have confirmed that when dealing with these levels of DNA, the chemical source or its transmission mechanism cannot be confirmed. It should also be remembered that Hanratty's trousers, with a semen stain on the fly, were examined in the 1961 laboratory, at about the same time as Miss Storie's knickers, and were also exhibited and handled in the committal hearing. This could, therefore, be one potential source of contamination. As noted earlier, Dr Evison will give evidence that washing utensils in water, as was the practice in 1961, does not remove DNA. In view of the unknown provenance of this piece of evidence, I don't believe anyone can scientifically discount the possibility of contamination, though that is just what Dr Whitaker has done here.

> MR JUSTICE LEVESON: Could I ask a converse question. Could you help us, please, on this possibility: there is an incidence of intercourse leaving semen on knickers, which semen is then utterly destroyed by the passage of time, or because we do not see traces of it in these results.

> WHITAKER: If I could just present again from my experience: I have dealt with an awful lot of very old forensic cases in which semen has been preserved on microscope slides. We have also, through our research work, done what we called 'ageing studies' where we look at how viable it is to get profiles from sperm

samples which have been stored going back 30 years. Providing the conditions are dry and not too hot, then I would fully expect to get profiles from old sperm heads, regardless of the length of time they have been stored.
Does that answer your question?

LEVESON: Yes, it is a combination of two aspects I am asking. First of all, the fact that you have found one set of results, but, secondly, that you have not found a mixture which would represent the semen of the rapist.

WHITAKER: I see your point. Again, when we talk about pre-assessment, you are quite right. For the result to have been achieved through a different route, the semen that we have visualised would have not had to worked [????] if it originated from somebody other than the appellant.

LEVESON: I think what you are directing to, and what I want to make sure I have the answer, is assume that, instead of the appellant, some third person who was the person who was guilty of the rape was being investigated. If semen were to get on knickers, and the piece that were to be cut out, as happened here by Dr Grant, had had semen on it from the rapist, would you be surprised, or not surprised if that semen was no longer giving traces, giving results?

WHITAKER: I would be surprised if it did not.

Why is there no mention here of the group AB semen? The FSS witnesses have been making what I believe to be contradictory statements, both in *Horizon* as well as throughout this hearing. At times, mention is made of the red fraction, or the group AB semen attributed to Gregsten, yet at other times, there is no mention of another semen stain or male profile. From the transcript alone it has become impossible to identify the validity of the evidence being presented. Yet, seemingly, the court was assured that no semen from the rapist – unless it was Hanratty –

had been found during the testing. On this unfortunate note I shall now move on to the testimony during the cross-examination.

Mr Mansfield spends several minutes laying out the apparent difficulties with the provenance of the samples from the knickers, then asks the following question:

> MANSFIELD: I am laying the groundwork for the question, if I may. The question I am leading to is this: there is no way of knowing, would you agree, from these notes, whether the piece that you looked at in the end, or had extractions looked at, which piece this is and whether it is the area with little sperm or an area with no sperm?
>
> WHITAKER: Correct ... .
>
> MANSFIELD: Their Lordships asked just before lunch about, if I can put it generally, the degradation of DNA; in other words, what might happen to it after it has been deposited. Of course, in the first place, we know that the knickers were not removed for some hours by the hospital when she finally arrived. We know that. Did you know that?
>
> WHITAKER: **I have had no pre-information to the case. I really did my results blind, so I did not compromise my interpretation.**

I would contend that Dr Whitaker's claim to have had no pre-information in the case is extremely dubious.

> MANSFIELD: Because in order to exclude contamination – I appreciate your point about looking at the results and being consistent with a particular scenario – over a 30 year period, you need to carefully analyse the various stages through which – I am taking the knickers as an example – the tiny piece of knicker has been maintained, indeed held, do you not?

> WHITAKER: In every case that we test in the forensic science laboratory, as I said before lunch, these issues are ones which we would consider. Those issues would not preclude us testing a sample but, in the interpretation of the DNA results and other results in the case, we would form an opinion based on every possible scenario. ...
>
> MANSFIELD: So you are not in any position, are you, to deal with whether anything happened either to the piece of fabric or to the handkerchief before they were both finally, as it were, seized and brought together after 1991 and then 1997? You are in no position to exclude it, are you?
>
> WHITAKER: No, and I do not think I have

I have seen nothing to indicate that Dr Whitaker considered the evidence from anything other than a point of view of accepting the respondent's premise. No examination of the undoubted opportunities for contamination had apparently been undertaken, other than to reject them outright. No explanation has been given for the rejection of contamination, other than the false claim that only one male DNA sample showed up in testing. From this transcript evidence, I believe it is clear he has not only excluded the possibility of contamination from his assessment, but also failed to provide a satisfactory scientific basis for that exclusion.

> MANSFIELD: Of course, the differential separation, if I can call it that, which involves centrifugation, is based on an assumption, is it not, that the supernatant liquid fraction will attract the epithelial cells and the pellet fraction will attract the heavier sperm cells?
>
> WHITAKER: Yes, in general terms.
>
> MANSFIELD: But that does not always occur, does it?

WHITAKER: No, sir, it does not.

MANSFIELD: In fact, in this case, one of the features are that the supernatant did give results for DNA commensurate or matching Mr Hanratty's?

WHITAKER: Yes, but this does not necessarily follow that that DNA came from intact sperm.

MANSFIELD: No. It may not. So, once again, one is having to be careful to, as it were, assess the possibilities for a contaminant DNA arriving on this fraction of fabric that may give rise to results both in the epithelial – I am going to call it the supernatant fraction – or the pellet fraction; are you not?

WHITAKER: The seminal fraction is designed to capture the sperm. My observations set out in the table show that more of that male profile, a lot more, was found in the seminal component. Therefore, also in casework it is not unexpected, and we appreciate that often sperm will break open; so that some of the male DNA is often more likely found in the epithelial fraction, not all the sperm will be intact.

It seems that in this case the supernatant liquid fraction, from either Mr Greenhalgh or Mr Bark – see Figure 2 – which normally collects the epithelial cells, apparently also collected DNA which, although a partial match only, was claimed to match Hanratty's. Dr Whitaker says this need not be from intact sperm. He also says a lot more of the male profile was found in the seminal component, and that male DNA from non-intact sperm is often found in the epithelial fragment. Unfortunately, the significance of this exchange remains unclear to me. I also confess to being unable to explain why Dr Whitaker, who did not run the pellet and supernatant tests according to the results from Figure 2, is being questioned about them. In view of the propensity for

FSS documentation errors being encountered in this case this could be another example of such mislabelling.

> MANSFIELD: Going back to this case, I think the description you had of the amount was it was at the lower end of the scale. Transference of half a nanogram from one part of an exhibit file to another is not an impossible scenario is it?
>
> WHITAKER: It is not impossible, but I do not think it is the best explanation of the results.
>
> MANSFIELD: I appreciate you may not see it as the best explanation I think, in fairness, this is not an explanation, do you agree, that you can exclude, even though you do not prefer it?
>
> WHITAKER: I do not think I have ever excluded it.

Dr Whitaker is claiming that secondary transference (contamination) is not the best explanation of the results. He claims, again, to have never excluded it as an explanation, but that he prefers another interpretation: that Hanratty is a rapist. It is his interpretation only. His report excludes it, so does his witness testimony, and subsequently so does the court, despite everything that has been detailed so far.

Later, during his re-examination by Mr Sweeney, we have the following exchange:

> SWEENEY: Could you explain to us, please, why it is your opinion that, even if it were contamination, it would have itself to be sperm?
>
> WHITAKER: I think I went through the points previously, but my rationale would go as follows. We have targeted an area where we would expect to find semen, given the details of the events. We visualise semen in that area. We have chemically selected for semen

in our DNA profiling tests. In that fraction we have obtained a male profile, which we would expect to find had it originated from the semen. All those points together, in terms of possible body fluids, my first choice would be that it had come from sperm.

Again, Dr Whitaker makes no mention of the group AB semen stain, purported to have come from Gregsten two days prior to the rape. Why is it not part of his explanation? Remember that the DNA source cannot be inferred when dealing with low template amounts of evidential DNA, as was confirmed by Caddy's review.

> SWEENEY: If what produced the appellant's profile was not sperm, but something else altogether, would you have expected the differential results that we have as between the pellet fraction and the supernatant fraction?

> WHITAKER: Yes, I would.

So, Dr Whitaker now seems to be saying that the differential results, obtained between the pellet and supernatant fractions, could also point to the appellant's profile not being sperm at all, but something else. Yet he had just said that he had obtained a male profile from the tests, which he considered to have been from sperm. He, therefore, appears to be immediately contradicting himself. Caddy and Krane confirm that at these levels the DNA sample type cannot be inferred. What is one to make of this? The reader should also note that Mr Sweeney does not point out this apparent contradiction and instead moves on immediately to the subject of buffer washes.

> SWEENEY: If we combine the absence of anything in the buffer wash with a predominant major male profile in the seminal fraction, but a predominant female profile in the epithelial fraction, what does all that taken together tell you in itself, and quite apart from the history?

> WHITAKER: The male profile has come from the semen, and the female profile has come from epithelial material, from the victim.

This final exchange infers that no contamination from Hanratty's sperm was likely because it would have come loose in the buffer wash. This may be a normal expectation, but these are not normal rape circumstances (by which I mean the evidence is forty years old), should such a thing be said to exist. It is worth noting that in evidence the next day, Dr Evison points out that buffer wash results, especially those from historical samples, do not behave in the consistent way assumed here by the FSS.

This concludes my perusal of the critical testimony of Dr Whitaker at this hearing. I am afraid that, after everything documented so far, I remain completely unconvinced of its scientific veracity. As it is the central plank of the remaining prosecution case, without which there would have been no case, and in view of how his similar claims were torn apart in the subsequent Sean Hoey case, its solidity seems distinctly questionable.

Wednesday, 24 April 2002

Dr Martin Evison's Evidence

Dr Evison is the only scientist called by the appellant's team to try and counter the evidence from the FSS witnesses for the respondent. I intend to discuss his evidence in some detail to show, firstly, the way his evidence was treated by Mr Sweeney and their lordships, but also to highlight where he gave examples of FSS errors to the court, which were subsequently ignored by the verdict.

The first thing I should point out is that the surname of this witness was misspelt throughout the whole transcript: it should be Evison, and not Everson. I have corrected the spelling of his name in this work, but everything else remains as written within the transcript. For brevity, I intend to examine only those parts of Dr Evison's testimony that have a bearing on the central tenet of this work.

> MR MANSFIELD: Have you a particular interest in DNA profiling, particularly on DNA profiling of aged products, in other words, some time ago?
>
> DR EVISON: Yes, I do. I was awarded a Bachelor of Science degree in genetics with honours in 1982. I completed a PhD degree in ancient DNA, awarded in 1987. **Since 1993, I have conducted research in the recovery of DNA from forensic and archaeological specimens, particularly using the technique now termed low copy number PRC.** [sic]

It appears that Dr Evison specialises in the recovery of DNA from archaeological specimens, apparently using the LCN technique.

Presumably, he has been brought in because of the point I raised earlier: that forensic recovery from a body buried for a period of nearly forty years is not the same as crime scene recovery forensics. Mr Mansfield's questioning does not cover this area, so this presumption might be mistaken. The other thing I find unclear is how his experience of LCN was obtained since, as we will see, he does not claim practical experience of the SGM or SGM Plus® methods. This may have stemmed from familiarity with one of the alternative low template DNA profiling methods, which I have not discussed, as they are not relevant to this case. But these are not similar techniques and I confess to being puzzled as to why Dr Evison would be referring to LCN. I would also ask you to consider what the development of these other techniques says about the general acceptance of the LCN technique among the scientific community, since these other laboratories have chosen not to use it. This should be borne in mind when considering the overall acceptance level of this controversial science.

> MANSFIELD: In addition to looking at the documentation about the history of the items, you have also studied the results that have been achieved on various occasions, 1995, 1997, 1998, in relation to the DNA profiling.
>
> EVISON: Yes, I have.
>
> MANSFIELD: And also examined the protocols as well as the practice that has been used in the laboratory, so far as you can ascertain?
>
> EVISON: So far as I can ascertain, yes, I have.

As I stated earlier, this exchange confirms that Dr Evison was unable to run his own tests; he had to rely on the documentation from the FSS. He also says that he examined the protocols and practice used in the FSS laboratory, "as far as he could ascertain", which must mean that this was not a fully comprehensive examination. The Reed ruling from 2009 stated that evidential samples should be divided into three aliquots, to allow defence experts to run their own confirmatory testing. Obviously, that did not happen here.

> MANSFIELD: In relation, therefore to that review, have you been able to exclude the realistic possibility of contamination in this case?
>
> EVISON: No, I have not been able to exclude the realistic possibility of contamination.

This immediate direction of questioning by Mr Mansfield raises some questions. For example, why is Dr Evison not being directed to the area of archaeological forensics, where his expertise lies? Also, why was the defence strategy of concentrating solely on the issue of potential contamination followed, to the detriment of pursuing other potentially more fruitful lines of questioning? Whatever the reasons, I believe these are unfortunate decisions on the part of Mr Mansfield.

The next exchange of interest concerns the testing on the knickers:

> MANSFIELD: So just take the knicker sample for a moment. What is the assessment about the total in nanograms of the DNA recovered?
>
> EVISON: I refer to the table, which I believe relates to Dr Whitaker's SGM Plus worth, which gives an estimated DNA total of about 0.38 nanograms, which I roughly estimate to equate to about 76 cells' worth of DNA. These are rough estimates, my Lords. It is that sort of figure. I should point out that was one of the best results in the analysis. Many of the other figures would fall below that figure.

This exchange, in which Dr Evison refers to Dr Whitaker performing SGM Plus® work on the knicker sample, is shortly to be attacked by

Mr Sweeney. To be fair to Dr Evison, he is taking a figure provided by Dr Whitaker and translating it correctly into a specific number of cells to answer this question. However, as we will see, that is not how Mr Sweeney puts it during cross-examination.

Next, we come to a potentially extremely important exchange:

MANSFIELD: The use of un-decontaminated utensils, what was the risk, in other words, in the laboratory in 1961, that they might use un-decontaminated utensils and which utensils?

EVISON: **It is my understanding that utensils such as scissors and forceps would be washed with water, which would not necessarily remove or destroy DNA. A simple wash with water would not, these days, be regarded as a reliable means of decontamination. A wash with some sort of detergent or chemical known to destroy DNA would be considered necessary.**

MANSFIELD: What about work surfaces as well as utensils?

EVISON: The same principle applies to the work surfaces. Again, these days they would be cleaned with a chemical that actually destroys the DNA. ... the exposure of DNA to ultraviolet light would also render it inert to subsequent analyses.

MANSFIELD: Droplets of aerosols, can you just explain that, please?

EVISON: **Yes. Water-borne DNA, I believe is an especially potentially potent source of contamination, especially if, for example, it came from a wash from a semen stain because the water-borne DNA in droplets or aerosols would be permitted to pass around the laboratory environment in the air by convection or in drafts or just through general movement of the atmosphere.**

Here is vital evidence regarding the real risk of contamination during the initial investigations at the Metropolitan Police Laboratories in late 1961 and early 1962. The points about washing utensils with water, and the risks of contamination from water-borne DNA need to be contrasted with the certainty, professed by the likes of Mr Mann and Dr Whitaker, that such contamination did not happen. For whatever reason, the bench ignored this testimony, and preferred the FSS position.

I shall now move on to consider Mr Sweeney's cross-examination of Dr Evison. I believe such hostile questioning is most likely to be indicative of the respondent being unsure of its case and wanting to fluster and wrong-foot the witness. It is yet another example of what I perceive to be questionable tactics to bolster the case against Hanratty.

SWEENEY: Dr Everson, when did you first come into the case?

EVISON: I am not sure if I recall precisely, but I believe I first became involved approximately in December last year, my Lord.

SWEENEY: What happened insofar as Dr Gallop is concerned, do you know?

EVISON: I am not sure I understand the question.

SWEENEY: She has been involved on behalf of the family in the work, as you are aware?

EVISON: Yes I am aware.

SWEENEY: Has she been involved in it with you or not?

EVISON: She has not been involved in it with me, no.

SWEENEY: Has Dr Lincoln been involved in it with you or not?

EVISON: I did not catch the name, would you mind repeating it?

SWEENEY: Do you not know Dr Lincoln?

SWEENEY: Yes, I recognise the name.

EVISON: Has he been involved with you, or not?

SWEENEY: Not with me, no.

Immediately, Mr Sweeney asks sets of questions, about two people with whom Dr Evison has not been involved. From the response I suspect that the question around Dr Lincoln will have been spoken in such a way as to make it impossible for Dr Evison to hear. This is an example of the weakness of a written transcript, as one is not aware of the body language and tone involved, but in this case one can, arguably, guess. Then having immediately wrong-footed Dr Evison, he goes in for the attack, as follows:

SWEENEY: **How much SGM and SGM Plus work have you, yourself, done?**

EVISON: **I have not done any SGM or SGM Plus work myself**. I have used another genetic system called the HLA complex, which is another highly variable genetic system not unlike SGR. [sic] I have also analysed the amelogenin system, which is the same system used in sexing in SGM and SGM Plus. I have also analysed the mitochondrial DNA system, which is a system also used in this analysis. Since 1993 I have conducted research in what has become called low copy PCR, which features in this analysis, and I have looked at 400 modern blood samples. I...

SWEENEY: You are struggling to reach the answer no, you have not done any SGM work, because that is the point of my question, because I am coming to another one directly concerned with that.

EVISON: Sorry.

SWEENEY: Miss Frazier told us yesterday that in fact she thought there were at least 400 cells present. Do you understand why she came to that figure, but you have quoted a figure of 76?

EVISON: Yes, I do. I believe Dr Frazier was referring to the sum total of the DNA in her extracts, and I believe I did make it clear in the amount I quoted that I was referring to the total produced in the SGM extract produced by Dr Whitaker.

SWEENEY: Do you not understand that, because the SGM Plus extract has in fact gone through four processes, each one of which reduces the cells available, those experienced in the field recognise that that figure should be multiplied by 4?

EVISON: I do not – I did not know that. I can understand the reasoning behind it. I should say that my intention is really to give my Lords a general view of the amount of cells or DNA present in the samples, and that the figure quoted by Dr Frazier with regard to 400 cells seems to be perfectly reasonable and not particularly different from the figure quoted, that I quoted for Dr Whitaker's results.

I would remind the reader of Frazier's testimony from the previous day, and the question put to Dr Evison by Mr Mansfield a little while before this exchange, that gave rise to the seventy-six number. He has just acknowledged that he has not done any SGM or SGM Plus® work, so Mr Sweeney immediately asks him a question about SGM Plus®, and ridicules him for not knowing the answer. This is just the unfair playground tactics which give our legal profession such a bad reputation. You may remember that Frazier gave no explanation for why this SGM Plus® test requires these four processes, and nor does Mr Sweeney. It is a requirement deserving of an explanation, since the DNA sample undergoes twenty-eight cycles of amplification in SGM Plus® testing, or thirty-four cycles in LCN, as a matter of course. As I stated when considering Frazier's evidence, I have been unable to unearth a similar default number for the SGM test itself, as this was over twenty years ago. I would again point out that these numbers, regardless of how they have been calculated, have not been arrived at by proper quantification, as per the recommendations of the Caddy report.

I am nevertheless moved to wonder why the defence called upon Dr Evison to be their expert witness in this case. I do not doubt his expertise, but in view of his lack of experience in SGM and SGM Plus® testing he seems not to be best placed to argue Hanratty's case. I suspect this was not unrelated to the already mentioned point that very few DNA scientists are available for the defence, as virtually all are based in laboratories working for the Crown. It is also worth noting that the respondent and the FSS have been presenting their evidence in a confusing and apparently contradictory manner. Their refusal to delineate LCN testing from ordinary SGM Plus® testing throughout has been exasperating. It would have required the 'Wisdom of Solomon' to avoid being confused by this stage of proceedings. I may be cynical, but I can't help feeling that a strategy to confuse the court was in play. How else can one view the confusing presentation of this evidence?

Following these exchanges, Mr Sweeney challenges Dr Evison about the handkerchief DNA evidence, in a lengthy attempt to get the latter to admit that it was nasal mucus from Hanratty. Dr Evison pointed out that it was not confirmed as a mucus stain, and that it was not impossible for Hanratty's DNA to have arrived through contamination. Bear in mind that, as was later acknowledged by Caddy, at low template levels it is not possible to prove scientifically what the DNA source material is, or even how it might have arrived. Any such statements of attribution are little more than speculation, although for the reasons previously outlined, I am inclined to believe it probably was Hanratty's DNA in the mucus on the handkerchief, even though as I've already pointed out it can never be scientifically proven. These exchanges went on for some time, during which no mention was made by either side that even if Hanratty had blown his nose on the handkerchief, it did not establish a connection between him and the murder weapon. This was a potentially fatal blow to Hanratty's case, since Dr Evison was pushed, by the Lord Chief Justice himself, to concede that direct transfer (by Hanratty blowing his nose on the handkerchief) rather than secondary transfer (i.e., by the handkerchief brushing against something containing Hanratty's DNA) was the most likely reason for the DNA being found.

I mention this exchange because it shows that the Lord Chief Justice is obviously aware that the mucus stain DNA could have come from Hanratty blowing his nose. Yet, in the judgment, the mucus stain evidence is only dealt with, in terms of being a result of contamination, which is discounted as being too unlikely.

SWEENEY: If we turn to the knickers, please. Do you agree or disagree with the evidence thus far that the buffer wash fraction would be expected to remove non-adhering material, i.e. not firmly adhering material?

EVISON: It may do, but we are dealing with very small numbers of cells, 400 or less, often down to numbers around 4 or 10 cells in a test. A number of other very sensitive tests, like the mitochondrial DNA, have failed on buffer washes. I think it is reasonable to suppose that, if there was any DNA there, they would have detected it even if the vast majority of it had been bound tightly to the material. The buffer washes are failing, and there is no great significance to that, other than there is not much material present in the specimens in the first place.

SWEENEY: **Can you not agree with the obvious: if there is material there which is not firmly adhering, the buffer wash is likely to remove it?**

EVISON: **In the context of these exhibits, given the low quantity of DNA, the fact that the buffer wash is not a particularly clean extract and probably will contain inhibiters, I do not accept as obvious at all, my Lord.**

SWEENEY: Have you ever done buffer washes for SGM or SGM Plus work yourself?

EVISON: Not with SGM and SGM Plus, but with the other tests that I mentioned earlier, I have, yes. I find it is really with quite recent material that a buffer wash will give a clear result.

Dr Evison sticking to his guns, despite Mr Sweeney's line of questioning, makes the important point I mentioned during yesterday's evidence: that buffer washes do not give consistent results when dealing with non-recent samples. This is in contradiction to the FSS assumption in this case. Possibly for this reason, Mr Sweeney quickly moves away from this potentially damaging testimony, to immediately ask the following question:

SWEENEY: What experience have you of rape cases?

EVISON: I have no experience of rape cases.

Again, this raises the question whether Dr Evison was best placed to act as the defence expert.

SWEENEY: Do you accept or not accept the evidence given by Dr Whitaker that his findings are precisely what he would expect if the major profile obtained from the pellet fraction was Valerie Storie's rapist?

EVISON: I accept that assertion. I feel I should say, in the context of this case, that there are other results from other attempts to differentiate the so-called epithelial fraction from the seminal fraction, and the other tests have not obtained such clear results So while I accept Dr Whitaker's assertion, I should point out some of the other tests do not give such clear results and, inasmuch as they give some result, they could be interpreted as showing a lack of correspondence with this assertion. Furthermore, the results with the poorer test, the SGM test, do not represent a weaker pattern of Dr Whitaker's results. The two poor results, if anything, might be interpreted as slightly disagreeing with it.

Here Dr Evison points out that while Whitaker's assertion is possible, it is not the *only* possible interpretation of the evidence. Again, Mr Sweeney quickly changes tack.

SWEENEY: If you go to Miss Frazier's document, please. Do you have that?

EVISON: The statement? Her results?

SWEENEY: No, her graphic results.

EVISON: Yes...

SWEENEY: **If we go to Dr Whitaker's work, we see the major profile is the appellant's and the minor bands present, three red and two, blue.**

EVISON: **Yes.**

Dr Whitaker made no mention of the 'red' fraction, possibly from Gregsten, but here is proof that he was aware of it. So, for him to assert that there was only one male profile in the result is potentially dishonest. A little later we have the following exchange, where Dr Evison explains the results that he feels are not in keeping with Dr Whitaker's interpretation:

SWEENEY: What other findings do you suggest in any sense cast any significant underlined question over those results?

EVISON: I think those results are consistent with the suppositions made by the scientists concerned. In that sense they are good results. I have also looked at (it may have been missed out in the transcript but there is no indication of that) two other similar tests, which are under the heading 'knickers re-extraction of 1995 tubes'. If you look at those results, we see that the fragment of knickers from the 1995 spinaroo epithelial fraction major contains the appellant's DNA, and we would normally expect, using the same reasoning that counsel has just described, to find that that would be Valerie Storie's DNA and it is not. The same goes for the second test, the second epithelial fraction, the supernatant referred as to the blue liquid from the 1995 extraction major. Again, that contains the appellant's profile where, following the same underlying logic, one would expect to find Valerie Storie's profile and we do not. So although I find the first two results satisfying, there are two other results which seem to contradict it. I, therefore, feel obliged to consider the broader picture and, therefore, to treat the first two results with a little bit of caution.

Dr Evison's erroneous acceptance of the claim that it is Hanratty's DNA, despite the science not confirming this, is like his refusal to countenance Hanratty blowing his nose on the handkerchief – another unfortunate and potentially critical mistake.

Mr Sweeney immediately changes tack and tries to undermine Dr Evison's credibility by claiming that, because he had not experienced the SGM techniques, he did not understand the effects of the re-extraction process:

SWEENEY: Dr Everson, given that you have never done SGM and SGM Plus work, are you not familiar with the effect of re-extractions on samples of this type?

EVISON: Re-extraction, I think, really refers to the recovery of DNA, not the analytical method –

SWEENEY: Are you not familiar with the physical consequences of re-extraction in these circumstances on this type of sample?

EVISON: Not in these circumstances exactly on this type of example exactly, but I have done a number of re-extractions, my Lords, and my experience is that one generally finds a cleaner DNA substrate present in the sample, and that this can lead us to generate results at times. At other times, unfortunately, there seems to be an overhead of DNA lost in the re-extraction process, and one can actually get sometimes poorer results following it. It is not always possible to predict which outcome will occur. ...

SWEENEY: You understand that I suggest that your caution comes from ignorance rather than knowledge. Insofar as the tests that we started with are concerned, the obvious answer is that which the Crown experts have given, is it not? In a test targeted to separate male and female cells by targeting the sperm heads in the pellet fraction, that which you have here is a classic result for the rapist in the major profile in the seminal fraction?

EVISON: The results of Dr Whitaker and the 1997 test of Dr Frazier do look like classic results of that kind, yes. Of course, we are not dealing with recent rape cases: we are dealing with material that was approaching 35 or 40 years old when it was analysed. So I am not sure how much suppositions based on modern analysis may hold in this sort of circumstance. They may hold very well, but we may be making assumptions which, in the circumstances, are not quite warranted. Although I think the results do show — are classic results from the type of test that you would expect, as counsel asserts, there are two other results which do not correspond well with it, and therefore I am merely suggesting that the results should be treated with a little bit of caution.

The attack came up short. Dr Evison makes two further critical points: firstly, that the FSS scientists are treating these results as though they were from a contemporary crime scene and, therefore, taking no account of the historical nature of the evidence, or its possible implications, and secondly, that they are also being selective in the way they are dealing with the results of the re-extraction process. Unfortunately, their lordships either didn't notice what was being said, or, for unclear reasons, chose to ignore it.

Then, we have another important exchange:

> SWEENEY: Equally, the finding of a small amount of DNA from the second male would be classically consistent with intercourse with someone else a couple of days or so beforehand?
>
> EVISON: So I gather.
>
> SWEENEY: Again, you are not in a position to dispute that?
>
> EVISON: I am not, no.

Surprisingly, Mr Sweeney chooses to bring up the fact that another male DNA profile was present, a fact he ignored at other critical times. Despite this, the court accepted the FSS contention that the only profile that counted was the one that supposedly came from Hanratty, but then by this stage, after nearly three days of confusing legal back and forth, they could easily have missed its significance.

> SWEENEY: Equally, finding the female's cells as the major cells in the epithelial fraction would [be] classically consistent with the test having achieved its purpose.
>
> EVISON: I can only re-iterate that that is what we find in two tests, but not what we find in another two.
>
> SWEENEY: We are not going to cross swords on that again because I have made my point. What has happened to the rapist's DNA, if it is not the appellant's?
>
> EVISON: I think it is possible the rapist's DNA could have degraded to such a low level that it is not clearly represented in

the test results. **I suppose it could be asserted or supposed that some of the results in red, the partial profile, could actually reflect the remnants of the rapist's DNA or they may not. Those red partial profiles, the source of them cannot be positively identified.**

As can be seen in this exchange, the red partial profile, attributed to Gregsten, was not positively identified. It is interesting that Mr Sweeney does not dispute that assertion, which would seem to confirm its veracity. He immediately changes the subject, yet again, to talk about the petticoat. Since Dr Evison was fully aware that the profile was not confirmed to belong to Gregsten, why did he not make more of its presence? He seems to have been tentatively considering the possibility that it could have belonged to the rapist, yet unfortunately chooses not to take this thought any further.

A short while later, Dr Evison gives the following explanation for how a contamination event in keeping with the results could have occurred:

SWEENEY: If contamination occurred .... If it was semen, why has it survived and the real rapist's DNA all but disappeared?

EVISON: This is an important issue, and I have given some thought to it. There are a number of factors that could affect this situation. If the contaminating DNA from the appellant had been stored in a form which reduced its rate of degradation relative to the DNA in the sperm from the rapist on the piece of fabric on the knickers this would allow, over the course of time, for the appellant's contaminating DNA to have been potentially available in significantly greater quantities. ... If, for example, the glass vial that was found on Lewis Nickolls' file had in fact contained liquid from a wash of semen from James Hanratty's trousers – which I think is not an unreasonable issue to consider – then a considerable source of James Hanratty's DNA could have been present on the file in a sealed glass vial.

There are a number of factors that affect DNA breakdown: moisture is one, exposure is another, because of oxidative damage to the DNA; and microbial attack is another.

If the vial did contain a wash of semen from James Hanratty's trousers, and it was sealed in the vial in a solution of roughly neutral Ph, so it was not particularly acid or particularly alkaline, it was sealed so it was not exposed to the atmosphere, so there would have been little or no oxidative damage to the DNA, and the solution had little or no microbial content and there would have been no microbes to digest the DNA, then that source of DNA could have stayed in considerable quantity over a considerable period of time.

The DNA from the rapist on the knickers, however, would have been exposed to oxidative damage, ... to microbial attack and it would have continued to degrade. Of course the epithelial cells from Valerie Storie would have been subject to similar attack. Normally one would expect the DNA in the sperm to be better protected. However because with DNA degradation there is a very massive fall in the early stages and then it peters out to a low level, the amount of DNA from the rapist and the amount of DNA from the epithelial cells would have, after a period of time, come to approach each other's level. ...If the deferential [*sic*] in breakdown continues to occur, eventually we would get to the point where Valerie Storie's DNA might be at a level or an even higher level than that from the rapist.

There is a reason why I think it is possible that epithelial cell DNA was better protected, and that is because although epithelial cells are more vulnerable once the DNA is released it would be free to bind to the fabric of the knickers, and, therefore, be better protected; whereas the DNA in the sperm heads would actually become more vulnerable over the course of time as the sperm heads themselves deteriorated. ... a reasonable explanation for the results ... consistent with contamination or innocent transfer being the explanation.

Dr Evison suggests that contamination could have come from a semen sample that was stored in a mysterious broken vial, (apparently, fragments of a glass vial were found in the container with the knicker sample). This fact had been discounted by Roger Mann from the FSS in his earlier testimony. He also explains how the real rapist's DNA could have been eventually overridden to be no longer visible, with evidence of this age.

As we know, the court chose to rely on Mr Mann's opinion to discount this evidence. It should be noted that Mr Mann had no first-hand experience of the possible actions, or reasons for those actions, of the scientists working at the police laboratory in 1961: his supposed experience went back only to 1968, and it was not explained what role he would have been performing then. He claimed to have never seen a vial storing liquid on such an evidential file. There was, however, no dispute that glass remains that appeared to come from a vial were present in the file when it was found. He came up with no alternative hypothesis for the presence of this glass.

I shall conclude with this exchange between the Lord Chief Justice and Dr Evison:

WOOLF: There is also the fact that the cross-contamination, so far as the knickers are concerned, is semen with semen?

EVISON: That is one possible scenario, my Lord.

WOOLF: You do not accept the view of the prosecution scientists that it was semen that was giving the DNA results in the case of the knicker?

EVISON: To say I do not accept it – well, it is not my view. My view is that it is a perfectly reasonable assertion –

WOOLF: Do you accept it or not?

EVISON: A scientist would say do some more tests.

WOOLF: What I am asking you is do you accept it or not?

EVISON: As an absolute, no, I do not accept it.

WOOLF: What does that mean? Does that mean that it is more likely than not?

EVISON: More likely – I suppose I would answer that it is more likely than unlikely.

WOOLF: Would you agree it is more likely than unlikely that the explanation for the results is that Hanratty was in fact the person whose positive semen was on the knickers?

EVISON: That depends upon a lot of information that I do not have access to my Lord.

WOOLF: What I want is your view, whether it is more likely than less likely?

EVISON: Well if the vial had contained semen –

WOOLF: No, what I want you to answer yes or no: is it more likely or less likely that Hanratty was the source of the semen on the knickers because he was the rapist? I want your expert opinion to help the court. Do you say it is more likely or less likely?

EVISON: On the basis of the evidence I have seen, which is by no means all of it, I would answer that it probably is more likely, but there is a reasonable, real and serious possibility that contamination accounts for the results.

WOOLF: What about the handkerchief; do you agree it is more likely that the explanation, so far as the handkerchief is concerned, is that it was because Hanratty was the source of the mucus on the handkerchief that the handkerchief gave the results it did? Again, I repeat, I want your help. It is the duty of the expert in coming to court to help the court.

EVISON: I see that, and I have endeavoured to fulfil that obligation, my Lord. Again, I would answer that, given the evidence I have seen in relation to this exhibit, I suppose it is more probable – it is more probable that it is from James Hanratty's mucus. But, again, there is a real potential for innocent transfer accounting for the result.

WOOLF: Thank you very much.

I shall leave it to the reader to decide whether they feel that this line of questioning is proper for the circumstances pertaining here. It is clear, that the Lord Chief Justice, is, at the very least, under the mistaken impression that the DNA sample attributed by the FSS to Hanratty is his. This is a failure by all the expert witnesses, including Dr Evison, to point out the real status of a DNA match, which was part of their fundamental duty to the court. We know from the verdict handed down that the court preferred the FSS evidence to that of Dr Evison. This just reinforces the importance of the appellant's team unfortunately insisting on two contamination events and missing the real level of significance of the handkerchief DNA evidence.

The remainder of the transcript covers two further areas. The first deals with the testimony of Detective Chief Superintendent Roger Matthews, who was mentioned in the first chapter as having been asked by Scotland Yard, on behalf of the Home Office, to review the case prior to its handover to the CCRC. He flatly contradicted the opinion of the Hawser report and considered Hanratty innocent. His testimony in this court was completely ignored by their lordships. Thereafter, the transcript covers the lengthy, and eventually unsuccessful, legal arguments from Mr Mansfield that the court should not admit the DNA evidence on an arcane point of law. Neither part appears to have any relevance to the question of the validity of the science employed to convict Hanratty, so I shall not review them here.

Conclusion

My aim when I began this work was to confirm that James Hanratty had been proved 'beyond reasonable doubt' to have been a killer and a rapist since that is the burden of proof in our criminal courts. I hoped to satisfy myself, firstly, that the DNA evidence to convict Hanratty was not open to doubt, and secondly, where such evidence runs counter to other evidence before it, the court had considered both sets of evidence fairly and had arrived at a verdict that could be justified and supported. Unfortunately, on both counts I can only conclude that the Court of Appeal's handling of the Hanratty case in 2002 failed abjectly.

If it were not for the strange legal principle, that an appeal can only be brought based on new evidence not previously considered by another court, the Court of Appeal might have been forced to look at the copious glaring issues with which this case abounds. This way of working means that when a previous court fails to consider evidence correctly, and delivers a flawed version of justice, the opportunity to right this wrong is lost, seemingly forever. It puts the onus on the injured party to provide further evidence of wrongs not previously considered. I maintain that such a system is fundamentally unjust.

This is especially the case with the rulings by the Court of Appeal, which seems to be accountable to no one for its actions. I know that we now have a Supreme Court as the final arbiter, but the legal hurdles to be cleared, and the costs involved in reaching that stage, make the overturning of such rulings nigh on impossible. When, as in Hanratty's case, the Court of Appeal fails, in my mind, to deliver a justifiable verdict, who has responsibility for holding it to account and, more to the point, by whom are they, in their turn, held to account? You might consider the famous quote from Roman poet Juvenal: "Quis custodiet ipsos custodes", roughly translated as "Who guards, the guards themselves?" In other words, who is watching over those who have judicial authority over us? The maintenance of this peculiar principle is an anomaly that seriously needs correcting by the authorities.

The court also missed the critical assumption – inherent in the way the handkerchief evidence was presented – that erroneously linked Hanratty to the murder weapon, and in fact used this handkerchief evidence as the deciding factor in dismissing the appeal. This was a fundamental and scientifically unjustifiable overstatement of the value of any supposed DNA finding on this evidence. In addition, I believe the court made no attempt to validate any of the evidence brought by the FSS witnesses. I thought it was noticeably much more critical and involved in the testimony of Dr Evison, which it then rejected, while merely accepting the FSS witness statements and those of Mr Sweeney, regardless of how many times these raised more questions than they answered.

If I consider again the key piece of evidence in favour of Hanratty's innocence, known as the Liverpool alibi, I am afraid that I can see no rational explanation for this scenario other than the one I put forward. No physical mechanism existed to enable him to travel from Liverpool to Dorney Reach in something like two and a half hours. Were *all* the witnesses lying or mistaken? I have racked my brain for an explanation that allows Hanratty to be in both places but have concluded that none existed. Even today, unless you have access to military transport or a private helicopter, you could not make the journey in the time. In terms of long odds, I would say that Hanratty having access to such transportation methods would be off the scale, and not even the prosecution at his trial claimed this which, considering some of their other claims, speaks volumes. For whatever reason, the court decided that this was not a bar to him having achieved this feat and didn't even cite it as evidence worthy of comment.

Unfortunately, instead of concentrating on this one simple question, the courts up to and including the 2002 appeal have, seemingly, become side-tracked or bogged down by other issues. They all apparently missed the pivotal nature of this scenario. The case is, therefore, actually very simple. Can anyone explain how James Hanratty could have been in

Dorney Reach to hijack that car based on the evidence for the Liverpool alibi? If they cannot, then any other evidence supposedly pointing to his guilt, including the interpretation of the DNA evidence, must be incorrect. As I hope to have shown, the odds of the DNA interpretation, and especially the discounting of contamination, being wrong are far more likely than anyone other than an expert would have realised. It is far more likely than all the witnesses to the Liverpool alibi being mistaken. At the very least, the Court of Appeal in 2002 should have considered the evidence that supported his being innocent, against that which supported his guilt, not that it did.

By not doing so, it not only condemned Hanratty unjustly, but it also gave the green light to all subsequent courts to treat contradictory evidence in the same manner. The implications of these actions, for the proper functioning of our justice system, remain immense. I have no explanation for this. As it is, the potential for miscarriages of justice continues unabated, despite the findings in the Sean Hoey trial. Why has there been this ridiculous saga of judicial obduracy for so long?

I fully understand and support the need for the legal system's functioning to be outside of direct political control, but this case has highlighted many reasons for why some form of oversight is desperately needed. After all the taxpayer is funding this system and, as this case has shown, can be badly let down by its actions. There are serious questions for our politicians and the judiciary to answer here.

Unfortunately, this is as far as the transcript evidence will take me in assessing the merit of the case against James Hanratty. Since the documentation necessary to move this case any further forward remains hidden from public scrutiny, with no explanation forthcoming, I must reluctantly conclude this investigation into this highly dubious case and place my findings into the public domain. I hope you can understand why I am far from convinced that the DNA evidence has proven him to have been the assailant in this case. Just because an authoritative figure or body proclaims a fact, it does not necessarily mean it is true.

I know that by publishing these findings I shall be vilified by the copious stakeholders for the 'Hanratty was guilty' side of the argument, not least our judicial and political authorities. My motivations for this work are not personal kudos or financial gain. I just want my findings engaged with constructively by those who can take them forward. If my work contains mistakes, I want them found and corrected, but above all I want this case, and the many issues arising from it addressed urgently and properly.

I hope this work will have given those who have always believed in his guilt pause for thought, and the opportunity to consider the wisdom of Wilson's aphorism regarding their motivations. Belief is not knowledge; it only exists in the face of doubt.

Finally, there is one constituency here that has suffered more than most at the hands of our judicial system; all those unheeded victims of its deliberations who belong to the families of the wrongfully accused and the wrongly convicted. I am thinking here of people like the Hanratty family, who have had to live for decades with the aftermath of an unspeakable wrong done to them by a corrupt and incompetent police force and a mysteriously obdurate legal and political establishment. You could argue that their continued suffering exceeds even that of their helpless relative who met the executioner's noose that April day.

Who will speak for them?

Points for the Criminal Cases Review Commission

Even though the CCRC must work within the woeful legal framework that applies in the UK, most particularly the principle that seems to bar an appeal revisiting previously erroneously considered evidence, I believe the following list summarises the potentially applicable areas that should form the basis of another approach to the Court of Appeal to overturn this longstanding miscarriage of justice. I am listing them in the order in which they have been first documented in this work, rather than in order of importance.

1) For Hanratty to have been guilty requires an explanation of how he could have travelled from central Liverpool to Dorney Reach in less than three hours, a feat which even today would require access to a helicopter. Dismissal of this means that all the unconnected witnesses to his presence in Liverpool either lied or were mistaken.
2) The BBC *Horizon* programme stated that some of the DNA testing in the case involved thirty-four cycles of PCR amplification and was therefore the highly contentious and experimental FSS developed LCN test. The judgment referred to it as the standard SGM Plus® only and it was never acknowledged during the evidence transcripts, so it seems to me to have been withheld from the court.
3) The murder weapon was a .38 Enfield that managed to fire seven shots before reloading, according to trial evidence documented in the 2002 judgment. This raises doubts about

how the weapon was modified to achieve this, as all three weapons given this designation only had six-round cylinders, and about the attributes of the weapon and its connection to the crime that have not been clarified to date.

4) The 2002 hearing judgment believed that the handkerchief nasal mucus stain was Hanratty's, which is not scientifically supportable, but more importantly that it proved he wrapped the purported murder weapon. This is wrong. No connection to the murder weapon is established. To do so required DNA to have been found on the gun, which has not been done to date.

5) The Royal Statistical Society says statistics remains a specialised area and that our courts should ensure such evidence is only presented by appropriately qualified experts. The Hanratty appeal court accepted Dr Whitaker's statistical claims without an understanding of how they were calculated or what they meant. As in this case, claims of this type are often not based upon valid scientific principles.

6) Katherine Troyer's 2001 study of the Arizona State Criminal database completely undermines the basis of the RMP statistical claims used in our courts.

7) The calling of even a full DNA match does not confirm the DNA belongs to the defendant. The Hanratty evidential samples were partial matches at best, yet the judgment claimed it was proven to be his DNA. Dr Whitaker claimed on several occasions that the DNA was Hanratty's, although according to the judgment he implied there was some slight doubt, which must therefore have been in his written submission, again contradicting his verbal evidence. Also, the Reed judgment from 2009, which is used by courts as a reference case, is not aware of this fact and incorrectly states that a match means the sample is the defendant's, thereby misleading all subsequent courts which use Reed for guidance.

8) Dr Whitaker's statistical probability claims for the underwear evidence were not given as a Bayesian likelihood ratio calculation, as was required by the accepted standard process when dealing

with a mixed evidential sample. A proper examination of his probability claims was not done by the court to confirm that it was scientifically valid.

9) Professor Caddy's review in 2008 confirmed explicitly that the only way for the FSS LCN evidence to be scientifically acceptable was if the pre-test quantification step was performed. Failure to do this invalidated the results, as the step is needed to ensure the test kit is properly calibrated. The FSS only started to do this in 2009, after that review. Therefore, the post exhumation and other Hanratty evidence testing, which used LCN, should not have been accepted by the court, nor indeed should any low template testing between 2001 and 2009, if not preceded by quantification.

10) All testing that involves samples at, or near, stochastic threshold levels should be run at the very least twice to ensure the electropherogram is reproducible and not subject to inconsistencies. Dr Whitaker claimed to have rerun the testing in Hanratty, but the electropherograms need to be reviewed by an independent expert to ensure the second test was run and that his interpretation claims are valid.

11) The FSS refused to engage with the international forensic science community to agree DNA interpretation standards. This is a fundamental problem with all such evidence, as without a reliable scientific basis for any interpretation, how can it be objectively demonstrated to be anything more than just an opinion?

12) The Reed judgment confirms that the FSS admitted to considerable stochastic problems with LCN profiles, which is hardly indicative of a reliable technology. This is another key reason for this science proving so controversial among international forensic experts. The Hanratty hearing was never informed of any doubts concerning the reliability of this testing.

13) No scientific research has been published into how to differentiate between semen deposited through intercourse

and semen deposited through contamination to support Dr Whitaker's claim that he could tell the difference by experienced eye. Don't forget this evidence was microscopic and at least forty years old.

14) Meakin and Jamieson's paper from 2013 confirms that it is not possible to reliably infer the mode of transfer of a sample at these low template levels. Caddy, in 2008, confirmed that the biological source of a sample cannot be inferred at low template levels. This contradicts Dr Whitaker's claim that the DNA evidence proved Hanratty was a rapist.

15) The status of the validation testing performed on the FSS LCN kit before its use in Hanratty has never been established. To have relied upon the SGM Plus® kit manufacturer's validation testing would be unethical. The acknowledged reliability issues are indicative of lack of proper validation before use.

16) The SGM and SGM Plus®/LCN pre-exhumation testing gave a different reading at the D21 locus with no explanation for the difference, yet both claimed they matched Hanratty. Rachel Frazier's testing was also experimental though this was not mentioned at the 2002 hearing. Why were the FSS running non-standard tests? How long had this practice been going on and were the judicial authorities aware?

17) Dr Whitaker's evidence in the Sean Hoey (2007) trial was demolished by experts for the defence, resulting in the prosecution case being dismissed and all low template criminal trials being abandoned while the Caddy review was carried out. His work was highly criticised by the judge, which is another reason for questioning his claims in the Hanratty case.

18) The samples tested from Hanratty's body after exhumation were a composite with no explanation provided as to why this was. This must raise further doubts about the discriminatory power of these evidential samples, which were nowhere near the standard required in current forensic cases.

19) Evidence of a group AB sample, assumed to belong to Gregsten from an earlier bout of sexual intercourse, was found by

Rachel Frazier during her testing of Valerie Storie's knickers, yet Dr Whitaker claimed to find no male sample other than Hanratty's and based his conclusion of Hanratty being the rapist on the claim that no other male sample was present on the knickers.
20) FSS paper by Peter Gill (the co-developer of LCN with Dr Whitaker) and others from 2000 states that laboratory-based contamination can never be completely excluded, which weakens the discounting of this even more.
21) Dr Whitaker's dismissal of contamination on the knickers was a circular argument that showed no evidence of an assessment of the likelihood of contamination at all.

This list is not fully comprehensive, but I hope it will provide the CCRC with enough of a stimulus to revisit this case. If that happens this work will not have been in vain.

Bibliography

Books

Paul Foot, (1988), *Who Killed Hanratty?*, Penguin
Lord Russell of Liverpool, (1966), *Deadman's Hill: Was Hanratty Guilty?*, Tallis Press
Bob Woffinden, (1999), *The Final Verdict*, Pan Books

Television

BBC *Horizon*, (2001), bbc.co.uk/science/horizon/2001/a6murdertrans.shtml

Websites

The British and Irish Legal Information Institute (bailii.org)
DNA View: dnaview.com
Forensic Bioinformatics: bioforensics.com
Forensic Science Investigation Unit: forensicunit.weebly.com
Inference: inference.org.uk
Law Commission: lawcom.gov.uk
The Official Home of UK Legislation: legislation.gov.uk
National Archives: nationalarchives.gov.uk
Parliament Publications: publications.parliament.uk
Royal Statistical Society: rss.org.uk
BBC Science Focus Magazine: sciencefocus.com
Wikipedia: en.wikipedia.org/wiki/James_Hanratty

Journals and PDFs

Brian Caddy, Graham Taylor, Adrian Linacre, 'A Review of the Science of Low Template DNA Analysis', (2008), https://assets.publishing.

service.gov.uk/government/uploads/system/uploads/attachment_ data/file/117556/Review_of_Low_Template_DNA_1.pdf

Dongya Yang, Camilla Speller, 'Technical Tips for Obtaining Reliable DNA Identification of Historic Human Remains', (2006), *Technical Briefs in Historical Archaeology*: 1 pp. 11-15

Georgina Meakin, Allan Jamieson, (2013), 'DNA Transfer: review and implications for casework', *Forensic Science International Genetics*: 7 (4) pp. 434-443

Itiel Dror, David Charlton, (2006), 'Why Experts Make Errors', *Journal of Forensic Identification*: 56 (4)

Jennifer N. Mellon, (2001), 'Manufacturing Convictions: Why Defendants Are Entitled to the Data Underlying Forensic DNA Kits' – *Duke Law Journal*: Vol 51, pp. 1097-1137

Jonathan Whitaker, E. Cotton, Peter Gill, (2001), 'A comparison of the characteristics of profiles produced with the AMPFlSTR(R) SGM Plus(TM) multiplex system for both standard and low copy number (LCN) STR DNA analysis', *Forensic Science International*: 123 (2-3): pp. 215-223

Peter Gill, Jonathan Whitaker, C. Flaxman et al., (2000), 'An investigation of the rigor of interpretation rules for STRs derived from less than 100 pg of DNA', *Forensic Science International*: 112 (1): pp. 17-40

S. Rand, M. Schurenkamp, Carsten Hohoff et al, (2004), 'The GEDNAP blind trial concept part II. Trend and Developments', *International Journal of Legal Medicine*: 118, pp. 83-89

Scientific Working Group on DNA analysis methods: *Guidelines for STR Enhanced Detection Methods*, 2014

Scientific Working Group on DNA analysis methods: *Interpretation Guidelines for Autosomal Enhanced STR Typing by Forensic DNA Laboratories*, 2017, revised 2021

William C. Thompson, Simon Ford, Travis Doom et al, (2003), 'Evaluating Forensic DNA Evidence: Essential elements of a competent defense review' parts one and two, *The Champion*, 27 (3), pp. 16-25 and (4) pp. 24-28

References

Chapter 1
1. Criminal Procedure and Investigations Act 1996, legislation.gov.uk/ukpga/1996/25/contents
2. Paul Foot, (1988), *Who Killed Hanratty?*, p. 425
3. Public Records Act 1958, legislation.gov.uk/ukpga/Eliz2/6-7/51/contents

Chapter 2
1. Bob Woffinden, (1999), *Hanratty The Final Verdict*, pp 120-123; Foot, pp. 189-191
4. *Ibid* pp. 191-195
5. *Ibid* p. 195
6. *Ibid* p. 196
7. *Ibid* p. 198
8. *Ibid* p. 200
9. *Ibid* p. 210
10. *Ibid* p. 209
11. *Ibid* p. 428

Chapter 3
1. BBC *Horizon* bbc.co.uk/science/horizon/2001/a6murdertrans.shtml
2. Forensic Science Investigation Unit: forensicunit.weebly.com/forensic-timeline.html
3. Peter Gill, Jonathan Whitaker, C. Flaxman et al., (2000), 'An investigation of the rigor of interpretation rules for STRs derived

from less than 100 pg of DNA', *Forensic Science International*: 112 (1): pp. 17-40
4. Jonathan Whitaker, E. Cotton, Peter Gill, (2001), 'A comparison of the characteristics of profiles produced with the AMPFlSTR(R) SGM Plus(TM) multiplex system for both standard and low copy number (LCN) STR DNA analysis', *Forensic Science International*: 123 (2-3): pp. 215-223
5. Scientific Working Group on DNA Analysis Methods, *Guidelines for STR Enhanced Detection Methods*, media.wix.com/ugd/4344b0_29feed748e3742a5a7112467cccec8dd.pdf

Chapter 4

1. The Court Of Appeal Judgment in the 2002 hearing Hanratty, R v [2002] EWCA Crim 1141 (10 May 2002) https://www.bailii.org/ew/cases/ewca/crim/2002/1141.html
2. Woffinden, p. 293
3. en.wikipedia.org/wiki/Enfield_No._2
4. Foot, p. 134

Chapter 5

1. Regina v Lorraine, Harris, Raymond Rock, Alan Barry, EWCA Crim 1980 (21 July 2005), bailii.org/ew/cases/EWCA/Crim/2005/1980.html
2. Mark Anthony Dallagher, EWCA Crim 1903 (25 July 2002), bailii.org/ew/cases/EWCA/Crim/2002/1903.html
3. Regina v Gerald Luttrell, Rakinder Jheeta, Nicholas Beagley (aka Richardson) et al, EWCA Crim 1344 (28 May 2004), bailii.org/ew/cases/EWCA/Crim/2004/1344.html
4. House of Commons Science and Technology *Seventh Report* publications.parliament.uk/pa/cm200405/cmselect/cmsctech/96/9602.htm
5. Law Commission, 'Expert Evidence in Criminal Proceedings', lawcom.gov.uk/project/expert-evidence-in-criminal-proceedings/
6. The Criminal Procedure Rules 2020, legislation.gov.uk/uksi/2020/759/contents/made

7. 'Expert Evidence In Criminal Courts – the Problem', speech given to the Forensic Science Society by Lord Justice Leveson (16 November 2010) webarchive.nationalarchives.gov.uk/ukgwa/20131202213129/http://www.judiciary.gov.uk/media/speeches/2010/speech-lj-leveson-expert-evidence-16112010

Chapter 6

1. Dr B. Mahendra, (2002), *New Law Journal*, Vol 152 No 7044, inference.org.uk/sallyclark/NLJ.html
2. Charles Brenner, 'Arizona DNA Database Matches', (2007), dna-view.com/ArizonaMatch.htm
3. James Curran, 'Are DNA Profiles as rare as we think? Or Can we trust DNA statistics?', rss.onlinelibrary.wiley.com/doi/full/10.1111/j.1740-9713.2010.00420.x
4. William C. Thompson, Simon Ford, Travis Doom et al, (2003), 'Evaluating Forensic DNA Evidence: Essential elements of a competent defense review' parts one and two, *The Champion*, 27 (3), pp. 16-25 and (4) pp. 24-28, bioforensics.com/download-articles/
5. Dongya Yang, Camilla Speller, (2006), 'Technical Tips for Obtaining Reliable DNA Identification of Historic Human Remains', *Technical Briefs in Historical Archaeology*, 1: pp. 11-15 pure.york.ac.uk/portal/en/publications/technical-tips-for-obtaining-reliable-dna-identification-of-historic-human-remains(e91f544d-a259-4198-8e71-f8bfdad9fcc9).html
6. Luis Villazon, *BBC Science Focus Magazine*, sciencefocus.com/the-human-body/how-much-skin-does-a-human-shed-in-their-life/
7. Brian Caddy, Graham Taylor, Adrian Linacre, (2008), 'A Review of the Science of Low Template DNA Analysis', assets.publishing.service.gov.uk/government/uploads/system/uploads/attachment_data/file/117556/Review_of_Low_Template_DNA_1.pdf
8. S. Rand, M. Schurenkamp, Carsten Hohoff et al, (2004), 'The GEDNAP blind trial concept part II. Trend and Developments',

Chapter 10

1. Lord Russell of Liverpool (1966), *Deadman's Hill: Was Hanratty Guilty?*, Tallis Press
2. Gill, Whitaker, Flaxman, 'Interpretation rules for STRs

Index

Acott, Detective Superintendent Robert, 14–16, 20, 22, 27, 44, 51
   car mileage calculations, 44
   letter to Liverpool CID, 14
   sweetshop witness lack of proper disclosure, 15–16
Adenine, 72
Adversarial forensic techniques, 62
Adversarial legal system, xiiii
Aliquots, 91, 92, 171
Alleles, 73–6, 85–8, 99, 100, 104–109, 110, 121, 132, 144–5, 150, 152–3
Allelic Drop-in, 87–8
Allelic Drop-out, 87–8
Aliquot, 91 *see* Reed, Regina vs
Alphon, Peter Louis, 2, 44, 49, 123, 124, 126, 129–31, 142
Amelogenin, 69, 103–104, 107–108, 121, 138–9, 143, 174
Ampthill magistrates court, *see* Committal Hearing
Anti-Contamination, *see* contamination of DNA evidence
Aphorism, 8, 81, 100, 114, 192
   see Wilson, Robert Anton

Appellant, xiii, 24, 38, 48–50, 56, 91, 125–9, 131–4, 138, 142–4, 146–7, 151–3, 162, 167, 169, 179–80, 182–3, 187
   see also Hanratty, James
Archer Street, 18
Ashworth, Dawn, 33
Autosome, 72–3, 104
A6 Murder Committee, 4

Baker Street, 18
Bark, John, 27, 32, 103–106, 122, 135, 143–4, 149–50, 165
   testing results, 103–106
   testimony in court, 136–7
Bayes, Reverend Thomas, 67
Bayes' theorem, 67–9, 74, 77, 79, 99, 132, 159–60
   likelihood ratio (LR), 67, 99, 132, 159, 160, 194
   notation, 67–8
Bedford, x
Bedfordshire, 1
Bedfordshire Constabulary, 12
'Beyond Reasonable Doubt' jury guidance, xii, 9, 22, 58, 189
Bindman, Sir Geoffrey, 7
Bindmans LLP, 102
Birthday Problem, 70–1

Blackhall, Edward, 44
Bleed-Through, 88
  see also Spurious Peaks
Blood Group, 9, 26, 49, 51
  type AB, 51
  type O, 26, 53
  type O secretor, 49
Bonython, South Australia Supreme Court, 61
Boundary Road Finchley, 17
British and Irish Legal Information Institute, 37
British Broadcasting Corporation (BBC), xi, 24
  Horizon program, xi, xii, 24–35, 39, 44, 107, 112, 116, 133, 139, 160, 162, 193
  transcript extracts, 26–35
  claim of connection to murder weapon, 29, 116
Broadway House Hotel, 18
Buccul Swab, 104, 107, 121, 138
Buffer Wash, 148, 167–8, 177–8
  consistency of results, 177–8
Burtol's Cleaners, 17
Butler, R.A. (Rab), 4

Caddy, Professor Brian, 77, 79, 82–3, 85, 91, 95–6, 101, 113, 118, 139, 157, 159, 161, 167, 176, 195, 196
  review paper, 77, 79, 82–3, 91, 96, 101, 113, 118, 139, 157, 159, 161, 167, 176, 195, 196
  findings, 82–3, 85, 91, 95, 101, 157, 159, 161, 167, 176, 195–6
  quantification of sample, 82–3
  recommendations, 83, 91, 95, 113, 139, 176
Callaghan, James, 4, 5
  letter to Paul Foot, 5
Carlton Road, 11, 14–15, 21
Caucasian, 74, 76–7
  see also Population Types
Cetus Corporation, 28
Chapman, Jessica, 33
Charlton, David, paper, 81
Christie, John, 4
Chromosome, 70, 72–3, 104
Chromosomal Locus (loci), 25–6, 31, 69–71, 73–6, 85–7, 90, 94, 104, 108–109, 132, 144–5, 150–3, 196
Combined Probability of Inclusion (CPI), 99
Committal Hearing, (Ampthill), 16
Composite DNA Sample, 29, 32, 78, 130, 144–5, 196 *see also* Hanratty, James
Contamination of DNA Evidence, 9, 30, 32–3, 35, 38, 50–3, 55–8, 66, 79, 80, 82, 87, 89, 92, 95, 101–102, 110, 112, 115, 119–20, 122, 129, 133–5, 150, 154–7, 159–61, 163–4, 166, 168, 171–3, 176–7, 183, 185–6, 187, 191, 196–7
  Anti-contamination, 83
  contamination types 100–101
  decontamination, 172
Control Sample test results, 85, 127, 132–3, 147–8

Court of Appeal, xi, xiii, 4, 7, 8,
  23–6, 31–2, 35, 37–8, 55–7,
  59, 62, 65, 66, 79, 82, 84, 90,
  96, 99–100, 102, 109–110, 112,
  114, 134, 189, 191
  consideration of case for
    Hanratty, 38, 40–1, 43–8
  consideration of DNA evidence,
    40, 49–56
  consideration of Hawser report,
    37–8
  judgement in Reed, 90–101
  number of shots fired, 42–3
  overstatement of handkerchief
    evidence value, 55–6
  proceedings, xii, 5
  rationale for proclaiming guilt,
    38–40, 55–6
  transcripts, 58, 112–89
  verdict summary, 37–40
  verdict in full, 40–56
Cowley, David, 16
Cowley family, 16, 19
Cowley's Sweet Shop, 11, 14–7,
  19–23, 45–7
Criminal Cases Review Commission
  (CCRC), xi, 3–4, 7–8, 24, 41,
  187, 193–7
  grounds for appeal in 2002, 41
  further points to consider, 193–7
Crown Copyright, 37
Crown The, xiii, 4, 68, 176, 181 see
  Respondent
Cytosine, 72

Dallagher, Mark, – Regina v., 61
Daubert Standard, 60–1

Daubert v Merrell Dow
  Pharmaceuticals, 60
Deadman's Hill, 1, 24
Decontamination, *see* contamination
  of DNA evidence
Developmental Validation Studies,
  31, 83, 89, 92, 98, 105, 196
  see also Mellon, M. Jennifer
Dinwoodie, Mrs Olive, 14–17, 19,
  22, 45–6
  doubt over alibi date, 16
  identification of Hanratty, 14
  statement confirming alibi detail,
    16
DNA profiling 27–8, 33, 50, 53, 65,
  67–8, 73, 75, 76, 80, 84–111,
  118, 153–6, 158–60, 167, 169–70
  issues, 84–111
  invention, 27
  see also Jeffreys, Alec
DNA Evidence Presentation,
  121–30
  see also Sweeney, Nigel issues
    with, 130–5
Dorney Reach, 1, 10, 19, 21, 23, 66,
  120, 158, 190–1, 193
DQA1 (PCR Typing), 28
  see also Cetus Corporation
Dror, Itiel, paper, 81

Electropherogram, 25, 30, 34,
  75–6, 8–2, 85–8, 90–4, 98, 102,
  104, 106, 110–12, 118, 122,
  127, 132–4, 145, 155, 158–9,
  163, 164, 166, 171, 179, 195
  experimental control problems,
    85, 127, 132–3, 147–8

inconsistencies between matching profiles, 85
interpretation, 25, 30, 34, 82, 86, 90–1, 93–4, 98, 102, 110, 112, 118, 122, 145, 155, 158–9, 163–4, 166, 179, 191, 195
interpretation bias, 81, 85
interpretation standards, lack of agreement, 86, 97, 111, 195
mixed sample interpretation issues, 86
peak heights, see Relative Fluorescence Unit, 88
spurious peaks, 87–8
unreported contributors, 85
Electrostatic Detection Apparatus (ESDA) Testing, 41
Enfield No. 2 MK1, MK1*, MK1** .38 Revolver, 42, 193
see also Murder Weapon
Environmental Science and Technology journal, 78
Epithelial Sample Tests, 54, 103, 107, 108, 121, 124–5, 127–8, 132–3, 138–9, 147–8, 154–5, 164–5, 167–8, 178, 180, 182, 184
Euston Station, London departure times, 10, 13
'Evaluating Forensic DNA Evidence', 74–7, 81, 84–8
see also Krane, Professor Dan
Evans, Timothy, 4
Evison, Dr Martin, 53, 58, 63, 92, 115, 118–19, 140–1, 154, 161, 168–87, 190
Cross-examination by Mr. Sweeney, 173–85

examination by Mr. Mansfield, 169–73
questioning by Lord Woolf, 177, 185–7
Ewer, William, 2
Exhibit 26, Knickers, 9, 25, 26–7, 29, 32–3, 39–40, 49–52, 54, 56, 58, 66, 79, 97, 102–104, 107–110, 112, 119, 121–2, 126, 128–32, 135, 138–41, 143–51, 152–5, 158–68, 171, 177, 180, 183–6, 197
see also Storie, Valerie
Exhibit 35, Handkerchief, 2, 28–9, 31–3, 35, 39–40, 49–52, 54–6, 58, 103, 105–106, 112, 115–16, 119–20, 122–3, 125, 127–8, 130, 134, 139–40, 148–53, 164, 176–7, 180, 187, 190, 194
see also Nasal Mucus
Exhumation, 29, 78, 102, 110, 122, 130, 142, 143–4, 195–6
see also James Hanratty
Expert Witness, 59–65
duty to court, 59–60
principles governing evidence, 59–60
procedures defining rules governing duty to the court, 63–4
content of witness report, 63–4
qualifications, 61

Federal Bureau of Investigation (FBI), 35
Finchley Road, 17
Foot, Paul, xi, 4, 5–21, 24, 113–19, 123–9, 136–40, 142–68, 169–88

transcript of Court of Appeal
hearing, 113–19, 123–9,
136–40, 142–88
general observations on
transcript, 114–18
'Who Killed Hanratty?' book,
5–21
Ford, Barbara Ann, 15–17, 19, 22, 46
doubt over alibi date, 15–16
statement confirming alibi
detail, 15
timing discrepancies with Linda
Walton, 15
Forensic Institute, 101, 196
Forensic Science Regulator, 83,
93, 113
Forensic Science Service (FSS),
xii, 8–9, 25–6, 29–30, 33–5,
51, 79–80, 82–3, 89, 91–8,
102, 105, 113, 116, 118, 137,
139–40, 142, 146, 155–6, 170,
193, 195–7
case studies, 33–4
closure, 25, 33
documentation errors, 26
factsheet number 2, 25–6
factsheet number 6, 34, 155
Horizon program BBC, 26–35
Low Copy Number, DNA
profiling, xiii, 28–32, 34, 61,
65, 77, 79–80, 82–4, 89, 91,
94–98, 102–110, 113, 116–17,
130–5, 137, 142, 147, 151, 153,
155, 157, 159, 169–70, 175–6,
193, 195–7
acceptability controversy, 30,
32, 34–5, 82, 84, 98, 170, 195

see also Caddy Review
see also Hoey, Regina vs
developmental validation testing,
31, 83, 89, 92, 98, 105, 196
peer reviewed papers, 30
PCR primer sequence, 89–90
reliability issues, 97–8
pre-exhumation testing results,
102–110
post exhumation testing results,
122–34
Forensic Science Society, 65
France, Carol, 17–18, 20
France, Mrs Charlotte, 17, 20
France, Charles 'Dixie', 2–3, 5–7,
10, 17–18, 20, 22, 40, 42, 44,
55, 120, 152
murder weapon discovery, 2, 42,
44, 55, 120
murder weapon hiding place
conversation, 40
unexplained suicide and letters,
5–7, 10, 18, 40, 44, 120
Frazier, Rachel, 102–110, 121–2,
131–3, 135, 137–41, 150, 175,
179, 181, 196–7
testimony in court, 137–41
testing results, 102–103, 107–108,
121–2
Freedom of Information Act 2000, 6
Frye Standard, 60

Gallop, Dr Angela, 173
German DNA Profiling Group
(GEDNAP), 80
profiling error testing, 80
Gilbart, Justice Andrew, 63

Gill, Professor Peter, 34, 197
Gillbanks, Joseph, 12–13, 15–16
Glass Vial, 183–6
Gorman, Mr Justice, 20, 22, 48
  comment on alibi purchase claim, 22
Greenhalgh, Matthew, 103–104, 148, 165
Gregsten, Michael John, 1, 26–7, 42–4, 47, 51, 53–4, 97, 101, 107, 112, 125, 131–2, 139, 147, 159, 162, 167, 179, 183, 196
  blood type, 27, 51
  car, 1, 39, 41–5, 191
  car mileage, 43–4,
Gregsten, Mrs. Janet, 1–3
Guanine, 72

Handkerchief, 2, 28–9, 31–2, 35, 39–40, 44, 49–51, 54–6, 58, 103, 105–106, 112, 115–16, 119–23, 125, 127–8, 130, 134, 139–40, 148–53, 164, 176–7, 180, 187, 190, 194
  nasal mucus, *see* Exhibit 35
  pivotal role in verdict, 55–6, 112, 115, 190, 194
  relationship to murder weapon, 55, 112, 115–16, 190, 194
  testing results, 103, 105–106, 121–2, 127–8, 149–52
Hanratty, James, x–xi, xiii, 1–11, 13, 15–18, 21–2, 24–5, 28–33, 35, 38–41, 43–51, 53–7, 61–3, 65–6, 68–9, 74, 77–80, 82–5, 89–92, 94–5, 97, 98, 100–102, 104–13, 115–20, 122–35, 138, 141–8, 150–3, 155, 158–62, 165–9, 173, 176–7, 179–80, 182–4, 186–97
  see also Appellant
  Liverpool alibi, 10–22
  presence in London evidence, 17–19
  presence in Liverpool evidence, 12–17, 21
  Rhyl alibi, 10, 21
  connection to murder weapon, 2, 18, 2-9, 39–40, 44–5, 49, 55, 57, 106, 115, 116, 119, 120, 148, 176, 190, 194
  hiding place discussion, 9, 39–40, 44
  composite DNA sample, 29, 32, 78, 130, 144–5, 196
  defence case, *see* Sherrard, Michael
  execution, x–xi, 1–4, 7, 9–10, 18, 23, 40, 44, 120, 192
  exhumation, 29–32, 50, 78, 102, 105–106, 110, 122, 130, 142–5, 153, 195–6
  identification parades, 38–41, 43–4
  witness statements, 10–14, 17–19, 21
Hanratty senior, James, 103–104, 106, 124, 145, 153
  Inferred DNA Profile 103
Hanratty, Mary, 29, 31, 102–107
  DNA sample test results, 102–103, 108, 143
Hanratty, Michael, 29, 31, 102–107
  DNA sample test results, 102–103, 108, 143
Harding, Albert Cecil, 19–20, 46
  log-book contradiction of evidence, 20

Hardy–Weinberg Equilibrium
  Equation, 75–6
Harris, Lorraine, – Regina v., 59
Hawser, Lewis, 7–8, 22–3, 37–8, 48,
  57, 187
  report, 7, 22–3, 37–8, 48, 57, 187
Hendon Dog Track, 19
Heterozygote, 73, 75–6
Hillman, Dr Dentist, 18
Hirons, Harold, 44
Hoey, Sean, (Omagh bombing) trial,
  77, 97, 113, 118, 134, 141, 168,
  191, 196
  aftermath, 77, 113, 118, 141
  test rerunning, 97
Hogan, Paddy, 43
Homozygote, 73, 75
Home Office, 3–9, 187
Home Secretary, 3, 5, 7
  see also Butler R.A., Callaghan,
  James, Howard, Michael,
  Jenkins, Roy, Maudling, Reginald
Horizon Program, xi, xii, 25–36, 39,
  44, 84, 107, 112, 116, 133, 139,
  160, 162, 193
    see also British Broadcasting
    Corporation
House of Commons, 62
  'Science and Technology – Seventh
    Report', 62
Howard, Henry, 51–2
Howard, Michael: 'Criminal Procedure
  and Investigations Act' 1996, 3–4
Huntley, Ian, 33

Identification Parade, 38, 39, 40, 41
  see also Storie, Valerie
  see also Hanratty, James

Indo/Pakistani, 76, 77
  see also Population Types
International Journal of Legal
  Medicine, 80

Jamieson, Professor Allan, paper,
  101, 196
Jeffreys, Professor, Sir Alec, 27, 33
Jenkins, Roy, 4
Justice of the Peace, journal, 7
Juvenal, 189

Kempt, Robert, 21–2, 46, 47
Kerr, John, 43
Kings College London, 65
Kleinman, Emmanuel, 12, 16
Knickers, *see* Exhibit, 26
  see also Storie, Valerie
Knicker Pellet Profile test result,
  103–104, 142–4, 164–5, 167,
  178, 181
  see also Greenhalgh, Matthew
Knox, Amanda, 34
Krane, Professor Dan, 74, 75, 76,
  81, 84, 88, 117, 161, 167
  paper, 74, 75, 76, 81, 84, 161, 167

Law Commission, 62–3
  report, 62–3
LCN, xiii, 28–32, 34, 61, 65, 77, 79–
  80, 82–4, 89, 91–8, 104–105,
  108, 113, 116–17, 130–1, 133,
  135, 137, 142, 147, 151, 153,
  155, 157, 159, 169–70, 175–6,
  193, 195–7
  see also Forensic Science Service
Left Luggage Department at Lime
  Street Station, 11–13

International Journal of Legal Medicine, 118, pp. 83-89, link. springer.com/article/10.1007/s00414-003-0421-4
9. Itiel Dror, David Charlton, (2006), 'Why Experts Make Errors' *Journal of Forensic Identification*: 56(4) researchgate.net/publication/248440075_Why_Experts_Make_Errors

Chapter 7

1. Thompson, Ford, Doom et al, 'Evaluating Forensic DNA Evidence'
2. AmpFLSTR™ NGM™ PCR Amplification Kit' – thermofisher.com/order/catalog/product/4415021?SID=srch-srp-4415021#/4415021?SID=srch-srp-4415021
3. 'SWGDAM Interpretation Guidelines for Autosomal STR Typing by Forensic DNA Test Laboratories', 13 July 2021 – swgdam.org/_files/ugd/4344b0_3f94c9a6286048c3924c58e2c230e74e.pdf
4. Jennifer N. Mellon, (2001), 'Manufacturing Convictions: Why Defendants Are Entitled to the Data Underlying Forensic DNA Kits' – *Duke Law Journal*: Vol 51, pp. 1097-1137, scholarship.law.duke.edu/dlj/vol51/iss3/6/
5. Regina & David and Thomas Reed; Regina & Garmson, (2009), EWCA Crim 2698, bailii.org/ew/cases/EWCA/Crim/2009/2698.html
6. The Forensic Science Regulator, Response to Professor Brian Caddy's Review of the Science of Low Template DNA Analysis, Section 1.2.6, 7 May 2008 - assets.publishing.service.gov.uk/government/uploads/system/uploads/attachment_data/file/117557/response-caddy-dna-review.pdf
7. Regina v Sean Hoey, (2007) NICC 49, bailii.org/nie/cases/NICC/2007/49.html
8. Georgina Meakin, Allan Jamieson, (2013), 'DNA Transfer: review and implications for casework', *Forensic Science International Genetics*: 7 (4) pp. 434-443 pubmed.ncbi.nlm.nih.gov/23623709/

Chapter 8

1. Response to Professor Brian Caddy's Review

Left Luggage Assistant with Withered or Turned Hand, 11, 14
  see also Stringer, Peter
  see also Usher, Peter
Leicester Square Underground Station, 19
Leicester University, 27, 33
Leveson, Mr, Justice Brian, 23, 37, 57–8, 65, 120, 161–2
Likelihood Ratio (LR), 67, 99, 132, 147, 159–60, 194
  see also Bayes' Theorem
Lime Street station, Liverpool, 12–14, 21, 46
  arrival times, 13
Lincoln, Dr 173, 174
Liverpool, 9–10, 13–15, 17, 19, 20–22, 25, 36, 38, 41, 45–6, 48, 55, 57–8, 66, 78, 102, 119–20, 158, 190–1, 194
Liverpool alibi, 9–23, 36, 38, 41, 45–6, 48, 57–8, 66, 78, 102, 119–20, 190–1
  see also Hanratty, James
Liverpool Police CID, 13–15
Locus (loci), see Chromosomal locus
Low Copy Number, see LCN
  see also Forensic Science Service
Low Template, DNA Analysis, 30, 79–80, 83, 94, 96, 112–13, 160, 167, 170, 176, 195, 196
  see also Caddy, Professor Brian
Luttrell, Gerald, – Regina v., 62
Lyons Cafe, Lime Street Liverpool, 11, 21

Mann, Linda, 33
Mann, Roger, 26, 33, 35, 53, 173
  BBC Horizon Program statements, 26, 33
  discounting contamination, 173, 185
  experience, 185
Mansfield, Michael, QC, 48, 50, 52, 115, 129, 155, 163–6, 169–73, 175, 188
  cross-examination of John Bark, 136–7
  cross-examination of Jonathan Whitaker, 163–6
  examination of Martin Evison, 169–73
Mantell, Lord Justice Charles, 37, 129
Matthews, Detective Chief Superintendent Roger, 7, 187
Maudling, Reginald, 4
McNally, Terry, 11
Meakin, Georgina, paper, 101, 196
Mellon, Jennifer N. paper, 88–90, 98
  developmental validation studies, 89
  PCR primer sequence, 89–90
  VWA locus differing between test machines, 90
Metropolitan Police Laboratory, 27, 51, 79, 104, 173
Mitochondrial DNA, 78, 104, 174, 177
Mixed DNA Samples, 30, 69, 77, 86–7, 96–99, 147, 152, 159, 195
Molecular Photocopying, 28
  see also Polymerase Chain Reaction

Multi Locus Profiling, 25
Murder Vehicle, 1, 39, 41–4, 191
   mileage discrepancy, 44
Murder Weapon, 1–2, 9, 18, 28,
   39–40, 42, 44–5, 49, 52, 55,
   57–8, 106, 112, 115, 116,
   119–20, 122, 148, 153, 176,
   190, 193, 194
   see also Enfield No2 MK1
   hiding place on 36A London bus,
     2, 9, 28, 39, 40, 42
   evidence anomalies, 42, 55
   connection to Hanratty, 44, 45, 49,
     55, 57–8, 112, 115–16, 119, 120,
     122, 148, 153, 176, 190, 194

Nanogram (ng), 30, 86, 92–4, 96,
   136–7, 140–1, 157, 166, 171
Nasal Mucus evidence, *see*
   handkerchief
   see also exhibit 35
New Law, Journal, 7
News of the World, 37
Nickolls, Dr Lewis, 51–2, 183
Noise Peaks, *see* Spurious Peaks
Nuclear DNA
   anti-contamination measures,
     83, 172
   cross-contamination, 89, 185
   degradation, 53, 78, 86–7, 134,
     142, 154, 163, 182–4
   evidence contamination, 9, 30, 32–3,
     35, 38, 50–3, 55, 56–8, 66, 79–80,
     82, 87, 89, 92, 95, 100–102, 110,
     112, 115, 119–20, 122, 129,
     133–5, 154–61, 163–4, 166, 168,
     171–3, 176–8, 185–7, 191, 196–7

evidence provenance, 52, 58, 66,
   79, 120, 133–4, 154, 161, 163
full match claim, 25, 26, 56, 70,
   73, 77–8, 84, 98, 99, 106, 110,
   130, 151, 153, 194
   not same as confirmation, 73
international interpretation
   standards, 88, 97, 111, 195
method of deposition and
   transfer, 100–101
missing alleles, 74, 87, 99, 100
Nucleic Acid bases, 72
Nucleotides, 72
partial match, 72–4, 84, 87,
   99–100, 122, 131–2, 138, 151,
   165, 183, 194
profiling, 25–35, 50–1, 53, 68,
   70–7, 79–80, 82, 84–111, 113,
   118, 121–2, 124–33, 135,
   138–9, 142–62, 165, 167,
   169–70, 178–83, 195
profiling issues, 84–111
quantification, 82–3, 90–2, 176
   see also Caddy report
sample analysis and interpretation
   errors, 30, 35, 82, 84–111, 156
sample transferal, primary,
   secondary, tertiary, 85, 100–
   101, 166, 177, 185, 187, 196
source material, 79, 101–102, 106,
   112, 159–61, 167, 172, 176,
   183–4, 196
storage and handling, 52, 79, 80,
   134, 162, 183, 185
testing reliability, 31, 83, 87, 89,
   92–3, 95–8, 105, 108, 130, 132,
   195, 196

see also Mellon, Jennifer N
unreported contributors to
electropherogram, 85
Nudds, William, 2–3, 10, 18

Omagh Bombing trial, 77
  see also Hoey, Sean

Paddington Station, 10
Palace Theatre, Shaftesbury
  Avenue, 19
Partial Profile Matches, *see* Nuclear
  DNA
PCR, 28–32, 82–4, 89–90, 93, 98,
  116, 139, 141, 156, 174, 193
  see also Polymerase Chain
  Reaction
Peak Heights, 85–6, 88
Peer Reviewed Papers for LCN, 30
  see also FSS
Phone Hacking Scandal, 37
  see also News of the World
Picogram (pg), 30, 79, 82, 86, 95, 96,
  97, 137, 140, 141, 155, 156, 157
Pitchfork, Colin, 33
Polymerase Chain Reaction, 28, 89
  amplification, 28
  positive, cross-referencing, 139
  primer sequence, 89
Polymerase Enzyme, 89
Polymorphic, 73
Population Types, 74, 76, 77
  Caucasian, 74, 76, 77
  Indo/Pakistani, 76, 77
Postcard Stamp Evidence, 103, 106,
  122
  testing of, 106

Prosecution Case, 3, 9–10, 12, 15,
  17, 18, 20, 22, 23, 38, 40, 41,
  42, 45, 46, 47, 48, 49, 60, 62,
  68, 74, 81, 85, 112, 159, 168,
  185, 190, 196 *see* Graham
  Swanwick
Pryce, Ann, 18
Public Records Act 1958, 5–6
Pull-up, 87, 88 *see* Bleed-Through

Random Man Not Excluded
  Probability (RMNE), 99
Random Match Probability (RMP)
  calculation, *see* Statistical
  Probabilities, 68, 69–72, 74–78,
  98, 147, 194
  evidence contradicting, 71–2, 194
  see Katherine Troyer
  heterozygote formula, 75
  homozygote formula, 75
  power of probability claims,
    69–70, 74–7
Reed, Reed and Garmson, Regina
  vs., 90, 91, 92, 93, 94, 95, 97,
  98, 100, 137, 150, 170–1, 194,
  194
  aliquot handling, 91, 92, 171
  exculpatory evidence, 49, 87, 99,
    100
  full profile match evidence value,
    98, 100
  LCN test reliability, 97–8
  mixed sample handling, 96–7
  partial profile match handling,
    99–100
  quantification process, 90–1
  rerunning of tests, 95–6

statistical probabilities, 98
stochastic threshold levels and handling, 92–3
transferal of DNA, 100–101
Rehearsal Club, Soho, 18
Relative Fluorescence Unit (RFU), 88
    see also Spurious Peaks
Respondent, xiii, 38, 52–4, 113, 115–18, 120, 122, 135, 141, 143, 148, 164, 169, 173, 176
    see also Sweeney, Nigel
'Review of the Science of Low Template DNA Analysis', 77, 79, 82–3, 85, 91, 96, 101–102, 113, 167, 195–6
    see also Caddy, Professor Brian
Reynold's Billiard Hall, Lime Street, Liverpool, 21
Rhyl, 10, 21, 38
    alibi, 21, 38
Royal Statistical Society, 68, 194
    evidence presentation recommendations, 68
Russell of Liverpool, Lord, 24, 154
    'Deadman's Hill: Was Hanratty Guilty?', 24
Ryan, J., 2, 13, 45

'Satisfied They Are Sure' jury guidance, xii
    see also 'Beyond Reasonable Doubt'
Scientific Working Group on DNA Analysis Methods, 35, 88
    see also SWGDAM
Scotland Road, Liverpool, 11, 14, 20, 45

Second Generation Multiplex (SGM) test, 25, 27–8, 31, 93, 102–107, 121, 123–4, 130, 131, 137, 140–1, 170, 174–6, 178–80, 196
    Autosome loci,
        TH01, 102–103, 107–108, 121, 138
        D21, 102–103, 107–108, 121, 138
        D18, 102–103, 107–108, 121, 138
        D8, 102–103, 107–108, 121, 138
        FGA, 102–103, 107–108, 121, 138
        VWA, 102–103, 107–108, 121, 138
Second Generation Multiplex Plus (SGM Plus®) test, 26, 28–31, 34, 69–71, 73, 84, 89, 91, 93–4, 96, 103–105, 107, 113, 116, 118, 121, 126–8, 130–1, 132–3, 137, 142, 147, 151, 153, 157, 170, 174–6, 178, 180, 193, 196
    additional Autosome loci,
        D2, 103, 107–108, 121
        D3, 103, 107–108, 121
        D16, 103, 107–108, 121
        D19, 103, 107–108, 121
    developmental validation studies, 31, 83, 89, 92, 98, 105, 196
    PCR primer sequence, 89–90
Seminal Fluid, 27, 49, 51, 102, 107, 121, 122, 124–5, 128, 131, 138–41, 165, 167, 178, 181
    Group AB, 27
Seminal Sample Test, 102, 107, 121, 122, 133, 138–9
Sherrard, Michael QC., 16, 48
Short Tandem Repeat (STR), 25–7, 30, 31, 73, 104, 136, 143, 148

Short Tandem Repeat (STR/QUAD) profile test, 27, 31, 104, 136, 143, 148
Simpson Dr. Keith, 42
Single Locus Profiling (SLP), 5
Skillett, John, 43–4
Speller, Camilla, paper, 78
Spurious Peaks, 87–8
  stutter peaks, 87
  noise peaks, 87
  pull-up or bleed-through, 88
  RFU, see Relative Fluorescent Unit, 88
Statistical Probabilities,
  Bayes' theorem, 67–9, 74, 77, 79, 99, 132, 147, 159–60, 194
  Classical analysis, 67
  Frequentist analysis, 67
  LCN discriminatory power, RMP, 68, 70–2, 74–7, 98, 147, 194
  SGM discriminatory power, 25, 31
  SGM Plus discriminatory power, 26, 31, 70
Stochastic Threshold, 86, 92–8, 110, 195
  artefacts *see* spurious peaks
  allelic drop-out or drop-in, 87
Storie, Valerie, 1–2, 9, 25–9, 35, 39–43, 47, 49, 51–4, 58, 66, 79, 97, 102, 104, 107–108, 112, 119–20, 123–27, 130–2, 134, 138–9, 142, 147, 148, 153–5, 158, 161, 178, 180, 184, 197
  account of the crimes, 41–3
  identification parade, 2, 39–41, 57

knicker extraction, 102–103, 107–108, 121, 131–3, 138, 143–50, 152, 171–2
knickers, 9, 25–6, 29, 32, 35, 39–40, 49–52, 54, 56, 58, 66, 79, 97, 104, 107–110, 112, 119–20, 122, 124, 126, 128–32, 135, 139–41, 151, 153–4, 158–63, 171, 177, 180, 183–6, 197
vaginal epithelial sample, 54, 103, 107–108, 121, 124–5, 127–8, 132–3, 138–9, 147–8, 154–5, 164–5, 167–8, 178, 180, 182, 184
Stringer, Peter, 12–13
  customer names not taken, 12
  overtime frequency and length, 13
  working hours, 12
Supernatant Liquid Fraction, 103, 143, 164–5, 167, 180
Supreme Court, 189
Sutherland Avenue, 44
Swanwick, Graham, QC., 12, 19–20, 22
  journey time from Liverpool to Dorney Reach, 19
  purchase of alibi claim, 20
  sweetshop alibi headache, 17
  target practice in Vienna Hotel room, 45
Sweeney, Nigel, QC., 54, 115–19, 121–35, 138–60, 166–8, 173–85, 190
  see also Respondent
  cross-examination of Martin Evison, 173–85
  DNA evidence presentation to court, 123–35

examination of Rachel Frazier in court, 138–141
examination of Jonathan Whitaker in court, 142–162
implied significance of handkerchief evidence, 115, 120, 123, 130, 139
re-examination of Jonathan Whitaker, 166–8
SGM Plus instead of LCN, 116
SWGDAM, 35, 88
  concerns with LCN, 35
  minimum RFU recommendation, 88
Swiss Cottage, 17

Tarlton Avenue, 11, 14
  see also Carlton Road
The Crown xiii, 4, 37, 68, 176, 181
  see also Respondent
Thymine, 72
Train Times, 10, 13,
  see also Euston Station
  see also Lime Street Station
Trower, James, 43–4
Troyer, Katherine, 71–2, 194
  Arizona criminal DNA database findings, 71

UK National DNA Database (UKDNAD), 72–3
Usher, Peter, 12–14, 22
  customer names taken, 12
  discrepancy of name taken, 12–3
  meeting with Hanratty, 12–13
  timing discrepancy, 13
  overtime frequency and length, 13
  working hours, 12

Vienna Hotel, 2, 10, 18, 44–6
  cartridge cases recovery, 2
  delay in discovery, 44
  target practice claim, 45

Walton, Linda, 15–17, 22
  timing disagreement with Barbara Ford, 15
  witness statement, 15–17
Wells, Holly, 33
Whiffen, Detective Chief Inspector Harold, 12
Whitaker, Dr. Jonathan, 29, 31, 34–5, 50, 53, 75, 97, 101, 103–108, 110, 113, 116–19, 122, 130–35, 141–63, 166–8, 171–3, 175, 178–9, 181, 194–7
  Cross-examination by Mr Mansfield, 163–6
  examination by Mr Sweeney, 142–62
  Horizon program, 31
  interpretation of DNA evidence, 50, 53, 101, 103, 105, 110, 122
  involvement in Hoey case, 77, 112–13
  post-exhumation composite DNA testing and results, 31, 144, 152–3, 195

pre-exhumation DNA testing
and results, 103–105, 107–109,
121, 143
re-examination by Mr Sweeney,
166–8
statistical claims, 31–2, 75, 77
Wilson, Robert Anton, 8, 81, 110,
114, 192

Woffinden, Bob, xi, 3–4, 7, 19, 24
'Hanratty: The Final Verdict' book
3, 7, 19, 24
Woolf, Lord Chief Justice Harry,
37, 58, 112, 123–4, 126, 128,
138–9, 160, 177, 185–7

Yang, Dongya, paper, 78